Social and Sexual Revolution

WORKS BY
BERTELL OLLMAN

Alienation: Marx's Conception of Man
in Capitalist Society

Studies in Socialist Pedagogy
(Co-editor with Theodore Mills Norton)

"Class Struggle"
(the first Marxist board game)

Social and Sexual Revolution

Essays on Marx and Reich

Bertell Ollman

South End Press   Boston

The essays drawn together in this book first appeared, often in a somewhat modified form, in the following places:

"Towards Class Consciousness Next Time: Marx and the Working Class," *Politics and Society* (Fall 1972).

"Marx's Use of 'Class'," *American Journal of Sociology* (March 1968).

"Marx's Vision of Communism: A Reconstruction," *Critique* (Summer 1977).

"Marxism and Political Science: Prolegomenon to a Debate on Marx's Method," *Politics and Society* (Summer 1973).

"On Teaching Marxism," *Insurgent Sociologist* (Summer 1976).

"The Marxism of Wilhelm Reich or the Social Function of Sexual Repression," *The Unknown Dimension: European Marxism Since Lenin*, edited by Karl Klare and Dick Howard (New York: Basic Books, 1971).

"Social and Sexual Revolution," Introduction to *Sex-Pol: Writings 1929-1934*, edited by Lee Baxandall (New York: Random House, 1972).

"Reply to Stolzman's Critique of 'On Teaching Marxism'," *Insurgent Sociologists* (Summer 1977).

"Reply to Mussachia's Critique of 'Social and Sexual Revolution'," *Monthly Review* (November 1974).

"Comment on Kelly's 'Alienation'," *Political Theory* (Summer 1973).

"Review of Miliband's *Marxism and Politics*," *American Political Science Review* (Spring 1979).

"Of Marxism and Universities," *New York Times Op Ed* (June 16, 1978).

"Review of Henri Lefebvre's *Sociology of Marx*," *American Journal of Sociology* (January 1969).

Library of Congress Catalog Card Number: 78-71204
ISBN 0-89608-080-3
ISBN 0-89608-081-1

Contents

Introduction

"In 1975 there were 39 million workers in the 'prime' 25 to 44 age bracket.... In 1990, there are expected to be 60.5 million workers in this bracket."[1] The *New York Times,* which recently provided these striking statistics, also quoted a number of "experts" who predict that this extraordinary bulge in the most active and demanding section of the labor force will bring in its train a great intensification of industrial conflict. There aren't enough jobs to go around now, certainly not enough well paying and interesting jobs. A continuing capitalist slump together with further progress in automation is likely to exacerbate this situation. How will the Vietnam generation and their slightly younger brothers and sisters—people familiar with anti-war agitation, Watergate corruption, civil rights struggles and other tradition bending and authority breaking activities—react to the terrible frustration of their expectations that is likely to result? Will this worsening situation lead to class consciousness on a mass scale? On the answer to this question, perhaps more than to any other, depends the future of American socialism in this century.

Class consciousness, the ability of a class to grasp its interests and act upon them, is one of the last subjects treated in most Marxist works for non-Marxists, just as it is one of the first to come up in discussions among Marxists. Since the interests of which classes become conscious (or don't become conscious, as the case may be) are objective, rooted in actual conditions, it is essential to know these conditions in order to understand what it means to be conscious of them. And, for Marx, such conditions include the whole social setting in which a class resides, the various forces driving and restraining it, together with its interaction with opponent classes. When non-Marxists discuss the workers they seldom get beyond the psychology of the workers they actually know or have read about. Marxists, on the other hand, rightly stress the conditions and actions which make workers what they are, provide opportunities for them to express themselves and—as society changes—permit and provoke new modes of thought and behavior. Without the larger context provided by Marxist analysis, inquiring after the consciousness of any group leads inevitably to psychological reductionism.

Yet, among ourselves, among comrades who take Marx's analysis of capitalism more or less for granted, there is frequent discussion of working class consciousness as a problem. Knowing why and how the workers' situation is worsening and the pressures for change that this creates is not the same as knowing how the workers will respond to these pressures. What is lacking? How can we study it? How can we affect it? It is chiefly to these questions—asked in this context—that the essays collected in this volume are directed. In the past, Marx and most Marxists have usually responded to the failure of the workers to revolt in situations where this was considered likely by revising their estimate of objective conditions (capitalism has further to develop, etc.). An alternative approach, one associated more with Lenin than with Marx, puts the blame on inadequate political organizations and/or strategies. While much can be learned from these approaches, they do beg the question of what the workers themselves are like and are capable of. In focusing more directly on the workers, I do not mean to deny or belittle the value of studies that approach workers' consciousness from the vantage points of changing conditions or existing political formations, but rather to supplement them with the processes of becoming class conscious that only emerge from study of the real people involved.

Though written at various times over the last ten years and represented by what appear to be quite different titles, the essays in this book are all concerned with class consciousness. The most detailed discussion of the subject is found in the opening chapter, "Toward Class Consciousness Next Time: Marx and the Working Class." After detailing Marx's own views, I distinguish between several interrelated barriers to working class consciousness and suggest how they can be and are being overcome. The chapters that follow are, in a sense, further attempts to lift some of these barriers. Chapter 2, "Marx's Use of 'Class'," examines the problem of determining who exactly are the workers, and indicates how this problem can be resolved. Chapter 3, "Marx's Vision of Communism," offers the fullest reconstruction of Marx's views of the future available in English in the hope that we can yet bring workers to grasp socialism as a potential inherent in our present society (and not in the practice of a foreign power). Chapter 4, "Marxism and Political Science: Prologomenon to a Debate on Marx's Method," sets out the steps involved in dialectical thinking and doing dialectical research. Chapter 5, "On Teaching Marxism," offers a case study of how one Marxist professor deals with some of the problems inherent in teaching Marxism in a capitalist university setting.

The two essays on Reich come out of the same problematic. Chapter 6, "Social and Sexual Revolution," places Reich's work in the context of Marx's materialism and theory of alienation, while chapter 7, "The Marxism of Wilhelm Reich: Or the Social Function of Sexual Repression," is more concerned with Reich's relationship to Freud. Yet, central to both essays is Reich's contribution to our understanding of class consciousness, especially the effect of sexual repression in undermining peoples' ability to make rational judgements. I might not have included these general essays on Reich in a book of more specialized articles on Marxism if this subject had received fuller treatment elsewhere. Unfortunately, this is not the case, certainly not in the English speaking countries—with the result that Reich's unique contribution to the discussion of class consciousness has yet to be fully appreciated and/or effectively integrated into socialist political strategies.

Non-Marxist readers of this book should be careful not to lose sight of my assumptions, of the Marxist theories I take for granted in explaining others, or they will end up with a distorted picture of Marxism. It also helps to already have some grasp of the labor theory of value, the materialist conception of history, and Marx's theory of alienation, for it is from within these theories that the main questions I've tried to confront in this work emerge and acquire their importance: why haven't the majority of workers in advanced capitalist countries become class conscious? What role does Marx's vision of the future play in helping us understand and transform the present? What is dialectical method and how does one use it? How should one teach Marxism? For those acquainted with Marx's theories, these questions demand immediate attention, since finding satisfactory answers is often the difference between treating Marxism as an ideology or as a science, which is to say between using its principles as a defense for sectarianism or as a guide to effective political practice.

Notes
1. *New York Times,* June 25, 1978, pp. 1, 34.

Social and Sexual Revolution

I. Marx

1.

Toward Class Consciousness Next Time: Marx and the Working Class

Why haven't workers in the advanced capitalist countries become class conscious? Marx was wont to blame leadership, short memories, temporary bursts of prosperity, and, in the case of the English and German workers, national characteristics.[1] In the last fifteen years of his life he often singled out the enmity between English and Irish workers as the chief hindrance to a revolutionary class consciousness developing in the country that was most ripe for it.[2] The success of this explanation can be judged from the fact that it was never given the same prominence by any of Marx's followers. Engels, too, remained unsatisfied. After Marx's death, he generally accounted for the disappointing performance of the working class, particularly in England, by claiming that they had been bought off with a share of their country's colonial spoils.[3] The same reasoning is found in Lenin's theory of imperialism, and in this form it still aids countless Marxists in understanding why the revolution Marx predicted never came to pass in the advanced capitalist countries.

Despite these varied explanations (or, perhaps, because of them), most socialists from Marx onward have approached each crisis in capitalism with the certainty that this time the proletariat will become class conscious. A half-dozen major crises have come and gone, and the proletariat at least in the United States, England, and Germany are as far away from such a consciousness as ever. What has gone "wrong?" Until socialists begin to examine the failure of the proletariat to perform its historically appointed task in light of their own excessive optimism, there is little reason to believe that on this matter at least the future will cease to resemble the past. It is the purpose of this essay to effect such an examination.

II

"Men make their own history," Marx said, "but they do not make it just as they please; they do not make it under circumstances chosen by themselves, but under circumstances directly encountered, given and transmitted from the past."[4] In his writings, Marx was primarily concerned with the circumstances of social and economic life under capitalism, with how they developed and are developing. His followers have likewise stressed social and economic processes. As is apparent from the above quotation, however, the necessary conditions for a proletarian revolution were never mistaken for sufficient conditions: real, living human beings had to react to their oppressive circumstances in ways that would bring needed change. The theoretical link in Marxism between determining conditions and determined response is the class consciousness of the actors.

The mediating role of consciousness is sometimes hidden behind such statements as: "The question is not what this or that proletarian, or even the whole of the proletariat at the moment considers its aim. The question is what the proletariat is, and what, consequent on that being, it will be compelled to do."[5] But compelled by what? Marx responds by "what the proletariat is." However, what the proletariat is is a class of people whose conditions of life, whose experiences at work and elsewhere, whose common struggles and discussions will sooner or later bring them to a consciousness of their state and of what must be done to transform it.[6] Though industrial wage earners are in the forefront of Marx's mind when he speaks of the proletariat, most of what he says holds for all wage earners, and he generally intends the designations "proletariat" and "working class" to apply to them as well.

Class consciousness is essentially the interests of a class becoming its recognized goals. These interests, for those who accept Marx's analysis, are objective; they accrue to a class because of its real situation and can be found there by all who seriously look. Rather than indicating simply what people want, "interest" refers to those generalized means which increase their ability to get what they want, and includes things such as money, power, ease, and structural reform or its absence. Whether they know it or not, the higher wages, improved working conditions, job security, inexpensive consumer goods, etc., that most workers say they want are only to be had through such mediation. Moreover, the reference is not only to the present, but to what people will come to want under other and better conditions. Hence, the aptness of C. Wright Mills' description of Marxian interests as "long run, general, and rational interests."[7] The most long run, general, and rational interest of the working class lies in overturning the exploitative relations which keep them, individually and collectively, from getting what they want.

Becoming class conscious in this sense is obviously based on the recognition of belonging to a group which has similar grievances and aspirations, and a correct appreciation of the group's relevant life conditions. For workers this involves divesting themselves of many current delusions—the list is as long as the program of the Democratic party—and acquiring a class analysis of capitalism akin to Marx's own. Such class consciousness also includes an *esprit de corps* that binds members of the class together in opposition to the common enemy.

As a social relation, class consciousness can also be seen to include the social and economic conditions in which recognition of class interests occurs (or can occur). Consequently, any large-scale exposition of this theory would have to involve an analysis of major developments in capitalism—ranging from the factory floor to the world market—from Marx's time to our own. In providing the beginnings of such an analysis, Marxist writers have tended to underplay the psychological dimensions of the problem. Rather than denying their important contribution, my own focus on the individual worker is best seen as an attempt to redress the imbalance.

Finally, the step from being class conscious to engaging in action aimed at attaining class interests is an automatic one; the latter is already contained in the former as its practical side. It makes no sense in Marx's schema to speak of a class conscious proletariat which is not engaged in the activity of overturning capitalism. Workers bursting with revolt stage revolts, or at least prepare for them by participating in the work of a revolutionary party or movement. The revolution takes place when "enough" workers have become class-conscious, and, given the place and number of the proletariat in modern society, its success is assured. The essential step, therefore, is the first one. If class consciousness is to play the role Marx gave it of mediating between determining conditions and determined response it must be taken in a broad enough sense to include this action component.

Another approach to class consciousness is offered by Lukacs who defines it as "the sense become conscious of the historical situation of the class."[8] By conceptualizing consciousness as a part of a class's objective conditions and interests, Lukacs can treat theoretically what is only possible as if it were actual. However, if workers always possess class consciousness because they are members of a class to which such consciousness attaches, then we are not talking about real workers or, alternatively, "consciousness" applies to something other than that of which real workers are conscious. In any case, if all workers are class conscious, in any sense of this term, we can no longer distinguish between those who are and those who are not, so that nothing concrete in the way of revolutionary activity follows from being class conscious. Lukacs only succeeds in avoiding our problem by begging the question.

A similar misconception, and one widespread in Marxist circles, has "class consciousness" referring to the workers' general resentment and feeling of being systematically cheated by the boss, where any aggressive action from complaining to industrial sabotage is viewed as evidence. Here, too, all workers are seen to be more or less class conscious, and, as with Lukacs, such consciousness leads nowhere in particular. Though obviously components of class consciousness, resenting the boss and the insight that he is taking unfair advantage are not by themselves sufficiently important to justify the use of this concept.

Nor is "class consciousness" a synonym for "trade union consciousness" as Lenin seems to suggest in *What Is To Be Done*, where he ties together the "awakening of class consciousness" and the "beginning of trade union struggle."[9] Despite this suggestion, an important distinction is made in this work between "trade union consciousness," or recognition of the need for unions and for struggle over union demands, and "socialist (or Social Democratic) consciousness," which is an awareness on the part of workers of the "irreconcilable antagonism of their interests to the whole of the modern political and social system."[10] Class consciousness, as I have explained it, has more in common with Lenin's notion of socialist consciousness, and Lenin, on one occasion, even speaks of "genuine class consciousness" with this advanced state of understanding in mind.[11]

III

For Marx, life itself is the hard school in which the workers learn to be class conscious, and he clearly believes they possess the qualities requisite to learning this lesson.[12] In so far as people share the same circumstances, work in identical factories, live in similar neighborhoods, etc., they are inclined to see things—the most important ones at least—in the same way. They cannot know more than what their life presents them with nor differently from what their life permits. However, the less obvious aspects of their situation, such as their own objective interests, often take some time before they are grasped. What insures eventual success is the ability Marx attributes to people to figure out, in the long run, what is good for them, given their particular circumstances. For Marx, no matter how dehumanizing his conditions, an individual is capable of seeing where his fundamental interests lie, of comprehending and agreeing to arguments which purport to defend these interests, and of coming to the conclusions dictated by them. It is such an ability that Thorstein Veblen labels the "calculus of advantage."[13]

Rather than the proletariat's conditions serving as a barrier to such rational thinking, Marx believes the reverse is the case. The very extremity of their situation, the very extent of their suffering and deprivation, makes the task of calculating advantages relatively an easy one. As part of this, the one-sided struggle of the working class—according to Engels, "the defeats even more than the victories"—further exposes the true nature of the system.[14] The reality to be understood stands out in harsh relief, rendering errors of judgment increasingly difficult to make.

The workers' much discussed alienation simply does not extend to their ability to calculate advantages, or, when it does— as in the matter of reification—it is regarded as a passing and essentially superficial phenomenon. Marx maintained that "the abstraction of all humanity, even the semblance of humanity" is "*practically* complete in the full blown proletariat."[15] A loophole is reserved for purposive activity, which is the individual's ability to grasp the nature of what he wants to transform and to direct his energies accordingly. Marx held that productive activity is always purposive, and that this is one of the main features which distinguishes human beings from animals.[16] Class consciousness is the result of such purposive activity with the self as object, of workers using their reasoning powers on themselves and their life conditions. It follows necessarily from what they are, both as calculating human beings and as workers caught up in an inhuman situation.

The workers are also prompted in their search for socialist meaning by their needs as individuals. For Marx, society produces people who have needs for whatever, broadly speaking, fulfills their powers in the state in which these latter have been fashioned by society. These needs are invariably felt as wants, and since that which fulfills an individual's powers includes by extension the conditions for such fulfillment, he soon comes to want the means of his own transformation; for capitalist conditions alone cannot secure for workers, even extremely alienated workers, what they want. Job security, social equality, and uninterrupted improvement in living conditions, for example, are simply impossibilities within the capitalist framework. Hence, even before they recognize their class interests, workers are driven by their needs in ways which serve to satisfy these interests. And, as planned action— based on a full appreciation of what these interests are—is the most effective means of proceeding, needs provide what is possibly the greatest boost to becoming class conscious.

Though rooted in people's everyday lives, class consciousness is never taken wholly for granted. The main effort of socialists from Marx to our own time has been directed toward helping workers draw socialist lessons from their conditions. Marx's activity both as a scholar and as a man of action had this objective. Viewed in this light, too, the debate initiated by Lenin regarding the character of a socialist party has not been over *what* to do, but rather over *how* to do it. Essential, here, is that among socialists the conviction has always existed that sooner or later, in one crisis or another (with the help of this form of organization or that), the proletariat would finally become class conscious.

Both critics and defenders of Marx alike have sought to explain the failure of the working class to assume its historical role by tampering with his account of capitalist conditions. Thus, his critics assert that the lot of the workers has improved, that the middle class has not disappeared, etc., and, at the extreme, that these conditions were never really as bad as Marx claimed. His defenders have tried to show that it was relative pauperization he predicted, that big businesses are getting larger, etc., and, after Lenin, that imperialist expansion permitted capitalists to buy off their workers. Such rejoinders, however, whether in criticism or defense, miss the essential point that for the whole of Marx's lifetime the situation in the capitalist world was adequate, by his own standards, for the revolution he expected to take place.

Martin Nicolaus, in his widely read article, "The Unknown Marx," has argued that the mature Marx (Marx of the *Grundrisse*, 1858) put the socialist revolution far into the future, in effect after capitalism was thoroughly beset by problems of automation.[17] Though Marx does speak of such a possibility, that is not his first projection. Marx was dealing after all with trends in the capitalist economy, and particularly, though not exclusively, with their *probable* outcome. On the basis of his research, he not only hoped for but expected revolutions on each downturn of the economic cycle. In 1858, the year of the *Grundrisse*, he wrote to Engels, "On the continent the revolution is immanent."[18] And twelve years later he declared: "The English have all the material requisites necessary for a social revolution. What they lack is the spirit of generalization and revolutionary ardor."[19] Does this sound like a man who thought capitalist conditions were not sufficiently ripe for the workers to make a revolution? Though it is true that Marx became progressively less optimistic (and always took account of other possibilities) he never really believed he was writing for a century other than his own.

If it was not conditions which failed Marx, it could have only been the workers. More precisely, the great majority of workers were not able to attain class consiousness in conditions that were more or less ideal for them to do so. Marx's error, an error which has had a far-ranging effect on the history of socialist thought and practice, is that he advanced from the workers' conditions of life to class consciousness in a single bound; the various psychological mediations united in class consciousness are treated as one. The severity of these conditions, the pressures he saw coming from material needs, and his belief that workers never lose their ability to calculate advantages made the eventual result certain and a detailed analysis of the steps involved unnecessary.

IV

Class consciousness is a more complex phenomenon—and, hence, more fraught with possibilities for failure—than Marx and most other socialists have believed. With the extra hundred years of hindsight, one can see that what Marx treated as a relatively direct, if not easy, transition is neither. Progress from the workers' conditions to class consciousness involves not one but many steps, each of which constitutes a real problem of achievement for some section of the working class.

First, workers must recognize that they have interests. Second, they must be able to see their interests as individuals in their interests as members of a class. Third, they must be able to distinguish what Marx considers their main interests as workers from other less important economic interests. Fourth, they must believe that their class interests come prior to their interests as members of a particular nation, religion, race, etc. Fifth, they must must truly hate their capitalist exploiters. Sixth, they must have an idea, however vague, that their situation could be qualitatively improved. Seventh, they must believe that they themselves, through some means or other, can help bring about this improvement. Eighth, they must believe that Marx's strategy, or that advocated by Marxist leaders, offers the best means for achieving their aims. And, ninth, having arrived at all the foregoing, they must not be afraid to act when the time comes.

These steps are not only conceptually distinct, but they constitute the real difficulties which have kept the mass of the proletariat in all capitalist countries from becoming class conscious. Though these difficulties can and do appear in other combinations, I believe the order in which they are given here corresponds to the inherent logic of the situation and correctly describes the trajectory most often followed. What we find then is that most workers have climbed a few of these steps (enough to complain), that some have scaled most of them (enough to vote for working-class candidates), but that relatively few have managed to ascend to the top.

To begin with, if we accept Marx's portrayal of the proletariat's dehumanization as more or less accurate, it is clear that there are workers who simply cannot recognize that they have interests of any sort. They have been rendered into unthinking brutes ("idiocy" and "cretinism" are Marx's terms), whose attention does not extend beyond their immediate task.[20] Given the conditions which prevailed in Marx's time, many workers must have suffered from this extreme degradation. And, when treated like animals, they reacted like animals, tame ones. Marx, himself, offers evidence for such a conclusion in telling of occasions when the workers' already impossible lot worsened without raising any protest from them.

In 1862, during a depression in the English cotton trade, a factory inspector is quoted as saying, "The sufferings of the operatives since the date of my last report have greatly increased; but at no period in the history of manufacturers, have sufferings so sudden and so severe been borne with so much silent resignation and so much patient self-respect."[21] Even a member of Parliament from one of the worst affected areas cannot refrain from commenting, nor Marx from quoting, that in this crisis, "the laborers of Lancashire have behaved like the ancient philosophers (Stoics)." Marx adds, "Not like sheep?"[22]

What conclusion did Marx draw from these events, events which were by no means unusual? None at all. Despite his angry retort, his purpose in relating this incident was to show the conditions in which the workers were forced to live and work, and not how uncomplainingly they had submitted to these conditions. So bludgeoned by life that they cannot conceive they have any interests, many workers are condemned to submit to their earthly travail with as much thought as an ox before the plow. Admittedly, this malaise was more prevalent when the working day averaged fourteen hours than now when eight hours is the rule, but I am not convinced that it has completely disappeared.

For workers who recognize that they are human beings with interests, the next step in becoming class conscious is to see their interests as individuals in their interests as members of the working class. It is not immediately apparent that the best way to obtain a good job, more pay, better conditions, etc. is to promote the interests of one's class. On the contrary, the practical isolation that capitalism forces on all its inhabitants makes the very notion of shared interests difficult to conceive. It was Marx, himself, who noted that the individual in capitalist society is "withdrawn into himself, wholly preoccupied with his private interest and acting in accordance with his private caprice."[23] The character of the ensuing struggle is well brought out in Marx's definition of "competition," its all-purpose label, as "avarice and war among the avaricious."[24] Throughout society, calculator meets calculator in the never ending battle of who can get the most out of whom. "Mutual exploitation" is the rule.[25]

With so much indifference and hostility ingrained in the way of life and outlook of everyone, it is not surprising that the competition between workers for a greater portion of the meager fare which goes to them as a class is no less intense. Marx is eminently aware that, "Competition makes individuals, not only the bourgeoisie, but still more the workers, mutually hostile, in spite of the fact that it brings them together."[26] This competition first rears its head at the factory gate where some are allowed in and others are not. Inside the factory, workers continue to compete with each other for such favors as their employer has it in him to bestow, especially for the easier and better paying jobs. After work, with too little money to spend, workers are again at each other's throats for the inadequate food, clothing, and shelter available to them.

The cooperation that characterizes industrial labor hardly offsets the atomizing effect of so much inner-class competition.

The scales are even more unbalanced than this suggests, since the individual worker, without a conception of his identity in the group, is incapable of appreciating the essential links between his own labor and that of his co-workers. Cooperation is something of which he is only dimly aware. So it is that both his social activity and product are viewed as alien powers. To be able to see one's interest as a member of the working class under these conditions is no little achievement.

After workers realize they have interests, and class interests at that, it is essential that they adopt Marx's view of what these latter are. I accept that there are objective interests which accrue to a class in virtue of its social-economic position, and, also, Marx's understanding of what these are for the workers, including their overriding interest in transforming the system. However, his belief that most workers will sooner or later come to agree with us has received little support from history. Without a doubt, this is the step at which the great part of the proletariat has faltered.

When Samuel Gompers, the early leader of the AFL, was asked what the workers want, he answered, "More." And, as much as I would like to dispute it, this strikes me as an accurate description of how most workers have conceived of their interests then and now. Most workers who have grasped that they have interests as workers have seen them in terms of getting a little more of what they already have, making their conditions a little better than what they are, working a little bit less than they do. As limited, cautious men and women, the workers have little, cautious designs. Their horizons have been clipped off at the roots. As with most of their other personal shortcomings, this is a result of the alienation Marx so eloquently describes. It is simply that their conditions have so limited their conceptions, that these conceptions offer them little opportunity to break out of their conditions.

While Marx was aware that most workers did not share his view of their interests, he refused to acknowledge the real gap which separated the two positions, or to devote serious study to its causes and likely consequences. Thus, when Jules Guesde came to London to seek Marx's advice about an election program, Marx could write, "With the exception of some trivialities which Guesde found necessary to throw to the French workers despite my protest, such as fixing the minimum wage by law and the like (I told him: 'If the French proletariat is still so childish to require such bait, it is not worthwhile drawing up any program whatever')..."[27] But the proletariat, not only in France but throughout the capitalist world, were so "childish," and they remain so.

Marx's inability to grasp the staying power of the workers' trade union designs is due, in part, to his belief that the capitalists would not and could not accede to most of these demands; having got nowhere for so long, the workers would not fail to see that their real interests lay elsewhere. In part, he believed that whatever minor benefits they managed to force upon the capitalists could only be temporary, acquired in booms, in periods of rapidly expanding capital, and lost again in depressions. And, in part, he thought that whatever improvements withstood the test of time ,were so clearly insignificant that this fact would not be lost upon the workers themselves. These were the "crumbs" which, he said, do nothing to bridge the "social gulf" between the classes.[28] In capitalism, even when the workers get higher pay, this is "nothing but better payment for the slave"; it does not "conquer either for the worker or for work their human status and dignity."[29] The successes of the English Factory Acts in ridding capitalism of its worst abuses are treated in the same light.[30]

However, it is one thing for us to agree with Marx's characterization of such improvements as "crumbs" which do not win for the workers their "human status and dignity," and quite another to believe that most workers agree as well, or that they ever have, or that they ever will. On the contrary, the same conditions which so limit their horizons that a higher wage is considered the acme of their interests make it likely that a few dollars added to their pay packet will be regarded as a major success. In keeping with this Lilliputian perspective, rather than being disappointed with "crumbs," they will use their collective bargaining power to obtain more. Organized into unions, they have managed to retain many of the gains made in prosperous times through the recurring crises, and, with the steady growth of society's absolute product, they have succeeded in acquiring a higher standard of living than Marx thought possible. Given the time and the patience, even pyramids can be built of crumbs. But most workers have never wanted anything else, nor have they ever conceived of their interests in other terms.

Once workers accept that they have class interests and that Marx is right about what these are, the step they must take is to consider these interests more important than ties of nation, religion, race, etc. In the *Communist Manifesto* (1848) Marx declared that the proletariat had already lost both religious and nationalist attachments.[31] This is one conclusion he was later forced to qualify, as least as regards English and Irish workers. The hopes for a growing proletarian brotherhood received an almost fatal setback by the chauvinistic behavior of the European working class during World War I. With such divisions firmly entrenched in the psychology of most workers, an all too frequent reaction in time of economic hardship has been to seek for scapegoats among their class. It is against those who compete with them for scarce jobs, against fellow workers who can be easily distinguished because of their nationality, religion, or race that much of their pent up ire is directed.

One does not have to offer a theory of where these prejudices come from and how they operate to hold that the weight Marx attached to them is seriously inadequate. Oddly enough, Marx provides the framework for such a theory in his account of alienation and the mystification which accompanies it, where we also learn that the tenacity of these prejudices is a function of the degree of distortion present. How could such deprived people be expected to operate with abilities they have lost? How could workers, who are manipulated more than any other group, overturn the results of this manipulation in their own personalities?

Besides causing conflicts among workers, the excessive attachment to nation, religion, and race is also responsible for a lot of inter-class cooperation, workers and capitalists of the same nation, etc., joining together to combat their alien counterparts.[32] In these circumstances, the hatred workers should feel for their exploiters, which is another requirement for class consciousness, is all but dissipated. The whole education, culture, and communication apparatus of bourgeois society, by clouding the workers' minds with noncontroversial orthodoxies, has succeeded in establishing numerous links between the classes on trivial matters. Aren't we all fans of the Green Bay Packers?

The workers, with relatively few exceptions—depending on the country and the period—don't really and deeply hate capitalists, because they cannot distinguish them sharply enough from themselves, because they have never been able to set off a sufficiently unencumbered target to hate. Whatever class mobility exists—this is a more significant factor in America than elsewhere—merely serves to compound the problem. And if some workers are aided in making this distinction by having a capitalist with a long nose or different colored skin, they are more likely to become incensed against his religion or race than against his class.

One excruciating result of such bourgeois successes is that workers, including socialist workers, often admire capitalists more than they hate them. Workers who live vicariously through their employer are not limited to those with a stunted conception of their interests. And their envy is not of a man who has more, but who is in some sense better. Such an admission is already contained in the widespread drive for respectability and prestige, for "status." Actions acquire status according to a particular social code, which is set and promulgated in every society by the ruling social and economic class. To be interested in acquiring status is to submit to the social code that determines it. It is to accept the legitimacy of existing society, and to admit, however feebly, that one's interests as a citizen are somehow superior to one's interests as a worker.

Marx and Engels were often made aware of this failing, which affected many of their own stalwarts, particularly in England. If Tom Mann, one of the truly outstanding leaders of the English working class, was—as Engels relates—"fond of mentioning that he will be lunching with the Lord Mayor," what could one expect of the others?[33] Yet, Marx and Engels always treated this "bourgeois infection" (Marx's term) as something skin deep and of passing importance.[34] My own conclusion from such evidence, which has not diminished with the years, is that the vast majority of workers, including some devotees of Marxist parties, have never really and decisively rejected the society which has despoiled them, but have always been more concerned to be accepted by it than to change it.

The next step up the ladder to class consciousness is that workers must have an inkling, however vague, that their situation can be qualitatively improved. It does no good to know what they need and to have the proper likes and dislikes if they believe that nothing can be done about it. For, in this situation, lotteries and football pools remain the only escape from the lot that has befallen them. We have all heard such rejoinders as "The world will never change" and "Rich and poor will always be with us." What is important to realize is that not only workers whose horizons stop at "more" are afflicted with this pessimism, but also many who share Marx's conception of their interests. Clearly, the relevant question is how could people who are so battered by their reality believe otherwise? A vision requires hope, and hope requires a crack in the ceiling, such as few good landlords in any society permit.

Frederick Lessner, a working-class acquaintance of Marx, says of his introduction to Weitling's book, *Guarantees of Harmony and Freedom,* "I read it once, twice, three times. It was then that it first occured to me that the world could be different from what it was."[35] But how many workers would read this kind of book work even once? Yet, it was only through such sustained mental effort that a man who became a model for his class could obtain a major prerequisite for engaging in socialist activity, the idea that a more just society can be constructed. More recently, disappointment with the Soviet experiment has served as another kind of block to the workers' imagination.

Once workers who have accompanied us so far accept that change for the better is possible, the next hurdle is becoming convinced that they have something positive to contribute to this effort. A widespread phenomenon in our time, which we can only assume was also present in Marx's day, is the feeling of powerlessness, the self-reproach that there is nothing one can do which matters. Most people simply feel themselves too small and the establishment which requires overturning too large and imposing to see any link between individual action and social change.

Each person must make his/her own decision whether to join others for political action, and must justify to him or herself and, perhaps, to his or her family the time and energy this new commitment will take. In this situation, even people with strong socialist views are prone to say, "One more, one less—it won't make any difference." Everything from going to vote to raising barricades is affected by this doubt. Socialist views come coupled with the duty to act upon them only where the individual is convinced that somehow or other, sooner or later, his or her participation will count. In Marx's day, many of the most restless spirits among the European proletariat immigrated to the New World simply because they did not believe there was anything they personally could do to improve the old one.

Assuming we cross this hurdle, we are now confronted with workers who have grasped what Marx takes to be their interests, who possess the proper attitudes toward co-workers and capitalists, who believe it possible to create a better world, and who think they can help effect this change—it is essential, next, that they consider the strategy advocated by Marx or their Marxist leaders to be the right one. Marx was thoroughly pragmatic when it came to the means for achieving social change, favoring the ballot where it could work and revolution where it could not.[36] Because national circumstances and traditions vary so greatly and because of the many peculiar "accidents" that cannot be systematized, Marx felt he was in no position to offer detailed advice, and, despite the reams written on Marx's theory of revolution, there is none. Most of his comments on this subject are very general, as when he says the "social disintegration" will be "more brutal or more human, according to the degree of development of the working class itself."[37]

Nor did Marx ever speculate on what is the proper kind of political party or movement to make the revolution. The First International was a loose coagulation of working-class unions, educational associations, and parties whose first aim was to promote class consciousness. This, as we will recall, is also how Marx saw his task. When enough workers became class conscious, they would know what to do and how to do it.

If Marx had no theory of revolution, he equally had no theory of democracy, and certainly felt no commitment to use "democratic" and "constitutional" methods. With his mixture of contempt and distrust for bourgeois democracy, his bias on the side of revolutions is a clear one. Once his followers were permitted to operate inside the constitution, however, many of them ceased thinking of their goals as outside it. For better or worse, they were determined to believe that it was possible to obtain what they wanted by obeying the rules (and even the customs) of the political game. What began as a tactical means became an end, displacing in the process their former end. Yesterday it was the Social Democrats and there are indications that the same metamorphosis is occurring in many Communist parties today.

Marx's correspondence is full of complaints against working class leaders, many of them close students of Marxism, for their tactical bungling, usually for engaging in compromising actions with the bourgeoisie. He most often attributes their mistakes to personal faults, and, in this way, manages to exonerate their following. Ernest Jones, the Chartist leader, is described as the general of an army who "crosses over to the camp of the enemy on the eve of battle."[38] The army, apparently, was ready to fight. Again, my conclusion is more severe, for the evidence has been compounded many times over since Marx's day. The rules and practice of the capitalist political game, with its perpetual promise of the half-loaf, poisons the socialist rank-and-file as well as their leaders.For the workers to take up revolutionary tactics, it is essential that they be completely disillusioned with all reformist leaders and methods. But, in democracies, such leaders and methods are generally able to secure a small part of what they promise. The result is that the workers are kept dangling, wed to solutions which they cannot solve; yet, temptation, and with it hope, never ceases.

One final step remains. Once workers grasp what they need as workers, who their friends and enemies are, that a better world can be created, what must be done to create it, possess the confidence that they have something to contribute and that by avoiding the trap of reformism they can succeed, what is still required is that they have the ability when the time comes to act. An imprisoned class consciousness that cannot be translated into revolutionary action is no class consciousness at all. Waiting for the German proletariat to provide a revolutionary initiative which never came, Rosa Luxemburg—whose politics ran a close parallel to Marx's own—paid for the delay with her life. Yet, in the aftermath of World War I, Germany probably had more workers who had climbed all previous steps than any capitalist country either before or since. But when the opportune moment for action arrived, most of them held back. This does not excuse the betrayal of the German Social Democrats who argued against rebellion and helped put down the outbreaks that occurred; it only helps explain, at least in part, their unfortunate success. Luxemburg's fate may very well have been Marx's had he lived in a more troubled land at a more troubled time. Or, would he have read the handwriting which had been on the wall since 1848 or thereabouts and become—a "Leninist"?

Marx's mistake was believing that understanding things correctly, in a way that calls for a particular action, necessarily leads to people taking this action. First of all, in the case before us, there is the very real fear of being hurt. Very few workers have the courage which comes with having nothing to lose, simply because they always have something to lose, their lives if nothing else. In recent years, of course, they have much more to lose, the growing number of objects which they have purchased. Because they have relatively few possessions, and ones they have worked very hard to obtain, the proletariat have become as petty as the petty bourgeoisie have always been about their goods. In this situation, the tendency is to look not at what one has to gain, but at what one has to lose in any radical change. This is the same affliction that the peasants have always suffered from.

But such last minute restraint can also be attributed to two related psychological mechanisms about which Marx knew very little. It has often been remarked how people in authority browbeat others to act against their recognized interests, how awe, respect, and habit combine to overturn the most rational conclusions. This falling into line under any circumstances is part of a syndrome which T.W. Adorno and others have popularized as the "authoritarian personality."[39] Rooted in the habit of taking orders, a habit which extends back to the earliest years of education and family training, it eventually succeeds in being felt as a duty. So great is the emotional compulsion to obey that the adult, who had been conditioned in this way, may actually feel physical pain when he disobeys.

How exactly this effect is created or the precise mechanism through which it operates cannot be gone into at this time. For my purposes, it is enough to state that it exists, and that the conditions in which most workers are raised—admittedly, more so in some cultures than in others—are only too well suited to producing authoritarian personalities. Thus in moments of crisis, many workers find themselves emotionally incapable of departing from long established patterns of subservience, no matter how much they rationally desire to do so.

The second psychological malfunction working to disrupt Marx's expectations is the security mindedness of the proletariat, what Erich Fromm has called their "fear of freedom."[40] People not only refuse emancipation because choosing against habitual patterns is painful, but because they irrationally fear what is to be chosen. What is new and unknown is more terrifying to many than the terror which is known. They think at least they have been able to live through the troubles they have had. How do they know they will be able to deal as well with the new troubles which await them?

People lack confidence in the future, essentially, because they lack confidence in themselves; but nothing in the lives of workers has enabled them to acquire such confidence. Again, those who are most in need of freedom are the very ones whose wretched, ego destroying existence has acted to make them afraid of freedom. In such straits, there will always be workers who desire to see the future conform to the past except at the limits of despair. This failing, admittedly, like the irrational need to obey, is more likely to afflict those who are not poised to act against the system. However, diseases—and what I have been describing are emotional diseases—generally have little respect for the political sophistication of their victims.

After removing workers for this, that, and the other shortcoming, and many for a combination of them (the actual combinations as I have indicated may vary), what is left? How many workers were class conscious in Marx's time or are now? How many could have become class conscious then or could become so now? How many workers who became class conscious were able to remain so (for if character alters, it alters in both directions)?

V

From the foregoing account, it appears that class consciousness is an extraordinary achievement of which very few workers at any time have shown themselves capable, and that there is little reason to believe this will change. Indeed, with greater inter-class mobility, increasing stratification within the working class, and the absolute (not relative) improvement in the workers' material conditions in our century, some of the factors which have helped bring about class consciousness where it did exist have lost much of their influence. The pessimistic import of such truths has led to the demise of more than one socialist and is at least partly responsible for the slight attention paid to problems of class consciousness by socialist writers.

Yet in trying to account for the past failures of the working class, my intention has not been to predict the future but to affect it. This is only possible, however, after frankly and fully admitting the real psychological as well as social barriers that exist to proletarian class consciousness. On the basis of the foregoing analysis, the problem with which socialists are confronted may be stated as follows: in order to have a revolution, there will not only have to be other severe crises in the capitalist system (these will occur), but a large segment of the working class will have to develop characteristics that will enable them to respond to one or another of these crises by becoming class conscious.

This manner of posing the problem is not affected by differences of opinion regarding how quickly class consciousness can arise. The French events of May 1968 found workers climbing many of the steps to class consciousness in short order (just as the aftermath found many of them quickly descending). Particularly impressive was the way workers initially rejected the gigantic wage increases won by their trade union leaders. Clearly, at this stage, a large number of workers wanted fundamental social change, though most were still uncertain as to what exactly that was or how to get it. The events of May were not only a result of preceding conditions and events, social, economic, and political, but as well of the ability of the most radical working class in any advanced capitalist country, with the possible exception of Italy, to respond as they did. And this response, when and to the limited degree that it occurred (whatever the guilt of the French Communist Party), is evidence of the speed at which under certain pressures the barriers to class consciousness can be overcome. We have not been dealing, however, with how fast workers can become class conscious, but with all such consciousness contains. While the complexity of this condition suggests slow or staggered development, it is clear that particular events can greatly speed the process.

It is time now to examine more closely the causes for Marx's own excessive optimism. Marx was forever expecting the proletariat to become class conscious, essentially because in his scheme for understanding people and society there is no niche put aside for their continued refusal to do so. We have already seen how the needs people have are conceptualized as one with the wants they feel for whatever it is that will satisfy these needs. Marx is aided (and perhaps even encouraged) in constructing this knot by the German language where *bedürfen* means both "need" and "want." As a result, Marx is inclined to believe that people want or will soon come to want that for which they have needs, or by extension, which serves as the means to acquire what they need. Yet, people may have needs for which they never consciously want relief, and others—as Freud has shown—of which they never become aware, and still others the means to the satisfaction of which they never directly want.

Marx's position that life activity is purposive brings him to a similar conclusion whenever the self is treated as the object. But, again, the necessity Marx finds is one he himself introduces into his concepts. In fact, people may act without purpose, without consciously seeking any particular development or goals. It was such faulty conceptualization which led Marx to treat conscious-ness, despite qualifications to the contrary, as the mental reflection of surroundings and kept him from correctly estim-ating the real gap between objective and subjective interests.

In this manner, the link between conditions and character— for all the space it gets in Marx's writings—remains undeveloped. The problem of the receptivity of character to new influences, its malleability, particularly relative to age, is nowhere discussed. Marx is obviously correct in holding that the individual is to a remarkably high degree the product of his society, and that by changing his living conditions we change him, but there are at least two questions that still have to be answered: are the changes which occur in character always rational, i.e., in keeping with the new interests that are created? How long does it take for new conditions to produce new people?

Marx believed that the effect of conditions on character was rational and relatively quick acting. The evidence examined in this paper argues against such beliefs. Before attempting to modify Marx's conceptual framework, however, we must first realize that very little that passes for irrationality here is sheer madness. For the most part, it is a matter of too little attention paid to some factors and too much to others, or of the right amount of attention paid too late. Given where his calculations should take him and when, the individual's response to his environment is distorted; he has become fanatical in his devotion to some needs and a cold suitor to others.

One factor, in particular, which has received less than its due in Marx's writings is the sexual drive. Young people are more interested in sex, devote more time to thinking about and trying to satisfy this drive, and are immensely more affected by it (by not having sex even more than by having it) than most adults, even after Freud, would care to admit. If one doesn't eat, one starves to death. But what happens if one doesn't satisfy the sexual drive, or does so only rarely, hurriedly, and with a lot of guilt? One doesn't die, but how does such abstinence effect the personality? Which qualities does it reinforce and which does it weaken? There are no conclusive answers, but it is my impression that sexual repression among the workers, as among other classes, has contributed significantly to their irrationality.[41]

By the right amount of attention paid too late, I have in mind the time lag which exists between the appearance of new conditions and resulting changes in character. Though Marx accepted the necessity of some such lag, he did not make it long enough; nor did he properly estimate the potential for mischief which this delay carried with it. People acquire most of their personal and class characteristics in childhood. It is the condition operating then, transmitted primarily by the family, which makes them what they are, at least as regards basic responses; and, in most cases, what they are will vary very little over their lives. Thus, even where the conditions people have been brought up in change by the time they reach maturity, their characters will reflect the situation which has passed on. If Marx had studied the family more closely, he surely would have noticed that as a factory for producing character it is invariably a generation or more behind the times, producing people today who, tomorrow, will be able to deal with yesterday's problems.

Even children, whose characters are more affected by existing conditions, don't become all these conditions call for, since the family, which is the chief mechanism through which society bears upon them, is staffed by adults whose outlook reflects the previous state of affairs. If, for adults, existing conditions come too late, for the young, who can do little about them in any case, they are reflected through a prism that both modifies and distorts the influence they would otherwise have. As a result, only in extreme cases do new conditions make people behave as they do (and these are generally young people), more often, old conditions determine their actions, and then, for the reasons given, this takes place in an irregular and distorted manner. In a society, such as capitalism, which is changing (albeit, in its superficial aspects) very rapidly, this means that the character of most people never catches up with their lives. They seem destined to be misfits, whose responses are forever out of date.

In order to allow for the irrationality which comes from this time lag, I would introduce into Marx's conceptual framework the idea of character structure, understood as the internalization of early behavior patterns, as organized habit. Our ideas and attitudes are more a product of what we do than of what we see or hear, and especially of what we do regularly from earliest years. Transformed into character structure, these patterns become a way of being that gets impressed on each new activity. Such characterological hardening of the arteries derives whence character derives, but is a product apart, exercising a relatively independent influence on how one will respond to future events and conditions.

The idea of character structure does little violence to Marx's basic framework; the interactions he describes go on as before, except that something now mediates between conditions and response, between needs and wants, between objective and subjective interests, between activity and consciousness, something into and through which the one must be translated to become the other. As such, character structure is both a product of alienation and, with the real conditions of life, a contributing cause of alienated activity. With the introduction of this new factor we can better explain why workers so often find their inclinations in conflict with the demands of the current situation, why they consistently misunderstand and are incapable of responding to it in ways that would promote their interests. We can better explain, too, why people today are driven to act in ways that mights have been rational a generation ago, in a war, a depression, or a boom which existed then but no longer does. The concept of character structure also helps account for the proletariat's "fear of freedom" and their submissiveness before authority, which are, after all, simply attempts to repeat in the future what has been done in the past. Finally, character structure helps to explain the distorting sentiments of nation, race, and religion, as well as the worker's pessimism regarding a better form of society and his own role in helping to bring it about by treating them as expressions of early behavior patterns that, internalized within the individual, have acquired a dynamic and power of their own.

Thus, whenever the system has been in crisis, when it was in the workers' interests to construct new solutions, their character structure has disposed them to go on seeking old nostrums, where they can continue to act as they have been and know how to. To be sure, new social and economic conditions did develop with the growth of imperialism, workers' movements were often cursed with poor leadership at critical moments of their history, and capitalists have sought to exacerbate national and racial antagonisms—all this, as Marxists rightly maintain, has served to inhibit the development of proletarian class consciousness. What those who accept Marx's analysis have seldom admitted is that the character structure of most workers has also been at fault. With the introduction of this concept into Marx's framework, workers must be viewed not only as prisoners of their conditions, but of themselves, of their own character structures which are the product of previous conditions.[42]

VI

The introduction of the concept of character structure into Marx's scheme, substituting a sense of retarded rationality for the sense of irrationality toward which so much of this study seemed to point, has great significance for a socialist strategy. If, as part of their alienation, workers cannot react to their conditions no matter how bad they get, in a rational manner, then all efforts to attain widespread class consciousness are doomed to failure. They are, that is, unless some manner can be found to affect their character structure during its formative years, to make sure that the behavior patterns internalized there never develop, or, more to the point, never acquire the degree of durability they now have. Looked at in this way, the focal point of a socialist strategy must be those conditions which most affect the young. For it is possible to alter the character structure of workers by fighting against its construction, by counteracting the disorienting influence of the family, school, and church, whatever in fact makes it difficult for the individual once he/she becomes an adult to make an objective assessment of his/her oppression and to act against it.

The concrete aims of radical activity, on the basis of this analysis, are to get teenage and even younger members of the working class to question the existing order along with all its symbols and leaders, to loosen generalized habits of respect and obedience, to oppose whatever doesn't make sense in terms of their needs as individuals and as members of a group, to conceive of the enemy as the capitalist system and the small group of men who control it, to articulate their hopes for a better life, to participate in successful protest actions no matter how small the immediate objective, and to create a sense of community and solidarity of all those in revolt. The purpose is to overturn (or, more accurately, to undermine) the specific barriers that have kept past generations of workers from becoming class conscious. Full class consciousness can only occur later on the basis of adult experiences, particularly in the mode of production. Making allowances for exceptions on both ends of the scale, what can be achieved now is essentially a predisposition to respond to the conditions of life in a rational manner, what might be called a state of preconsciousness. Capitalism willing, and capitalism is periodically willing, revolutionary effects will follow.

To insist on the necessity of altering character structure is not to argue that only new men and women can create a new society, but to reaffirm that changes in both people and conditions are needed for a socialist revolution to occur. The opposition between idealism (where people are held responsible for transforming society) and vulgar materialism (where conditions are) is, in any case, a false one. There is a constant, many-sided interaction going on, and the problem has always been how to capture (and conceptualize) the dynamics of this process so as to participate in it more effectively.

The conditions that now exist in the United States (more so than in other capitalist countries) are exceptionally well suited to the strategy I have been urging. In stressing the importance of social conditions in determining what people are and how they act, Marxists have not given sufficient attention to the fact that some conditions have a greater effect on what people are and others on how they act. This is chiefly because the people referred to in the two instances are not the same. Since we acquire the greatest part of our character when young, it is conditions which most affect the young that most affect what people are (or what they are a generation later when the once young have become adults); whereas adults are the subject of conditions, generally more extreme, which are said to affect how people act.

Recent events have thrown up a number of important new conditions which exercise their predominant effect on what people are. Among these are the Vietnam War in which the young were expected to fight as well as to believe, a pause in the cold war and with it in anticommunist ideology, an increasingly evident racism that goes counter to taught ideals, the hunger and suffering seen daily on television, frequent disruption of community services and schools, growing unemployment among the newly trained and among incoming skilled workers of all sorts, the pill and drugs, and the new obscurantist puritanism that has arisen to combat both. In each case, a pattern of behavior in which the older generation grew up and which, through its transformation into character structure, contributed significantly to a passive acceptance of their lot is changing into behavior that in one or more respects opposes adolescents to the existing social and political system. It remains for socialists, especially young socialists, to make the most of these conditions, not to instigate a youth revolt (whatever that is) or to create an auxiliary of the working class, but to help alter the character structure of the next generation of workers.

It is not possible for a paper that argues for a particular strategy to canvass all possible tactics that can be used to advance it. The choice of tactics requires detailed study of the time, place, and parties involved. In particular, one's chosen audience should be carefully studied in terms of the different barriers to class consciousness listed earlier in this paper, so that an educational effort can focus on where it is needed. Still, the strategy advocated here does suggest that the effort some radical groups are putting into high school "organizing" and publishing high school papers should be greatly expanded, especially in working-class districts, even at the expense of other activities in poor communities and among adult workers. Also, insofar as the aim is understood in the negative sense of breaking up existing behavior patterns, the hippies and Yippies—by holding up established ways and virtues to contempt and ridicule—may have as much to contribute as the more orthodox forms of protest. The means of keeping young people open to a rational calculus of advantages later in life may be quite different from those required to help them make the calculus itself. What exactly these means are needs further investigation, but for the moment I would not rule out any form of protest that increases or clarifies young people's discontent and their opposition to established authority.[43]

If the "revolution" is, as most socialists will admit, at a minimum decades away, then it is proper—given the conservative function of character structure and its greater malleability early in life—that we begin preparing for it among workers who will be around and relevant at the time. Samuel Gompers and his successors in the AFL-CIO sacrificed the revolutionary potential of the working class to the immediate needs of real workers; today, paradoxically, socialists with their limited means must pay less attention to real workers, certainly to workers over thirty (thirty-five?), so that they can help to develop a revolutionary working class.

Notes

1. Instances of such explanations can be found in Karl Marx, *Letters to Dr. Kugelmann* (London, 1941), pp. 107, 135; Karl Marx and Friedrich Engels, *Selected Correspondence,* ed. and trans. Dona Torr (London, 1941), pp. 249, 256-57, 350, 502; Karl Marx and Friedrich Engels, *Selected Writings I* (Moscow, 1951), p. 249; A. Lozovsky, *Marx and the Trade Unions* (New York, 1935), pp. 38, 58-59.

2. Karl Marx, *On Colonialism* (Moscow, n.d.), p. 201. See, too, *Selected Correspondence,* pp. 280-81.

3. Friedrich Engels, *Briefe an Bebel* (Berlin, 1958), pp. 82-83. See, too, Lozovsky, *Marx and the Trade Unions,* p. 61.

4. Karl Marx, "Eighteenth of Brumaire," *Selected Writings I,* p. 225.

5. Karl Marx and Friedrich Engels, *The Holy Family,* trans. R. Dixon (Moscow, 1956), p. 53.

6. Karl Marx speaks of the proletariat on one occasion as "that misery conscious of its spiritual and physical misery, that dehumanization conscious of its dehumanization and therefore self-abolishing." *Ibid.,* p. 52.

7. C. Wright Mills, *The Marxists* (New York, 1962), p. 115.

8. George Lukacs, *History and Class Consciousness,* trans. Rodney Livingstone (Cambridge, Mass., 1971), p. 73.

9. V.I. Lenin, "What is To Be Done?" *Selected Works,* 12 vols. (Moscow, n.d.), II: 77.

10. *Ibid.,* p. 53.

11. *Ibid.,* 88-89. For a useful survey of other interpretations of class consciousness see H. Wolpe's "Some Problems Concerning Revolutionary Consciousness," *The Socialist Register 1970,* ed. Ralph Miliband and John Saville (London, 1970), pp. 251-80.

12. According to Marx, "The contradiction between the individuality of each separate proletarian and labor, the conditions of life forced upon him, become evident to him himself, for he is sacrificed from youth upwards and, within his own class, has no chance for arriving at the conditions which would place him in the other class." Karl Marx and Friedrich Engels, *The German Ideology,* trans. R. Pascal (London, 1942), p. 78.

13. Thorstein Veblen, "The Economics of Karl Marx: II," *The Place of Science in Modern Civilization and Other Essays* (New York, 1961), p. 441.

14. Friedrich Engels, "Preface," Marx and Engels, *The Communist Manifesto,* trans. Samuel Moore (Chicago, 1945), p. 5.

15. *Holy Family* op. cit., p. 52 (my emphasis). For a discussion of the workers' alienation, see B. Ollman, *Alienation: Marx's Conception of Man in Capitalist Society* (Cambridge, 1971).

16. Though encased in another set of concepts, this is one of the main conclusions to emerge from Marx's discussion of natural and species powers in the *Economic and Philosophic Manuscripts of 1844* (henceforth referred to as *1844 Manuscripts*), trans. Martin Milligan (Moscow, 1959), esp. pp. 74-76, 156-58.

17. Martin Nicholaus, "The Unknown Marx," *The New Left Reader,* ed. Carl Oglesby (New York, 1969), pp. 105-6.

18. *Letters to Dr. Kugelmann, op. cit.,* p. 107.

19. *Selected Correspondence, op. cit.,* p. 118.

20. *1844 Manuscripts, op. cit.,* p. 71.

21. Karl Marx, *Capital III* (Moscow, 1959), p. 128.

22. *Ibid.,* p. 135.

23. Karl Marx, "Zur Judenfrage," Marx and Engels, *Werke I* (Berlin, 1959), p. 366.

24. *1844 Manuscripts, op. cit.,* p. 68.

25. Karl Marx and Friedrich Engels, *Deutsche Ideologie* in *Werke III* (Berlin, 1960), p. 395.

26. *German Ideology, op. cit.,* p. 58.

27. Karl Marx, *Letters to Americans,* trans. Leonard E. Mins (New York, 1953), p. 124.

28. Karl Marx, "Wage Labor and Capital," *Selected Writings I,* p. 91.

29. Karl Marx, *Capital I,* trans. Samuel Moore and Edward Aveling (Moscow, 1958), pp. 279 ff.

31. *Communist Manifesto, op. cit.,* p. 28.

32. *On Colonialism, op. cit.,* p. 301. In "Civil War in France" (1871), however, Marx still treats the German and French proletariat as if they were devoid of strong nationalist sentiment.

33. *Selected Correspondence, op. cit.,* p. 461.

34. *Ibid.,* p. 147. In 1863, Marx wrote to Engels, "How soon the English workers will free themselves from their apparent bourgeois infection one must wait and see." Engels had just written him, "All the revolutionary energy has faded practically entirely away from the English proletariat and the English proletariat is declaring his complete agreement with the rule of the bourgeoisie." *Ibid.*

35. Frederick Lessner, "Before 1848 and After," *Reminiscences of Marx and Engels,* no editor, (Moscow, n.d.), p. 50.

36. On one occasion, Marx maintains England, the United States and Holland are countries where socialism might come by "peaceful means." H. Gerth, ed., *The First International: Minutes of the Hague Congress of 1872* (Madison, 1958), p. 236.

37. Friedrich Engels, "Preface to English Edition," *Capital I, op. cit.,* p. 6.

38. *Letters to Americans, op. cit.,* p. 61.

39. T. W. Adorno, *The Authoritarian Personality* (New York, 1950). Marx had some conception of this failing as it applied to German workers. Of them, he says, "Here where the workers are under the thumb of bureaucracy from childhood on and believe in authority, in the constituted authorities, it is a foremost task to teach them to walk by themselves." Lozovsky, *Marx and the Trade Unions, op. cit.,* p. 42. In the same year, 1868, he writes to Engels, "For the German working class the most necessary thing of all is that it should cease conducting its agitation by kind permission of the higher authorities. A race so schooled in bureaucracy must go through a complete course of self-help." *Selected Correspondence, op. cit.,* p. 249.

40. Erich Fromm, *Fear of Freedom* (London, 1942), esp. pp. 1-19.

41. For an illuminating discussion of the role of sexual repression in helping to produce such irrationality, see Wilhelm Reich, *Mass Psychology of Fascism,* trans. Theodor P. Wolfe (New York, 1946), esp. pp. 19-28, 122-43.

42. Useful discussion of the concept of character structure can be found in Reich's *Character Analysis,* trans. T.P. Wolfe (New York, 1961), esp. 22 ff; and in Hans Gerth and C. Wright Mills, *Character and Social Structure* (London, 1961), pt. 2. I discuss this notion more fully in the last article in this book. Another attempt to revise Marx's conceptual scheme is found in Marcuse's distinction (though barely suggested in Marx's writings) between "true" and "false" needs. *One-Dimensional Man* (Boston, 1964), p. 6. Rather than having to overcome or undermine barriers rooted in character structure, Marcuse states the problem in terms of a struggle between two kinds of needs. In focusing on this broad distinction, however, the change-producing levers in human personality are disassembled. The same reconstruction leads Marcuse to overemphasize those elements in the population (particularly students) in whom liberating needs are dominant as agents of revolutionary change.

43. For further discussion of some of the tactics advocated in this paper, see Reich's "What is Class Consciousness?" *Sex-Pol: Essays 1929-1934, ed. Lee* Baxendall (New York, 1971). Though Reich devotes more attention to the problem of promoting class consciousness in adults than I feel is justified by his analysis of character structure, his stress on youth is unique in the serious literature on this subject. Reich's important contribution to Marxism in this area is summarized in my article, "The Marxism of Wilhelm Reich: Or the Social Function of Sexual Repression," republished as chapter 7 of this book.

2.

Marx's Use of "Class"

What are the classes into which Marx places the inhabitants of capitalist society? In *Capital,* he says that in developed capitalist society there is only a capitalist and a proletarian class.[1] The former, who are also called the bourgeoisie, are described in the *Communist Manifesto* as "owners of the means of social production and employers of wage labor." In the same place, the proletariat are said to be "the class of modern wage-laborers who, having no means of production of their own, are reduced to selling their labor-power in order to live."[2] But, though Marx believed European capitalism was sufficiently advanced for a Communist revolution to occur, he asserts elsewhere in *Capital* that three classes—capitalists, proletarians, and landowners— "consititute in their mutual opposition the framework of modern society."[3] For Marx, the landowner class is composed of owners of large tracts of land and is almost always feudal in origin. Has the standard by which Marx assesses class membership altered?[4]

Even where the basis for distinguishing classes appears to be a group's relations to the prevailing mode of production, the question is not the simple one of whether there are two or three classes, for Marx applies this label to several other economic units. Two outstanding examples are the petty bourgeoisie and the peasants. The former are small shopkeepers who own no means of production or, sometimes, a very tiny morsel, and employ at most a few workers; and the latter are the owners of small plots of land which they farm themselves. Their respective relations to the prevailing mode of production in capitalism are not those of the capitalists, the proletariat, or the landowners. Where, then, does Marx place small businessmen and peasants when he talks of society being made up of three classes? Also, it is not easy to draw the line between these classes. At what point does a small businessman stop being petty bourgeois and become a capitalist? How much land does a peasant have to own before he becomes a landowner?

Should we admit as classes all the groups mentioned, there are still other elements in the population that are difficult to place. Are farm laborers, for instance, proletarians or peasants? The inclusion of rural wage workers as prolerariat is required to give validity to Marx's claim that the proletariat contains the vast majority of people in capitalist society.[5] Marx quotes figures which show that factory workers were not a majority in England, and he must have been aware that this was even more true for Germany and France at the time.[6] On at least one occasion, Marx states explicitly that farm laborers are proletarians; yet, the whole weight of his treatment of the proletariat as workers in industry argues against this.[7] And, whenever Marx particularizes, it is of industrial workers that he speaks.

Beyond this, there is an indication that Marx sometimes extends the class of proletarians to include small-holding peasants as well, as when he states, "The owning peasant does not belong to the proletariat, and there where he does belong to it by his position, he does not believe that he belongs to it."[8] Marx's point is that because of his indebtedness to various capitalists, the mortgage on his property, etc., the peasant does not really own his plot of land, and is actually working for someone else. Bringing the peasantry into the proletariat may help account for Marx's division of capitalist society into two main classes; the landowners and the petty bourgeoisie, we can assume, have been swept under the rug of "capitalist." Most often in his writings, however, the peasants are referred to as a separate class whose distinctive qualities are aptly summed up in the phrase, "class of barbarians."[9]

Marx's contradictory attempts to categorize the intelligentsia is extremely revealing of the problems encountered in a straight economic division of society. Usually, he speaks of doctors, lawyers, journalists, professors, writers, and priests as "the ideological representatives and spokesmen" of the bourgeoisie.[10] Referring to petty bourgeois politicians and writers, Marx explains that what makes them representative of this class "is the fact that in their minds they do not get beyond the limits which the latter do not get beyond in life, that they are consequently driven, theoretically, to the same problem and solutions to which material interest and social position drive the latter practically."[11]

The relationship between the intelligentsia and the capitalist class is further clarified where Marx says the ideologists of a class are those "who make the perfecting of the illusion of the class about itself their chief sources of livelihood." This, he claims, is based on a division of labor inside the class between mental and physical work.[12] Though it would appear to be general, Marx carefully restricts his own application of this principle to the bourgeoisie. From comments such as these, the intelligentsia and the capitalists stand forth as brothers, similar at the core, who are merely specializing in different areas of capitalist "work."[13]

Though they are usually subsumed under the capitalist class, this does not preclude Marx, on occasion, from ascribing to the intelligentsia a status, not just as a class, but as a cluster of classes. In *Capital,* Volume I, for example, he speaks of them as the "ideological classes."[14] If Marx sometimes puts the intelligentsia among the capitalists and sometimes puts them on their own, he is obviously changing his criteria for deciding what constitutes a class.

Besides referring to capitalists, proletarians, landowners, petty bourgeoisie, and peasants, "class" is also used to refer to groups carved out of society on another basis than their relations to the mode of production. Such groups frequently contain members from two or more of the economic classes dealt with above. What Marx calls the "ideological class," for example, seems to be based on the role these people play in society at large, rather than in production. The ruling classes, another social unit found in Marx's writings, appears to have been marked out by the same measure: those individuals who take part in running the country or who help decide how it should be run are its members.[15] In Great Britain, the ruling classes are said to be composed of the "aristocracy," "moneyocracy," and "millocracy."[16] Thus, they include both capitalists and landowners, most of whom belong to the aristocracy. The "millocracy" refers to owners of factories which produce materials for clothing; and the "moneyocracy," or "finance aristocracy," refers to bankers and the like, who earn their entrance into the capitalist class as hirers of wage labor and by virtue of their monetary dealings with industrialists.[17]

Marx also speaks of a "lower middle class" which includes "the small manufacturers, the shopkeeper, the artisan, the peasant."[18] This class, it appears, picks up some members from all the economic classes mentioned earlier. What is the criterion by which Marx determines who belongs to the lower middle class? Judging by its membership, it could be income, power, or even distance from the extremes of involvement in the class struggle.

Elsewhere, the "middle classes" or "those who stand between the workman on the one hand and the capitalist and landlord on the other," are described as constantly growing in number and maintaining themselves increasingly out of revenues. They are also said to be a burden on workers and a social and political support for the power of the "upper ten thousand."[19] Here, it sounds as if it is officials of various sorts whom Marx has in mind in speaking of the "middle class."

One last example: what are we to make of the group Marx calls the "dangerous class," otherwise known as the *Lumpenproletariat,* which is said to be composed of "the social scum, that passively rotting mass thrown off by the lowest layers of old society"?[20] It is spoken of elsewhere as "a recruiting ground for thieves and criminals of all kinds, living on the crumbs of society, people without a definite trade, vagabonds, people without a hearth or a home."[21] By what standard does Marx judge membership in this class? It seems to be a gathering place for all the unemployed poor, though Marx's term, "dangerous class," suggests a certain action criterion as well. The *Lumpenproletariat* sell their services to the bourgeoisie, who use them as strikebreakers, labor spies, and fighters against the workers in times of revolution. Such are the actions which make them the "dangerous class."[22]

The plurality of criteria Marx uses in constructing classes is reminiscent of present day confusion on this subject. It is not enough to argue—as some have—that Marx's idea of class develops over time, for many of the complications we have drawn attention to are found in the same work or writings of the same period. If readers of this essay will check the citations which correspond to my footnotes 1, 3, 9, 14, and 17, they will see a sampling of the various and apparently contradictory uses of "class" in the volumes of *Capital*. The conclusion remains that, for a variety of purposes, Marx divides society up in as many different ways, speaking of the parts in each case as "classes."

Any attempt to explain Marx's practice must start with the admission that Marx uses this term loosely, often putting it forward as a synonym for "group," "faction," or "layer." This was only in keeping with the imprecise use of "class" which Rolf Dahrendorf informs us was typical of this period.[23] Where Marx speaks of "ruling classes," "groups" or "factions" could be substituted for "classes" without any alteration of the meaning. Marx himself uses "ruling class" and "ruling faction" interchangeably in one instance to refer to the same people.[24] "Groups" could also be substituted for "classes" without any change of meaning in the expression "ideological classes"; and either "group" or "layer" would serve for "class" where Marx talks of the "dangerous class." With all due allowance made for loose word usage, however, Marx cannot escape the more serious accusation of having a litter of standards for class membership and of changing them without prior warning.

The implications of this disorder for Marx's class analysis of society should not be carried too far, since Marx's tripartite division of society into capitalists, proletarians and landowners is the prevalent one, and it is also the classification most in keeping with his other theories. Hence, we may in fairness dub it the "Marxist system of classes." The other classes mentioned can be made more or less consistent with this division on the basis of hints Marx drops but nowhere develops. These hints are found in his expressions "subdivisions of classes" and "transition classes."[25] The former helps us comprehend occupational, income, and functional units within the three great classes based on differing relations to the prevailing mode of production. Millocracy, moneyocracy, and shipbuilders are all subdivisions of the capitalist class, just as skilled and unskilled workers are sub-divisions of the proletariat.

The concept of "transition class" can be used to justify leaving out of the more generalized presentations of the class system, those groups which are in the process of disappearing. Small-holding peasants and petty bourgeoisie are among the classes Marx sees disappearing in his own day.[26] A stumbling block to taking this way out is that "transition class" is a highly subjective concept even within Marx's own analytical frame-work; any class, after all, can be viewed as passing out of the picture, depending on the time span under consideration. We saw Marx claim that, in fully developed capitalism, only a capitalist and a proletarian class exist; therefore, if this is the period one has in mind, all other classes are transitional. After the proletarian revolution, however, the capitalist class, too, disappears; and, when communism arrives, the proletariat as well dissolves into the community. All references to "transitional classes," therefore, if they are to convey any meaning at all, must make explicit the time period under consideration.

Marx's only attempt to present a connected account of class appears at the end of Volume III of *Capital,* but unfortunately, he never completed it.[27] From these few paragraphs, we learn that wage laborers, capitalists and landowners constitute the three large classes of modern society. Yet, he admits that, even in England where capitalism is most developed, "the stratification of classes does not appear in its pure form. Middle and intermediate strata even here obliterate lines of demarcation everywhere (although incomparably less in rural districts, than in the cities)." He believes that developments in capitalist society are speedily reducing all such strata into the capitalist or proletarian class. The landowners, too, are shortly to go the same way. With the growing divorce between the means of production and labor, Marx sees all workers eventually becoming wage laborers. As for capitalists, the trend toward increasing concentration in industry enlarges the holdings of some just as it forces others into the proletariat.

Marx replies to his own question, "What constitutes a class?" with another, "What makes wage laborers, capitalists, and landowners constitute the three great social classes?" The fragment he left behind contains only the first part of his answer: "At first glance—the identity of revenues and sources of revenues. There are three great social groups whose numbers, the individuals forming them, live on wages, profit, and ground rent, respectively, on the realization of their labor-power, their capital, and their landed property." Marx recognizes that this standard also enables physicians and officials to be spoken of as "classes," "for they belong to two distinct groups receiving their revenues from one and the same source. The same would also be true of the infinite fragmentations of interest and rank into which the division of social labor splits laborers as well as capitalists and landlords—the latter, e.g., into owners of vineyards, farm owners, owners of forests, mine owners and owners of fisheries." Here the manuscript breaks off. When concentrating on the problem of class, Marx takes a stand against affixing this label to all kinds of social and economic groups which is something he himself was guilty of.

From our study of Marx's use of the term "class," we can suggest how he would have finished this account. The qualifications for constituting a class that capitalists possess and physicians do not are as follows: the capitalists have a direct operating relationship to the mode of production, while the physicians do not; the capitalists have distinct economic interests (the size of their profit) based on these relations which place them in conflict with the proletariat and landowners, the other two groups directly involved in capitalist production, while the economic interests of physicians—though leaning toward those of the capitalists in present society—are really compatible with the interests of any of the three great classes; the capitalists are conscious of their uniqueness as a class with interests that are opposed to those of the two other main classes in society, while physicians, even if they are conscious of themselves as a distinct group, do not view their interests as being opposed to those of others; the capitalists are organized in one or more political parties, which work to promote their interests, while physicians—despite their pressure group activity—have no such organization; and, finally, capitalists exhibit a general cultural affinity, a way of life and set of social values, which mark them off from the proletariat and the landowners, while physicians as a group have no such distinguishing features.[28]

A thread which runs through all of these criteria is the hostility a class displays for its opponent classes. Whether in work, politics, or culture, an essential defining characteristic of each class is its antagonism in this same sphere to others. For the capitalists, this can be seen in their hostile relations to the workers and the landowners at the point of production, in their political struggle to promote their interests at the expense of these classes, and in the cultural sideswipes they are forever directing against them. Of the bourgeoisie, Marx says, "The separate individuals form a class in so far as they have to carry on a common battle against another class: otherwise they are on hostile terms with each other as competitors."[29] This common battle is fought on as many fronts as there are criteria for constituting a class. On each front, it is the fact of battle itself which earns each side its label. Hence, Marx calls a society where only one class exists, such as occurs after the proletarian revolution, a classless society. Without an enemy, the antagonistic nature of the proletariat disappears and with it the designation "class." "Who is the enemy?" is a question that can be asked whenever Marx uses "class."

The secret of class in Marxism lies hidden in the socialist philosopher's conceptualization of it as a complex rather than a simple relation. In "class" Marx conflates a number of social ties (relations between groups based on various standards) which are generally treated separately. He views them as interacting parts of an organic whole, the society in question, such that development in any one necessarily affects (more or less, sooner or later) the others. The mistake made in virtually all treatments of this subject, a pit we could only climb out of after falling in ourselves, is to seek after a unidimensional meaning. But, by this maneuver, class is distorted to the number of major elements left unreported. The various criteria for establishing class, therefore, simply reflect the wealth of social relations that Marx sees bound up in it.

Only in advanced capitalism is it possible for a group to qualify as a class on all the criteria I have listed. Hence, Marx's assertion that class is a "product of the bourgeoisie."[30] To take just one instance, the absence of effective communication in earlier periods inhibits the exchange of information and contacts which is essential for class formation. An awareness of common interests as well as co-ordinated action to promote them are impossibilities for people living in scattered communities.

But if class is a product of capitalism, how can Marx speak of all history as the history of class struggle or refer—as he frequently does—to the distinguishing social divisions of previous epochs as "classes"?[31] To answer this query is also to demonstrate how he was able to refer to so many groups in capitalist society as "classes." It is simply that Marx applies this label if a group measures up to only some of the above standards. Which these are varies with his purpose in making the particular classification. This is the nub of the explanation for Marx's apparent confusion over class. If we want to discover the relevant criteria in each case, we must follow up our question, "Who is the enemy?" with one, "Why are they the enemy?" Nothing that has been said absolves Marx from the accusation of using "class" loosely, but it should help us comprehend what lies behind this usage.[32]

Whether it was proper of Marx to apply the label "class" on the basis of only a few of the relevant criteria is open to dispute, but that he could not wait for all of them to be satisfied before using this term is clear. Otherwise, he would have defined himself out of the running, for even the capitalists and the proletariat are occasionally seen to be without some of the requisite attributes. He says of the proletariat for example, "Thus the mass is already a class in opposition to capital, but not yet a class for itself."[33] The missing ingredient is class consciousness, the proletariat's comprehension of their life situation and their acceptance of the interests and enemies which accrue to it.

Elsewhere, Marx suggests the proletariat are not a class, because they lack a class wide political organization. In a letter to Kugelmann, Marx speaks of his program for the Geneva Conference of the First International as helping "the organization of the workers into a class."[34] In the *Communist Manifesto*, he specifically links this up with the formation of a political party.[35] Insofar as class consciousness remains the achievement of a few, and before such a party exists, the proletariat, even in

the most advanced capitalistic societies, lack two major qualifications for constituting a class.[36] A similar breakdown could be
made of the capitalists, and, in fact of all the groups Marx calls
"classes."[37]

There is a still more formidable objection to Marx's use of
"class." Besides changing his standards when moving from one
group to the next, the same group—as indicated by its popular
name—may be given its measure by a variety of standards.
Depending on his purpose, Marx may mean by the "proletariat"
all wage earners or "those who work," the simplest and largest net
of all.[38] Or he may mean those who pass one or any few of the
income, cultural, political, and social tests that have been listed.
With the shift in criteria, there is a shift, often of huge
proportions, in the number of people referred to. This explains,
of course, why some groups—peasants, rural workers, intellectuals, and shopkeepers being the prize examples—are sometimes
found in one class and sometimes in another. This objection
might have proved fatal for those wishing to comprehend Marx's
views about his contemporaries if certain trends were not
apparent in his use of class labels. Generally, Marx's comments
on the proletariat only apply to industrial wage earners, and his
descriptions of capitalists are usually meant for large merchants
and bankers as well as for the owners of the means of production.
These are the chief characters in Marx's realistic drama, *Capital.*

This brings us to the next and, for many, obvious question,
"How useful is Marx's concept of 'class'?" But, if our statement of
what Marx meant by "class"—garnered from his actual use of the
term—is correct, this question simply masks another more
profound one concerning the utility of Marxism itself. By
conceptualizing a unity of apparently distinct social relations,
"class" is inextricably bound up with the reality of the unity so
posited, that is, with the truth of Marx's own analysis. For the
interwoven criteria Marx used for understanding what constitutes a class represents the result of his empirical social studies.

It is only, in other words, because Marx found groups in his
society with different relations to the prevailing mode of
production, sets of opposing economic interests based on these
relations, a corresponding cultural and moral differentiation, a
growing consciousness among these groups of their uniqueness
and accompanying interests, and—resulting from this conscious-

ness—the development of social and political organizations which promote these interests that he constructed his peculiar concept of "class." Of overriding importance is that "class" in Marxism is not just a label for groups carved out of society on the basis of a discernable set of standards but expresses as well the involved interactions which Marx believed he uncovered between these standards.[39] When critics, such as R.N. Carew-Hunt, therefore, ask complainingly for Marx's definition of "class," they are asking, in effect, for the latter's analysis of capitalist class society; and it is understandable that Marx had difficulty in reconstituting this analysis in the form of a definition for "class."[40]

For those who accept Marx's version of capitalist social relations, the key concepts in which it is couched are second nature; "class" serves as a necessary vehicle for conveying what Marx taught. For those who do not share Marx's analysis, or something close to it, using his concept "class" can only distort what they have to say. We are not interested here in the utility of this concept as an aid in presenting Marxism when the purpose is to criticize the doctrine. Nor should our conclusion be taken as an argument against using the word "class" in some non-Marxist sense, as long as this is made clear. One can define the word "class" to suit practically any end, but it is altogether another matter to use Marx's concept "class" in ways other than he did himself.

Words are the property of language, but concepts—and "class" is both a word and a concept—belong to a particular philosophy (way of viewing the world) and share in all of the latter's uniqueness. As a concept, "class" cannot be detached from the structured knowledge it seeks to express and of which it is, in the last analysis, an integral part. Does Marx provide an adequate account of social relations in capitalism? It is on the answer to this question that the utility of Marx's concept of "class" hinges.[41]

As for those followers of Marx who try to construct a strict definition of "class" or of any particular class, who begin their studies with such definitions, and who often treat what class an individual or group (e.g., the managers) fall into as a problem to be solved, the preceeding analysis would make clear how far their approach has wandered from Marx'x own practice. For

Marx, the meaning of "proletariat," "capitalist," etc., develops as the analysis of these classes, especially of their interaction with one another, proceeds. Further, the meaning of these concepts along with the number of people included in each class varies somewhat with the problem under consideration and the focus (width or narrowness) with which he views it. Consequently, if class and the different particular classes are and cannot help but be some of the elements with which Marx begins his inquiry into capitalism, as complex relations which emerge through the course of his study, they are also versions of what is found. The distinction is well captured in E.P. Thompson's claim that "class is not this or that part of the machine, but the way the machine works once it is set in motion."[42] To offer a strict definition of "class" where brief, relative and conditional indications are called for undermines the effort to grasp the larger social movement within the developed notion of "class." It also illustrates the distance which separates what is popularly known as "class analysis" from Marx's dialectical method.

Notes

1. Karl Marx, *Capital* (Moscow, 1957), II, 348.
2. Karl Marx and Friedrich Engels, *The Communist Manifesto,* trans. Samuel Moore (Chicago, 1945), p. 12.
3. Marx, *Capital* (Moscow, 1959), III, p. 604.
4. The landowners are included as one of the "three great social classes" mentioned in Marx's Introduction to the *Critique of Political Economy* and are referred to as a separate class in a number of other places ("Introduction," *A Contribution to the Critique of Political Economy,* trans. N. I. Stone [Chicago, 1904], p. 305). In "The Eighteenth Brumaire of Louis Bonaparte," however, Marx treats them as a section of the bourgeoisie, claiming that "large landed property, despite its feudal coquetry and pride of race, has been rendered thoroughly bourgeois by the developments of modern society" (Marx, "The Eighteenth Brumaire of Louis Bonaparte" in Marx and Engels, *Selected Writings* [Moscow, 1951], I, 248).
5. Karl Marx and Friedrich Engels, *The German Ideology,* trans. R. Pascal (London, 1942), p. 69; Karl Marx, *Theories of Surplus Value I,* ed. S. Ryazanskaya, trans. Emile Burns (Moscow, 1969), p. 166. He also refers to the proletariat as "the mass of the people," in Karl Marx, *Theories of Surplus Value II,* ed. S. Ryazanskaya (Moscow, 1968), p. 115.
6. *Theories of Surplus Value I,* p. 201; for the relevant statistics on Germany, see Edward Bernstein, *Evolutionary Socialism,* trans. Edith Harvey (London, 1909), p. 106.
7. Marx says, "The capitalist tenant has ousted the peasant, and the real tiller of the soil is just as much a proletarian, a wage worker, as is the urban worker" (H. Meyer, "Marx on Bakunin: A Neglected Text," *Etudes de Marxologie,* ed. M. Rubel, (October, 1959), p. 109.
8. *Ibid.,* p. 108.
9. Marx, *Capital,* III, p. 793.
10. Marx, "The Class Struggles in France," *Selected Writings,* I, p. 129.
11. "Eighteenth Brumaire," *op. cit., p. 250.*
12. *German Ideology,* pp. 39, 40.
13. In the *Communist Manifesto,* the intelligentsia are referred to as the "paid wage-laborers" of the bourgeoisie (*Communist Manifesto,* p. 16). Marx's terminology here suggests a strong likeness between the intelligentsia and the proletariat. Nonetheless, the context makes it clear that their real place even here is within the capitalist class.
14. Marx, *Capital,* trans. Samuel Moore and Edward Aveling (Moscow, 1958), I, p. 446.
15. Of this class, Marx says, "the class, which is the ruling material force of society, is at the same time its ruling intellectual force" (*German Ideology,* p. 39). Though Marx uses the expression "ruling class" in ways which suggest a more functional definition, this statement does serve notice where the real power of any ruling class lies for Marx.
16. Marx, "The Future Results of British Rule in India," *Selected Writings,* I, p. 321.

17. Elsewhere, the latter group, or some part of it—the big money lenders and usurers—is labeled a "class of parasites" (*Capital,* III, p. 532).

18. *Communist Manifesto,* p. 27.

19. *Theories of Surplus Value,* II, p. 573.

20. *Communist Manifesto.*

21. "Class Struggles in France," *Selected Writings I,* p. 142.

22. Engels, it is worth noting, has even more referents for "class" than Marx, especially in *Germany: Revolution and Counter Revolution.*

23. Rolf Dahrendorf, *Class and Class Conflict in Industrial Society,* trans. by the author (London, 1959), p. 4.

24. "Class Struggles in France," *Selected Writings,* I, p. 130.

25. Marx, "The Bourgeoisie and the Counter-Revolution," *Selected Writings,* I, p.63; "Eighteenth Brumaire," *Selected Writings,* I, p. 253.

26. *Communist Manifesto,* p.16. Many groups, such as the petty bourgeoisie, fall into both of the above categories; they are a subdivision of the capitalist class and, for the period in which Marx is writing, a transition class as well.

27. Unless otherwise signified, what follows comes from *Capital III,* p. 862-63.

28. Whether the culture, way of life, and social values of capitalists really differ more from those of other sections of the population than the equivalent attributes of physicians is not at issue. All that concerns us is that Marx thought they did, for this belief was an important element in his construction of classes.

29. *German Ideology,* pp. 48-9.

30. *Ibid.,* p. 77. This is not to say that every capitalist society has a fully developed system of classes. Marx refers to the United States as a place "where although classes exist, they have not yet become fixed, but continually change and interchange their elements in constant flux" ("Eighteenth Brumaire," *Selected Writings I,* p. 232). Marx never adequately explains this exception.

31. He says, "The history of all hitherto existing society is the history of class struggles" (*Communist Manifesto,* p. 12). In a footnote to the 1888 English edition, Engels qualifies this where he says, "that is, all written history." He points out that in 1848 Marx and he did not know about the existence of primitive communism (*ibid.*). In any case, Engels' qualification does not affect our use of this statement.

32. To make his plurality of standards explicit, which we would have liked, would have made it necessary for Marx to tell more than he "had time for." It is simply that the requirements of getting on with his task of the moment forced him to subsume a great deal of the relations he was treating. On the one occasion when he sought to sketch out the main relations in "class," death intervened.

33. Marx, *The Poverty of Philosophy* (Moscow, n.d.), p. 195.

34. Marx, *Letters to Dr. Kugelmann* (London, n.d.), p. 19.

35. *Communist Manifesto,* p. 26.

36. These deficiencies are closely related. Increased class consciousness advances the cause of political organization by creating greater interest in it, while organizational activity heightens class consciousness through the propaganda it makes possible. Both deficiencies disappear with the further development of the capitalist mode of production: Marx says, "The organization of revolutionary

elements as a class supposes the existence of all productive forces which could be engendered in the bosom of the old society" (*Poverty of Philosophy*, p. 196).

37. The most explicit statements of this duality occurs in regard to the French small-holding peasants, of whom Marx says, "In so far as millions of families live under economic conditions of existence that separate their mode of life, their interests and their culture from those of other classes, and put them in hostile opposition to the latter, they form a class. In so far as there is merely a local interconnection between these small-holding peasants, and the identity of their interests begets no community, no national bond and no political organization among them, they do not form a class" ("Eighteenth Brumaire," *Selected Writings I*, p. 303). It appears that economically and culturally the peasants are a class, but as regards class consciousness and politics, they are not.

38. *Theories of Surplus Value III*, p. 63.

39. The interaction offered here is not meant to be complete, One whole area which has not been taken account of at all has to do with the role of class in Marx's theory of alienation. For a discussion of this aspect of class, see my book, *Alienation: Marx's Conception of Man in Capitalist Society* (Cambridge, 1976), ch. 29.

40. R. N. Carew-Hunt, *The Theory and Practice of Communism* (London, 1963), p. 65. As we have indicated, one possible exception to this rebuke is the short, unfinished chapter on class in *Capital III*, pp. 862-63.

41. It is our view that the same analysis could be made of Marx's other key concepts—"class struggle," "value," "surplus value," "freedom," "labor power," "alienation," etc. Like "class," each expresses an aspect of the social reality Marx believes he uncovered, and, like "class," the full meaning Marx attaches to these concepts can only be deciphered by examining how he actually uses them in his writings. All of them are equally unavailable to those who would use them to express non-Marxist views.

42. E. P. Thompson, "Peculiarities of the English," *The Socialist Register*, 1965, ed. R. Miliband and J. Saville (New York, 1965), p. 357.

3.

Marx's Vision of Communism

I

Marcuse argues that, in the middle of the twentieth century, utopia remains an impossible dream only to those theorists who use "the concept of 'utopia' to denounce certain socio-historical possibilities."[1] Every significant advance in wealth, technology and science extends the boundaries not only of the real but of the possible, of the ways this newly won potential can be realized. Today's production of goods and knowledge, together with accompanying skills, have transformed the utopias of an earlier time into practical alternatives to our everyday existence. Recognition of these trends and their meaning has led to a renewed interest in Marx's vision of the communist society.

Marx constructed his vision of communism out of the human and technological possibilities already visible in his time, given the priorities that would be adopted by a new socialist society. The programs introduced by a victorious working class to deal with the problems left by the old society and the revolution would unleash a social dynamic whose general results, Marx believed, could be charted beforehand. Projecting the communist future from existing patterns and trends is an integral part of Marx's analysis of capitalism, an analysis which links social and economic problems with the objective interests that incline each class to deal with them in distinctive ways; what unfolds are the real possibilities inherent in a socialist transformation of the capitalist mode of production. It is in this sense that Marx declares, "we do not anticipate the world dogmatically, but rather wish to find the new world through the criticism of the old."[2] Like the projections Marx made of the future of capitalism itself, however, what he foresaw for communism is no more than highly probable. Marx, whose excessive optimism is often mistaken for crude determinism, would not deny that some form of barbarism is another alternative, but a socialist victory—either through revolution or at the polls—is considered far more likely.[3]

Marx's communist society is in the anomalous position of being, at one and the same time, the most famous of utopias and among the least known. And, while no one disputes the importance of Marx's vision of communism to Marxism, the vision itself remains clouded and unclear. Responsibility for this state of affairs lies, in the first instance, with Marx himself who never offers a systematic account of the communist society. Furthermore, he frequently criticizes those socialist writers who do as foolish, ineffective, and even reactionary. There are also remarks which suggest that one cannot describe communism because it is forever in the process of becoming: "Communism is for us not a stable state which is to be established, an ideal to which reality will have to adjust itself. We call Communism the real movement which abolishes the present state of things. The conditions of this movement result from premises now in existence."[4]

Yet, as even casual readers of Marx know, descriptions of the future society are scattered throughout Marx's writings. Moreover, judging from an 1851 outline of what was to become *Capital*, Marx intended to present his views on communism in a systematic manner in the final volume. The plan changed, in part because Marx never concluded his work on political economy proper, and what Engels in a letter to Marx refers to as "the famous 'positive,' what you 'really' want" was never written.[5]

This incident does point up, however, that Marx's objection to discussing communist society was more of a strategic than of a principled sort. More specifically, and particularly in his earliest works, Marx was concerned to distinguish himself from other socialists for whom prescriptions of the future were the main stock-in-trade. He was also very aware that when people change their ways and views it is generally in reaction to an intolerable situation in the present and only to a small degree because of the attraction of a better life in the future. Consequently, emphasizing communism could not be an effective means to promote proletarian class consciousness, his immediate political objective. Finally, with only the outline of the future visible from the present, Marx hesitated to burden his analysis of capitalism with material that could not be brought into focus without undermining in the minds of many the scientific character of his entire enterprise.

Notwithstanding Marx's own practice and contrary to his implicit warning, in what follows I have tried to reconstruct Marx's vision of communism from his writings of 1844, the year in which he set down the broad lines of his analysis, to the end of his life. Assembling these varied comments the communist society falls into place like the picture on a puzzle. It is a picture in which many pieces are missing and others so vague as to be practically undecipherable. Yet, what is left is a more complete and coherent whole than most people have thought to exist. Despite some serious temptations, I have not gone beyond Marx's actual words in piecing together the components of the communist society. Gaps and uncertainties are left untouched. On occasion, however, when all the evidence points to a particular conclusion, I am not averse to stating it.

Is this effort to reconstruct Marx's vision of the future open to the same criticisms that kept Marx from presenting his own views on this subject in a more organized manner? I don't think so. No one today is likely to confuse Marxism, even with the addition of an explicit conception of communism, with other socialist schools whose very names are difficult to recall. Whether describing communism can help raise proletarian class consciousness is a more difficult question. There is no doubt in my mind that getting workers to understand their exploitation as a fundamental and necessary fact of the capitalist system, the avowed aim of most of Marx's writings, is the "high road" to class consciousness. It seems equally clear to me that the inability to conceive of a humanly superior way of life, an inability fostered by this same exploitation, has contributed to the lassitude and cynicism which helps to thwart such consciousness. Viewed in this light, giving workers and indeed members of all oppressed classes a better notion of what their lives would be like under communism (something not to be gleaned from accounts of life in present day Russia and China) is essential to the success of the socialist project.

As for only being able to know the broad outlines of communism, this is as true now as it was in Marx's time. But whereas presenting this outline then could only reflect negatively on Marxism as a whole, this is no longer the case, for the intervening century has brought pieces of Marx's horizon underfoot and made most of the rest—as I have indicated—easier to see and to comprehend. Still general and incomplete, the secret of the future revealed in Marx's masterly analysis of capitalist society is a secret whose time has come, and publicizing it has become another means of bringing the human fulfillment it portrays into existence.

II

Marx divides the communist future into halves, a first stage generally referred to as the "dictatorship of the proletariat" and a second stage usually called "full communism." The historical boundaries of the first stage are set in the claim that "Between capitalist and communist society lies the period of the revolutionary transformation of the one into the other. There corresponds to this also a political transition period in which the state can be nothing but the revolutionary dictatorship of the proletariat."[6]

The overall character of this period is supplied by Marx's statement that "What we have to deal with here is a communist society, not as it has developed on its own foundations, but, on the contrary, just as it emerges from capitalist society: which is thus in every respect, economically, morally and intellectually, still stamped with the birthmarks of the old society from whose womb it emerges."[7] This first stage is the necessary gestation period for full communism: it is a time when the people who have destroyed capitalism are engaged in the task of total reconstruction. As a way of life and organization it has traits in common with both capitalism and full communism and many which are uniquely its own. When its work is done—and Marx never indicates how long this may take—the first stage gives way gradually, almost imperceptibly to the second.

Our main sources for Marx's views on the dictatorship of the proletariat are the *Communist Manifesto,* the "Critique of the Gotha Program," and "Civil War in France," in which he discusses the reforms of the Paris Commune. In the *Communist Manifesto*, there are ten measures that workers' parties are urged to put into effect immediately after their victory over the capitalists. By viewing these measures as already accomplished, we can use this list as a basis for our picture of the first stage.

What Marx asks for are: "1) Abolition of property in land and application of all rents of land to public purposes. 2) A heavy progressive or graduated income tax. 3) Abolition of all right of inheritance. 4) Confiscation of the property of all emigrants and rebels. 5) Centralization of credit in the hands of the state, by means of a national bank with state capital and an exclusive monopoly. 6) Centralization of communication and transport in the hands of the state. 7) Extension of factories and instruments of production owned by the state, the bringing in cultivation of waste lands, and the improvement of the soil generally in accordance with a common plan. 8) Equal liability of all to labour. Establishment of industrial armies, especially for agriculture. 9) Combination of agriculture with manufacturing industries; gradual abolition of the distinction between town and country, by a more equable distribution of population over the country. 10) Free education for all children in public schools. Abolition of children's factory labour in its present form. Combination of education with industrial production, etc., etc."[8]

It is conceded that "these measures will of course differ in different countries," but in the most advanced countries they "will be pretty generally applicable." No matter the variation in means, and it appears these variations would be modest ones, the goals remain the same: "to wrest...all capital from the bourgeoisie, to centralize all instruments of production in the hands of the state...and to increase the total of productive forces as rapidly as possible."

These demands will be examined singly in order to reveal the full measure of change projected by each one: 1) "Abolition of property in land and application of all rents on land to public purposes." Rather than parcelling out estates and giving land to the people who work on it—the reactionary dream of all peasants—land becomes the property of the state, which uses the rent it receives for public purposes. Judging from Marx's treatment of the land question in "Civil War in France," farmers would pay less rent to the state than they paid to their former landlords.[9] Later in his life, faced with Bakunin's criticisms, Marx qualifies this demand: "the proletariat," he now says, "must take measures, as a government, through which the peasant finds his position directly improved, which thus wins him for the revolution; measures, however, which facilitate in nucleus the transition from private property in the soil to collective property, so that the peasant comes to it of his own accord, economically. But it must not antagonize the peasant, by, for instance, proclaiming the abolition of the right of inheritance or the abolition of his property: this is only possible where the capitalist tenant has ousted the peasant, and the real tiller of the soil is just as much a proletarian, a wage worker, as is the urban worker, and hence has directly, and not only indirectly, the same interests as he. One has even less right to strengthen small peasant property by simply enlarging the plots by the transfer of the larger estates to the peasants, as in Bakunin's revolutionary campaign."[10]

This apparent contradiction can be explained by the fact that here Marx is primarily concerned with tactics and with those peasants who work their own plots of land, while in the *Communist Manifesto* he was speaking mainly about non-owning peasants. The two positions can be reconciled as follows: before, during and immediately after the revolution care should be taken not to frighten the small land-owning peasants, while the landless peasants are to be collectivized at once on the estates of their former landlords and employers. Marx never wavered in his belief that if socialism is to "have any chance whatever of victory, it must at least be able to do as much immediately for the peasants, *mutatis mutandis,* as the French bourgeoisie did in its revolution."[11]

For Marx, the peasant, despite his numerous delusions, is

"above all a man of reckoning."[12] He could not fail to be attracted by the tax benefits and material comforts, work conditions and cultural life available on collectives. All this, it would appear, without depriving the small-holding peasant of anything he already has, are the arguments that will convince him to communize his property. Marx did not envision great difficulty in making this transition, nor that it would take much time.

2) "A heavy progressive or graduated income tax." Apparently, significant differences of income still exist at this stage, or, at least, at the start of it. Many enterprises are privately owned, and their owners probably make more than they would working in a factory. Moreover, in a full employment economy with a scarcity of many essential skills, there are still occupations that have to pay high wages in order to attract workers. The inequality of incomes, therefore, is economically necessary, but because it is also socially undesirable an attempt is made through the income tax to render the real gap as narrow as possible. With the increasing equalization of incomes, the progressive income tax soon becomes outmoded.

3) "Abolition of all right of inheritance." Differences between personal incomes are deplored but accepted as necessary. The disparity in family fortunes, however, is not acceptable, and is to be eliminated at the death of those who currently hold them. Even those modest fortunes which result from wage differentials cannot be bequeathed to one's children. How this is reconciled with the intention, stated earlier, of letting small-holding peasants retain their land until they themselves decide to join collectives is nowhere made clear. Nor do we know for sure what Marx includes among the things which cannot be inherited.

While discussing wages, Marx declares "nothing can pass to the ownership of individuals except individual means of consumption."[13] Something similar, no doubt, would be used to distinguish between what can and cannot be inherited. The purpose of the no-inheritance principle is to achieve wealth equality after the death of those now living. From this time forward, everyone begins life with the same material advantages, and equality of opportunity—an impossible dream under capitalism—is finally realized. What people acquire over and above this will be what they have earned through their own activity.

4) "Confiscation of the property of all emigrants and rebels."

This is a practical step intended not so much to aid the state in its drive towards public ownership as to serve as a warning to the bourgeoisie not to engage in counter-revolutionary activity. The proletariat's victory is not completed with the revolution, but must be fought over and won again with all those left-overs of the old society whose hostility impairs the process of social reconstruction. It is indicative of the humanity with which Marx confronts counter-revolutionaries that confiscation is the most severe punishment ever mentioned.

5) "Centralization of credit in the hands of the state, by means of a national bank with state capital and an exclusive monopoly." Carrying this measure into effect will deprive financiers of both their wealth and their power to direct the economy. With exclusive control of credit facilities, the state can decide what parts of the economy should be expanded and by how much. It will also enable the state to finance the "national workshops" that Marx calls for elsewhere.[14] Meanwhile, what are considered useless or socially harmful enterprises will be squeezed out of existence by withholding funds.[15] What is particularly striking about this demand is that it shows the degree of independence to be allowed individual enterprises, whether private or public. If all major decisions were made by some central authority, there would be no need for the state to use credit as a means of control.

6) "Centralization of communication and transport in the hands of the state." Like the previous one, this measure aims at depriving a few capitalists of their power to control the nation's economy, and allows the state to develop its internal communication system on the basis of social need. Another immediate result is that all transportation is made free to the poor.[16] Again, the need to specify that communication and transport are taken over by the state suggests that most fields of endeavour are not.

7) "Extension of factories and instruments of production owned by the state, the bringing in cultivation of waste lands, and the improvement of the soil generally in accordance with a common plan." The involvement of the state in the economy is not concluded when it takes over enterprises and gains control of others through its monopoly of credit facilities. The state cannot sit on the production laurels of the capitalist economy which preceded it, as imposing as these may be. With the aid of a plan, every effort is made to increase nature's bounty by rapidly

increasing and perfecting the means by which it is produced.

8) "Equal liability of all to labor. Establishment of industrial armies, especially for agriculture." The new order brings to an end the parasitic situation existing under capitalism, where the few who don't work are supported by the many who do. Everyone works in communism. Those who don't work don't eat: "Apart from surplus-labor for those who on account of age are not yet, or no longer able to take part in production, all labor to support those who do not work would cease."[17] The freedom to choose one's work is not affected, as some critics assert; just the privilege of choosing not to work is abolished. With everyone working, "productive labor ceases to be a class attribute," allowing Marx to claim that communism "recognizes no class differences because everyone is a worker like everyone else."[18]

In calling for the establishment of industrial armies, especially for agriculture, Marx is as concerned with changing the personalities of the people involved as he is with promoting greater economic efficiency.

9) "Combination of agriculture with manufacturing industries; gradual abolition of the distinction between town and country, by a more equable distribution of population over the country." One of the least known of the harmful divisions Marx sees in the human race is between man the "restricted town animal" and man the "restricted country animal."[19] We must remember that, for Marx, peasants are a "class of barbarians," whose way of existence he labels the "idiocy of rural life."[20] People in the country, therefore, need the city and all that it represents in the way of advanced technology and culture, just as people living in the city need the country, its fresh air, inspiring scenery, and toil on the land itself in order to achieve their full stature as human beings. The first stage of communism sees an attempt to create new economic arrangements which will allow people to spend time in cities as well as in the country. The importance Marx attaches to this development can be gathered from his claim that, "The abolition of the antagonism between town and country is one of the first conditions of communal life."[21]

Marx believes that the necessary means for healing the split between town and country have already been provided by the preceding mode of production: capitalism, he says, "creates the material conditions for a higher synthesis in the future, namely, the union of agriculture and industry on the basis of the more perfected forms they have each acquired during their temporary separation."[22] We are left to guess what this "higher synthesis" actually looks like, but it appears to involve moving some industries to the country as well as greatly expanding the amount of unencumbered land inside cities for parks, woodland, and garden plots. I suspect, too, that Marx would like to see the number of people living in any one city reduced, and more small and medium size cities set up throughout the countryside, resulting in "a more equable distribution of population over the country" and making possible the establishment of industrial armies for agriculture.

10) "Free education for all children in public schools. Abolition of children's factory labor in its present form. Combination of education with industrial production, etc., etc." In 1848, even elementary education had to be paid for in most countries, so we can easily understand why public education was a major reform.

By "public schools" Marx did not mean "state schools" as this expression is commonly understood. In his "Criticism of the Gotha Program," Marx opposes the Socialist Party's demand for control of "elementary education by the state." He says, "Defining by a general law the expenditure on the elementary schools, the qualifications of the teaching staff, the branches of instruction, etc., and, as is done in the United States, supervising the fulfillment of these legal specifications by state inspectors, is a very different thing from appointing the state as the educator of the people. Government and church should rather be totally excluded from any influence on the schools."[23] The people themselves, directly or through social organs still unspecified, will supply the guidelines of their educational system.

In Marx's time, working class children spent the greater part of each day slaving in factories. Clearly, this had to cease immediately. However, Marx did not believe that all this time was better devoted to classroom learning. This, too, would stunt the child's development.[24] Instead he favors an education that "will in the case of every child over a given age, combine productive labor with instruction and gymnastics, not only as one of the methods of adding to the efficiency of production but as the only method of producing fully developed human beings."[25]

III

Not all of the information Marx supplies on the first stage of communism fits neatly into the list of demands found in the *Communist Manifesto*: the state, conditions and hours of work, planning for production, and the distribution of what is produced remain to be discussed.

As an instrument of working class rule, the state in this period is labelled, in what has proven to be an unfortunate turn of phrase, the "dictatorship of the proletariat." Hal Draper has demonstrated that "dictatorship" meant something very different to Marx and his contemporaries than it does to most of us.[26] Marx did not use this concept to refer to the extra-legal and generally violent rule of one man or a small group of men. Before Hitler and Mussolini, the meaning of "dictatorship" was strongly influenced by its use in ancient Rome, where the constitution provided for the election of a dictator to carry out certain specified tasks for a limited period, generally in times of crisis. It was in opposition to Blanqui's elitist views on the organization of the coming workers' state that Marx first introduced the expression "dictatorship of the proletariat," and by it he meant the democratic rule of the entire working class (including farm laborers), which made up the large majority of the population in all advanced countries.

In capitalism there is the "dictatorship of the bourgeoisie" (political power is in the hands of the capitalists) and, despite the facade of popular rule, the mass of the workers have no real chance to participate in and affect government. In the dictatorship of the proletariat, on the other hand, political power is held by the great majority, and once the former capitalists and landlords get production jobs they become workers and take part in the political process with the rest of the population. The dictatorship of the proletariat, therefore, is actually more democratic than democratic governments in capitalist societies, even by the latter's own definition of "democracy."

The dictatorship of the proletariat comes in the wake of the revolution and exists until the onset of full communism. Broadly speaking, its task is to transform the capitalism left behind in all its aspects, material and human, into the full communist society that lies ahead. It functions as a "permanent revolution."[27] As a government, it has a singleness of aim as regards both the past, out of which old enemies are constantly reappearing, and the future, which it works for in a highly systematic way. Marx says, "as long as other classes, especially the capitalist class, still exist, as long as the proletariat is still struggling with it (because with its conquest of governmental power its enemies and the old organization of society have not disappeared), it must use coercive means, hence governmental means: it is still a class, and the economic conditions on which the class struggle and the existence of classes rest have not yet disappeared and must be removed by force, or transformed, their process of transformation must be speeded up by force."[28]

Where remnants of the old order remain, they are to be removed, the state using all the force necessary for this purpose. Marx's comments elsewhere on the abolition of inheritance, the confiscation of the property of rebels, etc., give an indication of the kind of measures he favored to do away with capitalists as a class. Should individual members of this class prove incorrigible, his statement on the role of the proletarian dictatorship seems to provide a justification for using more extreme means. Marx, however, apparently believed that the economic and social measures introduced by the new regime would be sufficient to transform most capitalists, and that physical violence would only be used against those who resorted to violence themselves.

Most of our details on the workers' government come from Marx's laudatory account of the Paris Commune. The Commune was not a true dictatorship of the proletariat, but it was a close enough approximation to allow us to abstract the general lines, if not the exact configurations, of the workers' state. Marx says the "true secret" of the Commune is that "It was essentially a working class government, the product of the struggle of the producing class against the appropriating class, the political form at last discovered under which to work out the economic emancipation of labor."[29]

How, then, was the Commune organized? "The Commune was formed of the municipal councillors, chosen by universal suffrage in the various wards of the town, responsible and revocable at short terms...The Commune was to be a working, not a parliamentary body, executive and legislative at the same time. Instead of continuing to be the agent of the Central

Government, the police was at once stripped of its political attributes, and turned into the responsible and at all times revocable agent of the Commune. So were the officials of all other branches of the administration."[30] The long arm of popular rule extended into the chambers of the judiciary, ending what Marx calls their "sham independence": "Like the rest of public servants, magistrates and judges were to be elective, responsible, and revocable."[31] We also learn that a clear line was drawn between church and state, and that the army, like the police, was disbanded and replaced by the armed people.[32]

The organization of the Paris Commune was to serve as a model not only for the other cities of France, but for small towns and rural districts as well. Marx says, "The rural communes of every district were to administer their common affairs by an assembly of delegates in the central town, and these district assemblies were again to send deputies to the National Delegation in Paris, each delegate to be at any time revocable and bound by the *mandat imperatif* (formal instructions) of his constituents. The few but important functions which still would remain for a central government were not to be suppressed, as has been intentionally misstated, but were to be discharged by Communal, and therefore strictly responsible agents... While the merely repressive organs of the old government were to be amputated, its legitimate functions were to be wrested from an authority usurping pre-eminence over society itself, and restored to the responsible agents of society. Instead of deciding once in three or six years which member of the ruling class was to misrepresent the people in Parliament, universal suffrage was to serve the people, constituted in Communes, as individual suffrage serves every other employer in search for the workmen and managers in his business. And it is well known that companies, like individuals, in matters of real business generally know how to put the right man in the right place, and, if they for once make a mistake, to redress it promptly."[33]

Marx's defense of the Commune's vision of frequent elections for all government functionaries, mandated instructions from their constituents, and their recall reflect his belief that people of all classes recognize, or can be made to recognize where their best interests lie and to act upon them. But is it really obvious that people usually know or can come to know who will represent their best interests in Parliament? Marx thought it was, and that to open up the channels for popular control, in the absence of capitalist brain-washing techniques, is enough to insure that these interests would be properly represented.

The citizens of the proletarian state, Marx believes, will be able to choose their leaders wisely, but what of the leaders chosen? In marginal notes he wrote into his copy of Bakunin's *State and Anarchism,* Marx gives us his answer to the kind of criticism of Marxism and Russian communism now associated with Milovan Djilas' *New Class.* Far ahead of his time, Bakunin warns that workers, "once they become rulers or representatives of the people, cease to be workers." Next to this comment, Marx writes, "No more than a manufacturer today ceases to be a capitalist when he becomes a member of the municipal council." Bakunin continues, "And from the heights of the State they begin to look down upon the toiling people. From that time on they represent not the people but themselves and their own claims to govern the people. Those who doubt this know precious little about human nature." Beside this, Marx writes, "If Mr. Bakunin were *au courant,* be it only with the position of a manager in a workers' cooperative, he would send all his nightmares about authority to the devil."[34]

Two significant conclusions emerge from this exchange: first, Marx believed people in the government do not have important interests which conflict with those of the class from which they come. Consequently, the elected leaders of the proletarian dictatorship will want to represent the workers correctly. Should the electors make a "mistake," which in this context could only refer to the faulty character of an individual office holder, it will be quickly rectified through the instrument of the recall. Second, to believe that workers elected to government will use their authority to advance personal ends is to have a "nightmare," which I understand in this context as a foolish and impossible dream. Marx is asserting, in effect, "The workers are not like that," or, to be more precise, "will not be like that when they come to power." Evidence that this is what has happened in present day communist countries cannot really be used to settle this dispute since the social, economic and political pre-conditions which Marx thought necessary have never existed in these countries.

So far we have been discussing the dictatorship of the proletariat as if it were the government of a single country. This may be the case immediately after the first revolution, but it is evident that Marx expects this government, within a short space of time, to become world wide. Capitalism establishes a "universal intercourse" between people, creates the same classes with identical interests in each country and connects them in such a way that no ruling group, whether capitalist or socialist, can succeed on less than a universal basis. Marx states, "Empirically, communism is only possible as the act of the dominant people, 'all at once' or simultaneously."[35] There is no need, therefore, to advise the workers' government on how to deal with the remaining capitalist powers, nor is there any need to provide for a standing army. Marx believed that all the people and means of production currently going to waste in military ventures would become available for useful work. Probably nothing is more responsible for the distortion Marx's vision of communism has undergone in Russia than the fact that the "world revolution" of 1917 succeeded only in a small part of the world.

IV

Marx's description of economic life in the new society is as general and incomplete as his discussion of its political forms. Still, the basic outline of what to expect is there. Inside the factory, an immediate result of the revolution is an improvement in working conditions. Marx attacked the capitalist system for "the absence of all provisions to render the productive process human, agreeable, or at least bearable," and it is clear that the dictatorship of the proletariat gives top priority to correcting this situation.[36] As well as an indictment of existing evils, the description of working conditions in *Capital* can be taken as a roll call of needed reforms. The aim of all action in this field is, first, to make work bearable, then agreeable, and finally, human.

Hand in hand with the "amelioration" of working conditions goes the shortening of the working day.[37] This is accomplished without any decrease in the total social product. In the only instance where figures are given, it appears that the working day will be cut in half. Marx explains how this is possible: "If everybody must work, if the opposition between those who do work and those who don't disappears...and if moreover, one takes count of the development of the productive forces engendered by capital, society will produce in 6 hours the necessary surplus, even more than now in 12 hours; at the same time everbody will have 6 hours of 'time at his disposition,' the true richness..."[38] In communism, it is not material objects but free time that is the substance of wealth. Another basis for Marx's optimism is seen in his claim that shorter work days will mean greater intensity of labor for the time actually at work.[39]

The very enormity of the cut in hours Marx proposes indicates how great, he believes, is the number of people not working or engaged in useless activity, (9/10 of the labor in the circulation process, for example, is said to be necessary only under conditions of capitalism), and also the extent to which capitalism has not taken advantage of its opportunities for technical progress.[40] How else could the revolution cut each worker's day in half while enabling society to produce more than before? In any case, it is clear that Marx's proletariat, unlike Lenin's, does not have to build the industrial base of capitalism before it sets out to build communism. The factories, machines, skills, etc., have been provided in abundance by the preceding era.

Also in the area of production, Marx's views on planning occupy a key position. The immediate aim of all communist planning, he claims, is the satisfaction of "social needs."[41] In deciding how much of any given article to produce, the planners have to strike a balance between social need, available labor-time and the existing means of production.[42] Although Marx recognizes that demand is elastic he never doubts that his proletarian planners—whose actual planning mechanisms are never discussed—will make the right equations.

As regards distribution in this period, Marx says, before each individual gets his/her share of the social product, society must deduct "cover for replacement of the means of production used up. Secondly, additional portions for expansion of production. Thirdly, reserve or insurance funds to provide against accidents, dislocations caused by natural calamities, etc."[43] These inroads into the social product will probably be much larger than their equivalents under capitalism. After society has taken this much out, it must again subtract, "First, the general costs of administration not belonging to production. This part will, from the outset, be very considerably restricted in comparison with present-day society and diminished in proportion as the new society develops. Secondly, that which is intended for the common satisfaction of needs such as schools, health services, etc. From the outset this part grows considerably in comparison with present-day society and it grows in proportion as the new society develops. Thirdly, funds for those unable to work, etc., in short, for what is included under so-called official poor relief today."[44]

Marx's belief that the costs of administration will diminish does not necessarily imply that there will be less government in the short-run, though his claim that these costs diminish "in proportion as the new society develops" does imply just this for the long-run. The transformation of the professional army into a people's army and the low wages paid to all government functionaries (the example for this was set by the Commune) offer sufficient reasons for the immediate drop in expenses of running a government.[45]

Despite all these inroads into the social product, the portion which goes to each individual is still larger than a worker's portion under capitalism.[46] Besides rapid economic growth, this new prosperity is explained by the fact that the outsized shares of the product which went to capitalists, landlords, army officers, bureaucrats, and many industries now considered wasteful are divided among everyone. What each person receives directly as his/her share in the total product plus the welfare, etc. he/she gets as a citizen gives him/her a material existence that is both secure and comfortable.[47]

So far we have spoken as if all the people living in the first stage of communism receive equal shares of the social product. But this is only true if they work the same amount of time, since the measure guiding distribution for most of this period—it is introduced as soon as it is feasible—is labor-time. Marx claims that each person "receives back from society—after the deductions have been made—exactly what he gives to it. What he has given to it is his individual quantum of labor... He receives a certificate from society that he has furnished such and such an amount of labor (after deducting his labor for the common funds), and with this certificate he draws from the social stock of means of consumption as much as constitutes the same amount of labor. The same amount of labor which he has given to society in one form he receives back in another."[48] The Commune's practice of paying everyone in government service, from members of the Commune downwards, the same worker's wages is declared to be a practical expression of the principle, "equal pay for equal labor-time."[49]

The uses of money are so limited in this period that Marx prefers to speak of "certificates" and "vouchers." Instead of money, what we have are pieces of paper which state how much labor-time one has contributed to the social fund. These simply entitle the individual to draw an equivalent from the fund in the form of consumption goods; means of production and social means of consumption—such as scenic land and trains—are not for sale. As Marx says elsewhere, "These vouchers are not money. They do not circulate."[50] Its circulation between all sectors in the economy has always been a major defining characteristic of money. Such limitations on the power and function of wage payments put an end to the money system as we know it.

After defending the principle of "equal pay for equal work time" as marking a notable advance on ideas governing distribution in capitalism, Marx dubs it a "bourgeois limitation." In the first stage of communism, "The right of producers is proportional to the labor they supply; the equality consists in the fact that measurement is made with an equal standard, labor." But he points out, "one man is superior to another physically or mentally and so supplies more labor in the same time, or can labor for a longer time; and labor, to serve as a measure, must be defined by its duration or intensity, otherwise it ceases to be a standard of measurement. This equal right is an unequal right for unequal labor. It recognizes no class differences, because everyone is only a worker like everyone else; but it tacitly recognizes unequal individual endowment and thus productive capacity as natural privileges. It is, therefore, a right of inequality, in its content, like every right."[51] The ideal system of distribution, which is foreshadowed in these remarks, would neither punish nor reward people for their personal characteristics.

Marx's picture of life and organization in the first stage of communism is very incomplete. There is no discussion of such obviously important developments as workers' control. We can only guess how much power workers enjoy in their enterprises and through what mechanisms they exercise it on the basis of the democratic processes Marx favors for politics.[52] Cultural institutions and practices are hardly mentioned. Nor is there much said about how conflicts between individuals, between groups, or between the masses and their elected leaders are resolved.

Perhaps more significant is the absence of a list of priorities for the measures favored. Politics is to a large extent the art of arranging priorities, but in what order are Marx's reforms to be tackled? Pointing out that this order is seriously affected by conditions in each country only serves to qualify the question; it doesn't answer it. One would be mistaken, therefore, to view what has been pieced together here as a blueprint of what to do and how to do it. It is but a vision, only one of the ingredients from which blueprints are made—and Marx would not have wanted it otherwise.

V

With the intensification and completion of the various aspects of life and organization associated with the first stage, the second stage of communism gradually makes its appearance. Communism, for we may now drop all qualifying prefixes, is as unlike its immediate predecessor as that society differed from capitalism; yet, the heritage of the first stage is present everywhere. As a framework structuring all other communist conditions and relations is the social ownership of the means of production. It is some time since this has been achieved, though it is not so long since it has been completely accepted. Remnants of capitalism no longer exist, neither in the mentality of the people nor in their conduct, depriving the political dictatorship of its main *raison d'etre*.

The wealth which capitalism left and which the first stage of communism multiplied many times over starts communism on its way with a super abundance of all material goods. Wide-scale planning has been enormously successful. Technology has developed to a plane where practically anything is possible.

Wastelands have been brought under cultivation; a multitude of modern towns have sprung up in the countryside; large cities have been renovated; the communication and transportation systems are as advanced as anything we now have (without actually picturing modern inventions in these fields, it is approximately this high degree of development which Marx had in mind); factories have become pleasant places in which to work. At work, where undoubtedly the hours have been shortened once again, people have gotten used to putting in the same amount of time and receiving equal pay. Elsewhere in society, the education of the young has proceeded to the point where everyone has been trained in factories as well as in classrooms.

All such developments are best viewed as constituting the foundations of communism. What, then, is communism? Marx's comments on the life and organization that come into being on these foundations, though even more general and less systematic than his comments on the first stage, offer a description of communism that can be summarized in six main points: 1) The division of labor, as Marx understands it, has come to an end, and with it the subjection of individuals to a single life task. People now feel the need and have the ability to perform many kinds of work. 2) Activity with and for others, at work, in consumption, and during free time, has become a prime want, and occupies most of the life of every individual. 3) Social ownership has been extended to cover all of nature from the land and the sea to the food each person eats and the clothes he or she wears. Individual ownership, private property in all its guises, has been abolished.

4) Everything with which a person comes into contact, which at this time means the entire world, becomes the product of his/her conscious efforts to bend things to his/her own purposes. Instead of submitting to chance as formerly, people, through their knowledge and control over natural forces, make their own chance. 5) People's activities are no longer organized by external forces, with the exception of productive work where such organization still exists but in the manner of an orchestra leader who directs a willing orchestra (the example is Marx's). As a part of this, restrictive rules are unknown; nor is there any coercion or punishment. The state, too, withers away. 6) The divisions we are accustomed to seeing in the human species along lines of nation,

race, religion, geographical section (town dweller and country dweller), occupation, class, and family have all ceased to exist. They are replaced by new and, as yet, unnamed divisions more in keeping with the character of the people and life of this period.

The individual's victory over the division of labor is, without a doubt, the central feature of communist society, just as it is the most difficult one for the uninitiated to grasp. In previous periods, the necessities of the production process as well as the social relations of production presented each person with a single job for life. He or she was either a worker, a farmer, a business-person, an intellectual, etc. This was so even in the first stage of communism, where the amelioration of this condition had already begun. The realities of one's class position made it impossible, both physically and from the point of view of opportunities and attainments, to do work which lay in the dominion of another class. A striking exception to this rule is found in the ancient world and Marx quotes Lemontey with obvious approval: "We are struck with admiration when we see among the Ancients the same person distinguishing himself to a high degree as a philosopher, poet, orator, historian, priest, administrator, general of an army. Our souls are appalled at the sight of so vast a domain. Each of us plants his hedge and shuts himself up in this enclosure. I do not know whether by this parcellation the world is enlarged, but I do know that man is belittled."[53]

If such varied activity was possible for a small privileged class in the ancient world, by the time of capitalism each class is shut up in its own enclosure; and inside each enclosure parcel-lation has continued unabated. The final turn of the screw is applied by "modern industry" where machines usurp the few human skills that remain leaving most men with the minute and highly repetitive operations involved in machine minding. In this situation, leisure activities can only be of the kind that come naturally, men having neither the time nor the opportunity to acquire special talents and tastes.

Life in communism is at the opposite extreme from what exists in capitalism. In the new society, people do many kinds of work where their ancestors used to do one. Both manual and intellectual activity form a part of every working day, for, according to Marx, "the antithesis between mental and physical labor has vanished."[54] Human kind is no longer divided into sheep and goats, and given their work tasks accordingly. The individual is declared rich in communism because he/she needs "the totality of human life activities."[55] And he/she enjoys them, to a large extent, just because they are so varied.

But the break with the parcellation of the past is more radical still. For in the new society, there are no more weavers, metal workers, coal miners, plumbers, farmers, factory managers, engineers, or professors. These labels are used to categorize people who are tied down to a particular occupation for life. In communism, the tie is unknotted, and each person takes part, at one time or another, in many if not most of these activities. Perhaps Marx's best known statement on this subject is his claim that "in communist society, where nobody has one exclusive sphere of activity but each can become accomplished in any branch he wishes, society regulates the general production and thus makes it possible for me to do one thing today, another tomorrow, to hunt in the morning, fish in the afternoon, rear cattle in the evening, criticize after dinner, just as I have a mind, without ever becoming hunter, fisherman, shepherd, or critic."[56] These are unfortunate examples to show how diversified a person's endeavors become, for they have led some to believe that life in communism is all play and no work—anyway, no factory work. But factory work, in the new social form which it takes in this period, is an activity to which all people devote some time. It is something which everybody, without exception, wants to do.[57]

Besides contributing to production, each individual also participates in cultural and scientific life, and not just as a consumer of other people's products but as a creator. We have met communist men and women as workers, farmers, hunters, and critics, and Marx now introduces us to the same persons as artists: "The exclusive concentration of artistic talent in some individuals and its suppression in the grand mass which springs from this, is a consequence of the division of labor... In a communist society, there are no painters, but men who among other things do painting."[58] Being a painter is to be subjected to the division of labor as much as if one only did weaving. Every person in communist society is relieved of the burden of narrowness which plagued his or her ancestors, weavers and painters alike, and given the opportunity to express him or herself in all possible ways.

What applies to painting also applies to science. The scientist, as someone who devotes his/her entire working life to science, is replaced in this period by the whole citizenry, who spend part of their time doing theoretical as well as practical scientific work. People in communism relate to other activities ranging from athletics to courting to musing on one's own in the same way.

Marx not only ascribes a world of activities to the communist person, but believes they will be very proficient in their performance. To achieve this is the aim of communist education.[59] At the same time, Marx recognizes that not all people will be equally good in everything they try. As regards painting, for example, he admits that only a few will rise to the level of Raphael. On the other hand, the quality of other people's work will be extremely high; and he maintains, all paintings will be original.[60] By "original" I take him to mean that each person's creatives efforts will be a true expression of his/her unique qualities. Marx would probably be willing to make a similar distinction between average and exceptional ability in science, farming, material production, etc., always with the proviso that those who lag behind are still extraordinarily good.

Even in communism, people do not have the time to become equally skilled in all tasks. There is just too much to do. Hence, those who spend more time learning surgery will be better surgeons in any social system. Furthermore, people will always possess different intellectual and physical capacities.[61] Marx does not dismiss heredity, though the nature of its effect is never revealed to us beyond the generalities of more and better. Yet, despite these admissions, the least gifted people in communism are spoken of as if they are more accomplished than Lemontey's heroes, and do each of their tasks with a high degree of skill.

To those who argue that skill is invariably a function of specialization, Marx would probably reply that, in so far as specialization involves learning a body of data and technique, communist people are specialists in many tasks. The exclusive quality which we associate with specialization is viewed as a social side effect that is destined to disappear. In the past, outstanding contributions to civilization were often the work of one-sided "geniuses," who—compared to their no-sided contemporaries—realized at least some of their potential. The difference is that the many-sided people living in communism are able to learn a great variety of skills quickly, and, hence, to develop a wide range of powers. Everything in their society is bent to facilitate these efforts, and the character of each individual—itself the product of communist conditions—insures that he/she is able to make the most of his/her opportunities.[62]

VI

Another major characteristic of communist society is the high degree of cooperation and mutual concern which is discernable in most human activities. One indication of this development is simply the increase in the number of things people do in common. Reference has already been made to the "industrial armies" which do the work formerly done by peasants on their own plots. Beyond this, Marx claims, "communal activity and communal consumption—that is activity and consumption which are manifested and directly confirmed in real association with other men—will occur wherever such a direct expression of sociality stems from the true character of the activity's content and is adequate to the nature of consumption."[63]

We are not told which activities have a "character" that requires they be done communally. Nor do we learn what types of consumption have a "nature" that requires communal consumption. Consequently, we don't really know how far Marx would extend his principle in practice. All we can be certain of is that cooperation will cover far more than it does today. Marx speaks, for example, of new "social organs" coming into existence which are the institutional forms of new social activities as well as the new forms adapted for old ones.[64]

Of greater significance than the spread of cooperation is the fact that it is qualitatively superior to what goes by the same name in earlier periods. Marx believed that production is social in any society since it is always carried on inside some relationship with other people. However, the cooperation involved varies from tenuous, unconscious and forced, to close, conscious and free. In communism, interdependence becomes the recognized means to transform the limitations set by what was until now unrecognized interdependence.

Because people at this time are "brought into practical connection with the material and intellectual production of the whole world," interdependence is world-wide and grasped as such.[65] These relations lead each individual to become conscious of humanity as part of him/herself, which is to say of him/herself as a "social being."[66] This is not only a matter of considering social interdependence as a facet of one's own existence, but of thinking (and therefore, treating) the needs of others as one's own, experiencing happiness when they are happy and sadness when they are sad, and believing that what one controls or does is equally their's and their doing, and vice-versa. Perhaps nothing in the communist society helps explain the extraordinary cooperation which characterizes this period as much as the individual's new conception of self, which, in turn, could only emerge full blown as a product of such cooperation.[67]

In discussing the first stage of communism, we saw that the satisfaction of social needs had become the accepted goal of material production. By full communism, this goal has sunk into the consciousness of each individual, determining how he or she views all the products of his or her work. Besides the sense of devotedness which comes from feeling oneself a part of a productive unit (and the productive unit a part of oneself), each person gives his best because he is aware of the needs of those who use his products (and because he conceives of these needs as his own). He realizes that the better he does the more satisfaction he gives.[68] Communist people's concern for their fellows as co-producers is matched by their concern for them as consumers of what they have helped to produce.

This desire to please is not associated with any sense of duty, but with the satisfaction one gets at this time in helping others. Assuming the role of a communist, Marx proclaims, "in your joy or in your use of my product, I would have the direct joy from my good conscience of having, by my work, satisfied a human need...and consequently, of having procured to the need of another human being his corresponding object."[69] We can approximate what takes place here if we view each person as loving all others such that he or she can get pleasure from the pleasure they derive from his or her efforts. This should not be so hard to conceive when we think of how close friends and relatives often get pleasure from the happiness they give each other. Marx is universalizing this emotion, much enriched, to the point where each person is able to feel it for everyone whom his/her actions affect, which in communism is the whole of society. Everywhere the individual recognizes and experiences the other as the "complement" of his/her own "nature" and as a "necessary part" of his/her own "being."[70] Aside from considerations of getting something done, people at this time also engage in communal activities for the sheer pleasure of being with others. Human togetherness has become its own justification.[71]

A third characteristic distinctive of the communist society is the replacement of private property by social ownership in personal as well as public effects.[72] Communism is spoken of in one place as "the positive transcendence of private property."[73] We have already seen the role social ownership of the means of production plays in the first stage of communism in enabling wide-scale planning, promoting equality and securing better working conditions. Small businesses, however, still existed at least at the beginning of the first stage, and articles subject to direct consumption were still owned as private property. Most people attached great value to the particular objects they used for these were not easy to replace, and, in any case, cost money (labor vouchers) which could be spent on something else. Under such conditions, cooperation did not extend to sharing all that one had with others, and the grasping attitude so prevalent today still had to be reckoned with, though probably less among the proletariat who had fewer material possessions to begin with, than among the small-holding peasants and the remnants of the bourgeoisie.

Private property, by its very nature, secures the owner special rights over and against all non-owners. It is essentially a negative notion, an assertion, backed by the full coercive force of society, that one person may exclude others from using or benefiting from whatever it is he/she owns, if so desired. It assumes the possibility—no, the inevitability—of a clash between what he/she wants to do with his/her objects and what others want to do with them. What happens, then, to the notion of private property in a society where no one ever claims a right to the things he/she is using, wearing, eating, or living in, where instead of refusing to share with others he/she is only too happy to give them what they want, where—if you like—all claims to use are considered equally legitimate? This is the situation in communism: the clash of competing interests has disappeared and with it the need to claim rights of any sort.

We have just seen how aware each communist person is of the effect his actions have on others and how concerned he is with their obtaining satisfaction, both because his own personal needs require it and because he has conceptualized himself as a social being of which they are integral parts. It is this which allows him to say, "The senses and enjoyment of other men have become my own appropriation."[74] Consequently, if one person has something another wants his first reaction is to give it to her. Of private property in land, Marx says, "From the standpoint of a higher economic form of society, private ownership of the globe by single individuals will appear quite as absurd as private ownership of one man by another."[75] In full communism, with human relationships as I have depicted them, private ownership of anything will appear equally ridiculous. It should be clear that it is never a matter of people depriving themselves for the sake of others. Consumption for all citizens is that which "the full development of the individual requires."[76] The community stores are replete with everything a communist person could possibly want. "To each according to his need" is the promise communist society makes to all its members.[77]

Private property has always been based, in a fundamental sense, on the existence of material scarcity. This applies to the dictatorship of the proletariat as well as to earlier periods. What one man or a few had could not be acquired by the many, because there simply was not enough to go around. Demand exceeds supply; those who Have use the idea of private property and the coercive power of the state to reinforce their position; those who Have Not compete for the social product with every means at their disposal from beggary to revolution. But, when supply is so plentiful that everyone can have as much of anything he wants just for the asking (and where the things wanted in earlier class societies because of the power and status they represent are no longer wanted), the social relationships that rest on existing scarcity are turned upside down. Who today would begrudge another person a drink of water, or, for that matter, all the water he wants? If water were scarce, however, those who had it would hoard it, or would charge a price for what they let others use.

Water would become an item of private property. In communism all material goods have become as abundant as water is today. Only on this foundation, can people view whatever they happen to be using at the moment as social objects, as products made by everyone for everyone. There is no longer "mine," "yours," "his," and "hers," but only "ours."

VII

Another unique attribute of communist society is the masterly control which human beings exercise over all the forces and objects of nature. Previously, people were chiefly objects of nature, and their happiness and often their lives depended on the vagaries of the seasons, the fertility of the soil, the adequacy of their mechanical power and skills, the demand for their work or products, and many other events and processes whose effects were equally uncertain. In communism, Marx declares the task "is to put in place of the supremacy of exterior conditions and of chance over individuals, the supremacy of the individuals over chance and objective conditions."[78] This is also referred to as "the casting off of all natural limitations."[79] These are limitations placed on people's activities by the sum of the non-human circumstances in which they find themselves, and what formerly, through ignorance, was labelled "natural law."

For Marx, the "laws of nature" which are said to govern us are "founded on the want of knowledge of those whose action is the subject to it."[80] There is no want of knowledge about nature in the new society. People understand their total environment, how it functions and what its possibilities are. Implicit in Marx's view is the belief that when communist people fully comprehend nature they will not desire anything which stands outside their effective reach. This belief, in turn, is based on his conception of how far people's reach actually extends in communism and accompanying assumptions regarding the creative potential of their cooperation. Marx is saying, in effect, that much of what people today want to do but cannot will be done under the ideal conditions of communism, that what remains are things which the extraordinary people of this time will not want to do, and most important, that what they will want to do which we do not (we caught a glimpse of what this might be in presenting the material prerequisites of communism) they will easily accomplish.

Yet, so complete is their grasp of the interconnnected parts which constitute communist reality that Marx foresees natural science and human science will become one.[81] It is in this sense too that he later says man "becomes able to understand his own history as a process, and to conceive of nature (involving also practical control over it) as his own real body."[82] What is involved here is becoming conscious of the internal relations between what are today called "natural" and "social" worlds, and treating the hitherto separate halves as a single totality. In learning about either society or nature, the individual will recognize that he is learning about both.

Communist people cannot change the climate (or can they?), but they can take all its effects into consideration and make their broader plans accordingly. As for the rest, Marx seems to believe that a united and cooperating humankind can dominate nature directly, and his conception of the productive potential of industry seems closer to the reality we expect for tomorrow than the one we have today. We are told that, "The reality which communism is creating is precisely the real basis for rendering it impossible that anything exist independently of individuals, in so far as things are only a product of the preceding intercourse of individuals themselves."[83]

As for those objects and processes not already a part of human intercourse, Marx declares, man "for the first time, consciously treats all natural premises as the creatures of men, strips them of their natural character and subjugates them to the power of individuals united."[84] Thus, the whole world is regarded through the eyes of a creator; everything people come into contact with is altered to suit their wide-ranging purposes; former barriers have been transformed into freeways; nothing is allowed to block their fulfillment, and nothing which can contribute to it is permitted to remain neutral. Viewing people's ties with nature as logically internal relations over which each person in conjunction with his or her fellows has now gained conscious mastery, Marx can claim that in communism "nature becomes man."[85]

Marx does not supply us with a map of communist topography, so we are left with the notion that physical changes are enormous without knowing in much detail what they are. We have already come across some of them, such as the spatial reorganization of town and countryside. Probably nothing shows the extent to which Marx foresaw human domination over nature better, however, than his comment that language will "submit to the perfect control of individuals."[86] I interpret this to mean that one language will replace the thousands now in existence (whatever limited cultural role many languages may continue to play), and that it will be specially adapted to permit clear expression to the extraordinary experiences, understanding, and feelings of the people of this time.

The key to the individual's newly arrived at domination over nature lies in the peculiar quality of communist cooperation. Marx labels cooperation in any historical period a "productive force," which is a way of saying that the form of social interaction as such is partly responsible for the quantity and quality of its products.[87] The difference is that in communism, where work in common is the rule and everyone gives himself fully to all his tasks, cooperation is a productive force of practically limitless potential. According to Marx, "It is just this combination of individuals (assuming the advanced stage of modern productive forces, of course) which puts the conditions of the free development and movement of individuals under their control."[88]

VIII

A fifth striking feature of communism is the absence of external rules and with it of all forms of coercion and discipline. Aside from work in factories and on farms, none of the activities people engage in at this time are organized by others, from outside; that is to say, there is nothing they must do and no predetermined manner or time restrictions they must follow in doing it. On the other hand, coordination is the minimal demand which social production *per se* makes on all its participants. Hence, some organization, headed by someone whose job it is to coordinate productive tasks, is required of every society. According to Marx, "in all kinds of work where there is cooperation of many individuals, the connection and the unity of the process are necessarily represented in a will which commands and in functions which, as for the leader of an orchestra, are not concerned with partial efforts, but with the collective activity. It is therefore a productive work which must be accomplished in any mode of combined production." He calls this "the work of general supervision and direction."[89]

However, even in production, the organization which Marx foresees in communism is a far cry from what exists today. Though factories and farms still possess managers, their duties are simply to coordinate the efforts of those who work under them; they act as leaders of an orchestra. Since people in communism are frequently changing jobs, we can assume that at one time or another almost everyone will serve as a manager. The orchestra which is being directed is always willing and enthusiastic, since its goals and those of the manager are the same, viz., to produce articles which satisfy social needs, to produce all that is required, of the best quality, in the shortest possible time and with the least amount of waste. In capitalism, workers do as little and as shoddy a job as they can get away with and their bosses are constantly after them to work even more and harder than they could if they were really trying. In communism, laziness, which Marx views as an historically conditioned phenomenon, would die a natural death.[90] "From each according to his ability" is a promise that no one at this time would think of breaking.[91]

In production where each individual works to the best of his/her ability, factory discipline with all its paraphernalia of fines, dismissals, threats, etc., has become obsolete. Marx claims such discipline "will become superfluous under a social system in which laborers work for their own account, as it has already become practically superfluous in piece-work."[92] Whenever workers recognize that by exerting themselves they can increase their share of the product, they do not have to be coerced to work. In communism, each worker-musician does his/her best to keep time with the rest of the orchestra.

What have we learned about work in communism? Without coercion and full of mutual concern, in pleasant surroundings and for relatively short periods each day (week?), people use the socially owned means of production to control and transform nature to satisfy human needs. Frequently changing tasks, they find both joy and fulfillment in their cooperation and its momentous achievements. Unlike Fourier, however, who compares work in communism to play, Marx says it will be earnest and intense effort as befits any truly creative activity.[93] Still—in an oft quoted phrase—Marx refers to production in communism as the "realm of necessity" and contrasts it with the "realm of freedom," or non-work activity, where the "development of human energy ...is an end in itself."[94] The fact is that whether communist people want to or not they have to do some work just in order to live: that they invariably want to is beside the point. If this qualification places work in the *realm* of necessity, however, it doesn't follow that work is an un-free activity. In his most forthright statement on this subject, Marx calls human freedom "the positive power to assert his true individuality."[95] Given the character of work in communism, including the degree of control over nature exercised in work, it is the equal of any other activity in bringing out and developing the unique potential in each human being. Consequently, Marx can speak of work in this period as the "activity of real freedom."[96]

If people in communism are so cooperative that the only productive organization is that minimum required by economic efficiency, then, we may expect that even this minimum will disappear in the non-work areas of life. In one listing, we learn that soldiers, policemen, hangmen, legislators, and judges are equally unnecessary "under proper conditions of society."[97] Without any need for coercion, the institutionalized means by which it is exercised can be eliminated.[98] This victory over external authority is a victory of the accusers as well as of the accused, for as Marx says, "punishment, coercion is contrary to human conduct."[99]

With the sole exception of production, all forms of organization adopted in the dictatorship of the proletariat serve in the role of Wittgenstein's ladder for communist people: they enable them to climb into communism, only to be discarded then they get there. Restrictive rules, coercion of all kinds, become worse than nuisances—they constitute actual obstructions—in a society which knows no clash of basic interests.

Perfect success is too much to ask from the full-time job Marx gives each communist person of being his brother's keeper. Consequently, whenever an individual fails in one of the tasks he has set himself or, through carelessness—we cannot conceive of any more wicked motive operating on him—breaks a norm or causes harm to others, he himself administers the punishment. Marx declares that "under human conditions, punishment will really be nothing but the sentence passed by the culprit on himself. There will be no attempt to persuade him that violence from without, exerted on him by others, is violence on himself by himself. On the contrary, he will see in other men his natural saviors from the sentence which he has pronounced on himself; in other words the relation will be reversed."[100] Given the social-mindedness referred to earlier, any significant lapse in a person's cooperative behavior will provoke feelings of guilt. Guilt is a burden that can only be removed by others. In communism, society's role has changed from punishing wrong-doers to reassuring and soothing them to help relieve their self-inflicted anguish.

We should not be surprised to learn that in these conditions there is no place for a state. Simply put, the state withers away because there is nothing further for it to do. The main work of the dictatorship of the proletariat was to destroy all remnants of capitalism and to construct the foundations for full communism. Laws, organization, discipline, coercion, etc., were all necessary to accomplish these ends. But now communism is the reality, and capitalism is history. Marx says, "When, in the course of development, class distinctions have disappeared, and all pro-duction has been concentrated in the hands of associated individuals, the public power will lose its political character. Political power, properly so called, is merely the organized power of one class for oppressing another."[101] What does a state without a "political character" look like? Marx rephrases this question to read, "What social functions will remain in existence there that are analogous to present functions of the state?"[102] Though he never gives a full answer, it is clear what his answer would be.

The three main functions of any state are legislation, adjudication, and administration. Of legislation, Marx says, in communism all forms of parliamentarism will be "ranged under the category of nuisances."[103] Legislatures are political expres-sions of the principle of majority rule which, in turn, is based on the assumption that on important matters people's opinions are bound to clash. They are battlefields of the class struggle, battlefields on which the ruling economic class, obtaining its majority by means fair and foul, legislates repeated defeats for the opposition. But the people of communism are agreed on all the subjects which could possibly come before a parliament. Where interests merge and decisions are unanimous it is not necessary to go through the formality of counting hands. Furthermore, all really major decisions, those bearing on the structure of communism itself, have already been taken by this time. People have what they want, that is, communism, and there is nothing for a legislature, whose main function is to make changes, to change. Whatever minor adjustments are required are best undertaken by the people on the spot, directly.

The judicial arm of government, too, is based on an assumption of necessary conflict between people. From the quasi-sanctification of a raised bench, the ruling class, in the person of some of its more pompous representatives, renders biased interpretations of one-sided laws. But if this conflict doesn't exist...? A typical case which comes before courts everywhere is a suit for injuries. In the communist society, a person who is harmed by another suffers no economic disadvantages because of it (he/she continues to take from the social stock whatever he/she needs); moreover, he knows that the person who struck the blow did not do it on purpose, and that the pain of a guilty conscience is as great or greater than the pain coming from the injury. Rather than insisting on revenge or compensation, our victim would probably join with co-workers and neighbors to ease the guilt of the person who injured him. All "claims for damages" will be dispensed with in this way, by the people concerned directly. The other cases which come before our courts today, those involving murder, robbery, kidnapping, forgery, etc., simply do not exist. They have been made either impossible, since everything people want is free and legal papers which secure special rights and powers don't exist, or unnecessary, since there is nothing people want that requires such anti-social measures. What, then, is the need for the courts?

The case of the administration is a bit more complicated. One main function of the administrative branch of government is to enforce the laws. In communist society, where there are no laws and where social norms are accepted and heeded by all, this function no longer exists. But another task remains which is comparable to the coordination provided by factory managers. In the area of production, communist society as a whole, like its individual enterprises, will require the general supervision of managers. Duplication as well as gaps in production and services have to be prevented. Coordinating efforts, therefore, will be needed at all the major crossroads of social life, wherever, in fact, a traffic director is useful in helping people get where they want to go.

Some might argue that this coordinating function conceals acts of legislation and adjudication, and that administrators are the new law-givers and judges of this period, but communism is unique in having administrators and administered who are striving to achieve the same ends. Their mutual trust and concern with one another are likewise complete. Consequently, the minor altercations and judgments required are accepted as expressions of a common will. Recall, too, that each individual has come to conceive of his fellows as parts of himself, as extensions of his nature as a social being, so even when he is not directly involved in administration he feels himself involved through his relations with those who are. Furthermore, since the activity of coordinating social life at its various levels is something everyone will undertake at some time or another, there is no special strata of administrators. To describe this state of affairs in terms of "legislature," "laws," "courts," etc., is extremely misleading. This work of administration, more properly of coordination, is the only function in communism which is analogous to the duties of a modern state.

Distributing these administrative tasks takes place through an election which Marx describes as a "business matter." Since everyone agrees on matters of policy, elections are probably uncontested. In any case, victory does not "result in any domination." We are assured that an election in communism has "none of its present political character." Elections are merely a way of passing administrative jobs around to people who are more or less equally equipped to carry them out. In these conditions, Marx is able to claim, "The whole people will govern; there will be no one to be governed."[104] Marx, however, prefers to play down the role of coordinating authority in the new society, emphasizing instead the power which comes through direct cooperation.

Could a complex industrial society be run in this manner? Marx believed it could not be run as effectively in any other.

After all, many of the worst administrative complexities are byproducts of present social organization and its accompanying attitudes. Most records, for example, are only kept to secure a limited number of people—the young, the old, the sick, veterans, etc.—rights which in communism are universal (or, as Marx would prefer, which have disappeared for everyone because they are no longer necessary for anyone). The extensive red-tape bureaucracies for which modern day "socialist" countries are noted do not offer any indication of what to expect when the special conditions Marx lays down for communism have been fulfilled. Likewise, a great deal of administrative calculation in government as elsewhere is devoted to getting people to obey rules they don't like, deciding what incentives to offer and how to punish slackers; manipulations connected with improving the position of privileged segments of the ruling class or trying to harmonize competing social interests are other components of existing complexity. With new aims and standards, and, above all, new communist people, most of what makes social administration an unfathomable labyrinth will disappear. Simple cooperation within each functional social unit together with single purpose coordination between them provides communism as an advanced industrial society with all the "administration" it requires.

IX

Sixth and last, communist society is also unique in the kind of human groups it has and doesn't have. The humankind we know is divided into various nations, races, religions, geographical sections (town dweller / country dweller), classes, occupations, and families. No doubt, for many people a world where these distinctions cannot be made is inconceivable. Yet, this is just the situation Marx introduces us to in communism. First of all, our globe is no longer divided into countries.[105] An approach to grasping what has occurred may be had by viewing the whole world as one nation. One should recognize, however, that the term "nation" has been imported from the vocabulary of another time. The world as a nation performs none of the functions associated with the nations of old. We have just seen how the state has withered away, there is no world parliament, world court, or world army, and—aside from some world managers to coordinate production on this macrocosmic scale—there is no world executive.

Both as a producer and as a consumer, the individual is profoundly affected by the disappearance of the state. Marx tells us that in their artistic endeavors—and everyone at this time engages in some type of artistry—communist people are no longer subjected to national limitations.[106] No longer bound by the experience, tastes, and tools of his locality, each person is able to express his emotions and thoughts in a universal manner. If art can free itself of the limiting effect of customs, so can material production and indeed everything else people do once the constraints of nationhood and nationalism are removed. I have already noted Marx's belief that everyone will eventually speak a single language.[107] The existence of such a language does not mean that lesser local languages and the distinctive cultures which accompany them will all disappear. Latin and Latin culture have enriched the lives of millions long after the decline of the Roman empire, and I expect the same fate awaits most other tongues and traditions which are now widespread.

The cosmopolitanism of people as producers is matched by their new cosmopolitanism as consumers. People are able to use and fully appreciate all manner of products. Of this period, Marx says, "Only then will the separate individuals be liberated from the various national and local barriers, be brought into practical connection with the material and intellectual production of the whole world and be put in a position to acquire the capacity to enjoy this all-sided production of the whole earth (the creations of man)."[108]

Religious divisions between people have also ceased to exist in communism with the demise of all mystical beliefs. Superstition has given way to science, and individual fear and weakness to the power of the community. What Marx calls "the witchery of religion" is no more.[109] Communist people are not atheists; this is a term Marx avoids because of its suggestion of being anti-religion. The truth is that religion has stopped being a matter of concern. People are neither for nor against it; they are disinterested. As with the state, religion simply withers away as its functions, particularly of explanation and compensation, disappear.

The distinction between city-bred and country-bred people also falls by the wayside in communism where the whole countryside is spotted with cities and cities are equally invaded by the countryside.[110]

Divisions between people on the basis of class were practically non-existent in the first stage of communism, where everyone was already a worker. In one place, Marx goes so far as to claim that with everyone engaged in productive work classes cease to exist.[111] Yet, we also know that a major task of the dictatorship of the proletariat is to control and convert remnants of the capitalist class, so not every "worker" in this transition period is an equal member of the proletariat.[112] Marx uses several criteria to assess class membership, and it is simply that the dictatorship of the proletariat is classless in some senses and not in others.[113] By full communism, all of Marx's criteria for a classless society have been met.

As for setting people apart because of their occupations, this went out with permanent occupations. Each person in communism engages in a variety of productive tasks.

Probably the least known of Marx's projections for communism has to do with the end of racial divisions. Marx did not enjoy floundering so deeply in the unknown; nevertheless, his single expression of opinion on this subject is very forthright. While discussing the effect of environment, Marx says, "The capacity for development of infants depends on the development of parents and all the mutilations of individuals, which are an historical product of ancient social conditions, are equally capable of being historically avoided. Even the natural diversity of species, as for example the differences of race, etc., are and must be checked historically."[114] Marx is not just referring to a few racial characteristics; his words are "the differences of race." No doubt, he saw some differences as easier to change than others, but if so this is nowhere stated. When we consider the quality of the cooperation which exists between all people in communism and their ready access to one another, it is not surprising that Marx envisioned a time—perhaps thousands of years hence—when all the world's races have blended into one.

If the least known of Marx's projections for communism is the end of racial divisions, probably the best known—and maybe for that reason the most distorted—is the abolition of the family.

Marx spoke of the "earthly family" being destroyed "both in theory and practice" in communism.[115] Some people have taken this to mean the end of all intimate relationships, free love, forced separation from children, and many other "immoralities," each more gross than the one before. Marx is guilty of none of these sins. To begin with, the form of the family that he claims will disappear is the bourgeois family. According to him, this is a form based on capital and private gain, in which economic advantage is the main reason for entering marriage, in which the male has practically all the rights, in which parents have almost total power over their children, and in which the stifling closeness between members of the family excludes most kinds of intimacy with other people.[116] The task of abolishing this form of the family had been begun by the bourgeoisie themselves when they forced conditions of life upon their workers which made it impossible for them to spend much time with their wives and children, and destroyed all privacy when they were together. It is in this sense that Marx maintains the family had practically ceased to exist among the proletariat.[117]

The communist alternative to the family is never stated very clearly, but it can be pieced together from Marx's scattered comments on this subject. Its main features appear to be group living, monogamous sexual relationships, and the communal raising of children. The group living aspect is apparent from Marx's contrast of the family with what he calls a "communal domestic economy."[118] All the advances of modern science are used to make living together as comfortable and harmonious as possible. Whether people eat in communal dining rooms, sleep in the same building, share household tasks, etc., is not disclosed, though I suspect this is the kind of thing Marx had in mind.

A great deal of the abuse leveled against communism has been directed at what is really a phantom of the bourgeois imagination. The abolition of the family and free love, that is indiscriminate sexual activity by both sexes, are almost always joined together in the minds of those who criticize communism. Marx, however, opposes sexual promiscuity (at least for adults) both for the society in which he lives and for communism. His hostility to the sexual antics of the bourgeoisie and the sarcasm with which he treats charges of the same in communism are clear evidence of this.[119] He also attacks the school he calls "crude communism" for having as one of its goals "the community of women."[120] Sex in his ideal society is always associated with love, and love of this kind appears to be an exclusive if sometimes temporary relationship between one man and one woman. The universal love which was alluded to in our discussion of cooperation in communism does not include engaging indiscriminately in the sexual act, for Marx acknowledges there will continue to be something like unrequited love and calls it a misfortune.[121]

To grasp Marx's views on this subject, it is necessary to see that he is wholly on the side of love and lovers, that he demands a full equality for both partners, and that he views sexual love in communism as the highest expression of the new kind of relationship which exists between all people in this period. In *The Holy Family,* that extended review of Eugene Sue's novel *Mysteries of Paris,* Marx sides time and time again with the most sensual characters, with those who can and want to love.[122] And in the *Economic and Philosophic Manuscripts of 1844* we learn that women have become men's equals in love as in all else, and that the type of mutual consideration which characterizes sexual love in communism has become the measure of perfection for all contacts with other people.[123]

The communal raising of children is never mentioned explicitly, but can be deduced from other aspects of communist life which seem to require it. For Marx, aside from minor differences due to heredity, a child's development is determined by his or her environment, an important part of which is the parental home. In capitalism, parents have considerable control over their children's health, education, work, marriage, etc., but, given the parents' own problems and limitations, this power is seldom used wisely. In communism, parents will no longer be allowed to exercise a destructive influence on their children. This does not mean that they will be forcibly separated from their young. Given communist sociality, that is without the pervading selfishness and emotional insecurity which characterize current parent-child relations, communist parents will want a community no less perfect for their children than the one they construct for themselves.

Not only children, of course, but adults as well require special conditions to realize their full human potential. We have already seen the importance Marx attaches to free time. Though he never deals with the drain children are on their parents, particularly on mothers, he surely was aware of it. Already living in the "communal domestic economy," the arrangement which seems best suited to permit self-realization of young and old alike is some kind of communal raising of children. Parents and children simply spend as much time together and apart as their respective development requires. Unlike today, however, the time together is no longer rooted in necessary work and customary duties, but in the same desire to satisfy common needs which characterizes all social contact in the communist society.[124]

It should be clear by now that Marx is far more precise about the social and other divisions which will disappear in communism than about what will replace them. Nations, religions, geographical sections, classes, occupations, races and families are to disappear, but what new social categories will emerge? Before attempting an answer it is important to specify that Marx viewed all such divisions as barriers to the direct contact between people and, therefore, to the fulfillment of human potential in so far as it requires this contact. With the overturning of these barriers, people can see, appreciate, and react to each other as individuals, rather than as members of the groups into which they were either born or educated. People can no longer be treated as instances of a kind when the kinds of which they are instances themselves disappear. Erasing social lines *per se,* then, is a major task of the dictatorship of the proletariat, and fusion of the once separate and distinct social categories is one of the surest signs that communism has arrived.

However, even communism contains boundary lines of a sort which allow some distinctions between people to be made. From what has been said, it would appear that these new subdivisions, like the social organs they contain, are consciously designed functional units which merely express the most efficient and humane ways of getting things done. The factory, the communal domestic economy, and the industrial army for agriculture are examples of the functional units into which communist society is divided. With people changing jobs as often as they do, however, it is unlikely that a person will carry one work place label for very long. I suspect that distinctions based on membership in communal domestic economies are of a more durable nature, since home groups are likely to be more pemanent than work groups.

These boundary lines in communist society are never barriers to direct human contact. For though they aid us in making passing distinctions between individuals, they do not really substitute for our understanding of them as people, as the corresponding attributes do in earlier periods. The difference is that everyone at this time possesses or could easily acquire the credentials for membership in any group. Thus, when discussing communism, Marx dismisses its particular associations and directs all his remarks to the species, to human beings who are forever dividing and re-dividing society in pursuit of human goals.[125]

X

Our reconstruction of communism is now complete, or as complete as Marx's diverse comments permit. As a way of life, communism develops in people extraordinary qualities which are themselves necessary for this way of life to operate. What are these qualities? On the basis of the foregoing account we can say that the citizen of the future is someone who is interested in and skillful in carrying out a variety of tasks, who is highly and consistently cooperative, who conceives of all objects in terms of "ours," who shares with others a masterful control over the forces of nature, who regulates his/her activities without the help of externally imposed rules, and who is indistinguishable from other persons when viewed from the perspective of existing social divisions. She (he) is, in short, a brilliant, highly rational and socialized, humane and successful creator. In a terminology preferred by a younger Marx, this is the accomplished figure who "brings his species powers out of himself" and "grasps the human nature of need," the same who "appropriates his total essence...as a whole man."[126]

Each part of this description of people in communism can serve as the full account once its relations with the whole are recognized. An individual could only engage successfully in so many activities if he cooperates with his fellows at every turn, treats all material objects as belonging to the group, enjoys the requisite power over nature, etc. In the same way, he can only exercise communist sociality if he is able to do a variety of tasks with the ease of an expert, treat objects as "ours," and the rest. Just as no aspect of communist life can arise independently, none of the qualities ascribed to communist people can emerge alone. As internally related parts of an organic whole, each assumes and is based on the presence of all. Marx's best known description of communism—that it is a classless society, a time when the division of labor has disappeared, and when private property has been abolished—are all to be viewed in this light.[127] Rather than partial, one-sided alternatives, these descriptions of communism (including each other as necessary conditions and/or results) are equally complete, the only difference being one of focus and emphasis within the totality.

The qualities and life Marx ascribes to the people of communism represent a complete victory over the alienation that has characterized humanity's existence throughout class society, reaching its culmination in the relations between workers and capitalists in modern capitalism. At the core of alienation is the separation of the individual from the conditions of human existence, chiefly his activities (particularly production), their real and potential products, and other people. As a result of class divisions and accompanying antagonisms, people have lost control over all social expressions of their humanity, grossly misunderstanding them in the process, coming eventually to service the "needs" of their own creations. Viewing whatever people do and use to satisfy their needs and realize their powers as elements of human nature, the progressive dismemberment of human nature (alienation) becomes identical with the stunting and distortion of potential in each real individual. The bringing together or reunification on a higher technological plane of the elements of human nature that earlier societies had torn asunder begins with the revolution, gains momentum in the dictatorship of the proletariat, and is only completed in full communism. To the extent that social life remains split up (separated by barriers of occupation, religion, family, etc.) and misunderstood in the first stage of communism, the people of this period can still be spoken of as alienated (which is not to say that the theory of alienation with which Marx captures the dynamics of a market society is still useful in explaining social change).

As opposites, alienation and communism serve as necessary

points of reference for each other. A theoretically adequate description of communism, therefore, would have to include an extended account of alienation. I have offered such an account elsewhere.[128] In the present essay, I have been content to sacrifice some theoretical adequacy to the demands of a simpler, more coherent vision.

The question that remains is how to evaluate Marx's vision of communism. Experience is not a relevant criterion, though the history of the species should make us sensitive to the enormous flexibility of human needs and powers. It is no use to say (though people continue to say it) that such a society has never existed and that the people Marx depicts have never lived. The communist society is the ultimate achievement of a long series of develop- ments which begin with the socialist appropriation of the capitalist mode of production. Its distinctive characteristics evolve gradually out of the programs adopted in the dictatorship of the proletariat and the new relationships and possibilities established. These characteristics cannot exist—and one should not expect to find them—before this context itself has developed in ways that the world has yet to experience. Likewise, the extraordinary qualities Marx ascribes to the people of com- munism could never exist outside of the unique conditions which give rise to them, and given these conditions the development of other qualities, certainly of opposing qualities, simply makes no sense. One can only state the unproven assumptions on which this expected flowering of human nature rests. These are that the individual's potential is so varied and great; that people possess an inner drive to realize all this potential; that the whole range of powers in each person can be fully realized together; and that the overall fulfillment of each individual is compatible with that of all others. Given how often and drastically the development and discovery of new social forms has extended accepted views of what is human, I think it would be unwise at this time to foreclose on the possibility that Marx's assumptions are correct.

There is really only one way to evaluate Marx's vision of communism and that is to examine his analysis of capitalism to see if the communist society is indeed present within it as an unrealized potential. If Marx sought, as he tells us, "to find the new world through the criticism of the old," then any judgment of his views on communism rests in the last analysis on the validity of his critique of capitalism. This is not the place for the extensive examination that is required but I would like to offer three guidelines to those who would undertake it: 1) capitalism must be conceptualized in terms of social relations, Marx's way of incorporating the actual past and future possibilities of his subject into his study of its present forms (this is the logical basis of Marx's study of history, including future history, as a process); 2) a Marxist analysis of today's capitalism should be integrated into Marx's analysis of late 19th century capitalism (the social relations from which projections are made must be brought up to date); and 3) one should not try to show that communism is inevitable, only that it is possible, that it is based on conditions inherent in the further development of our present ones. After all, communism is hardly ever opposed because one holds other values, but because it is said to be an unrealizable ideal. In these circumstances, making a case for communism as a *possible* successor to capitalism is generally enough to convince people that they must help to bring it about.[129]

Notes

1. Herbert Marcuse, *Five Lectures: Psychoanalysis, Politics and Utopia,* trans. J. J. Shapiro and S. M. Webber (Boston, 1970), p. 62.

2. Karl Marx, "Letter to Ruge," *Writings of the Young Marx on Philosophy and Society,* trans. and ed. L. D. Easton and K. H. Guddat (N.Y., 1967), p. 212.

3. Though Marx considered revolution the most likely possibility, he lists England, the United States and Holland as countries where socialism might be attained by "peaceful means." H. Gerth, ed., *The First International: Minutes of the Hague Congress of 1872* (Madison, 1958), p. 236.

4. Marx and Engels, *German Ideology,* trans. R. Pascal (London, 1942), p. 26. Engels, in a letter written shortly before his death goes so far as to say that it is impossible to provide details on communism "without falling into utopianism or empty phrasemaking." Marx and Engels, *Werke* XXXIX (Berlin, 1968), p. 195. Such a view of attempts to describe the future was also a part of Marx's Hegelian heritage. Hegel had said, "since philosophy is the exploration of the rational, it is for that reason the apprehension of the present and actual, not the erection of a beyond, supposed to exist God knows where, or rather which exists, and we can perfectly well say where, namely in the error of a one-sided, empty ratiocination." G.W.F. Hegel, *Philosophy of Right,* trans. T.M. Knox (Oxford, 1942), p. 10.

5. Marx and Engels, *Briefwechsel I* (Berlin, 1949), p. 348.

6. Marx, "Critique of the Gotha Program," *Selected Writings II* (Moscow, 1951), p. 21.

7. *Ibid.,* p. 21.

8. Marx and Engels, *Communist Manifesto,* trans. S. Moore (Chicago, 1945), pp. 42-3.

9. Marx, "Civil War in France," *Selected Writings I*, p. 476.

10. H. Meyer, "Marx on Bakunin," *Etudes de Marxologie* (October, 1959), pp. 108-9.

11. *Ibid.,*p. 109.

12. "Civil War," *Selected Writings I*, p. 476.

13. "Gotha Critique," *Selected Writings II*, p. 22.

14. Marx, Engels and others, "Forderungen der Kommunistischen Partei in Deutschland," *Werke V* (Berlin, 1959), p. 4.

15. According to Marx capitalism created a "vast number of employments, at present indispensable, but in themselves superfluous." Advertising, insurance, and the stock exchange are obvious cases of "industries" which would disappear in what Marx calls "the avoidance of all useless labour." Marx, *Capital I*, trans. S. Moore and E. Aveling (Moscow, 1958), p. 530.

16. "Forderungen der Kommunistischen Partei," *Werke V*, p. 4.

17. Marx, *Capital III* (Moscow, 1959), p. 826.

18. "Civil War," *Selected Writings I*, p. 474; "Gotha Critique," *Selected Writings II*, p. 22.

19. *German Ideology*, p. 44. Marx goes on to explain that "The town is in actual fact the concentration of the population, of the instruments of production, of capital, of pleasures, of needs, while the country demonstrates just the opposite fact, their isolation and separation."

20. *Capital III*, p. 793; *Communist Manifesto*, p. 18.

21. *German Ideology*, p. 44.

22. *Capital I*, p. 505.

23. "Gotha Critique," *Selected Writings II*, p. 32.

24. John Bellers, a 17th century English writer, is allowed to express their common view on this subject: "An idle learning being little better than the learning of idleness...Bodily labor, it's a primitive institution of God...Labor being as proper for the body's health as eating is for its living; for what pains a man saves by ease, he will find in disease...Labor adds oil to the lamp of life, when thinking inflames it...A childish silly employ...leaves the children's minds silly." *Capital I*, pp. 488-9.

25. *Ibid.*, p. 484. He also says that "technical instruction, both theoretical and practical, will take its proper place in working class schools." *Ibid.*, p. 488.

26. H. Draper, "Marx and the Dictatorship of the Proletariat," *Etudes de Marxologie* (September, 1962), p. 30.

27. Marx, Engels and others, "Weltgesellschaft der Revolutionaren Kommunisten," *Werke VII* (Berlin, 1960), p. 553.

28. Meyer, "Marx on Bakunin," *Etudes de Marxologie* (October, 1959), p. 108.

29. "Civil War," *Selected Writings I*, p. 473.

30. *Ibid.*, p. 471.

31. *Ibid.*

32. *Ibid.*, p. 470.

33. *Ibid.*, p. 472.

34. Meyer, "Marx on Bakunin," *Etudes de Marxologie* (October, 1959), p. 112.

35. *German Ideology*, p. 25.

36. *Capital III*, p. 86. Marx strongly approved of the factory laws passed by the Paris Commune. "Civil War," *Selected Writings I*, p. 478.

37. *Capital I*, p. 530.
38. Marx, *Theorien uber der Mehwert III*, ed. K. Kautsky (Stuttgart, 1910), pp. 303-4.
39. *Capital I*, p. 530.
40. *Theories of Surplus Value III*, p. 505.
41. *Capital III*, p. 854; Marx, *Poverty of Philosophy* (Moscow, n.d.), p. 70.
42. *Capital III*, p. 184.
43. "Gotha Critique," *Selected Writings II*, p. 20.
44. *Ibid.*, pp. 20-1.
45. "Civil War," *Selected Writings I*, p. 471.
46. *Capital I*, p. 530.
47. Marx says, "What the producer is deprived of in his capacity as a private individual benefits him...in his capacity as a member of society." "Gotha Critique," *Selected Writings II, p. 21.*
48. *Ibid.*, pp. 21-2.
49. "Civil War," *Selected Writings I*, p. 471.
50. *Capital II*, p. 358.
51. "Gotha Critique," *Selected Writings II, p. 22.*
52. For an interesting debate between those who see workers' control operating at this time and those who believe Marx favours centralized state ownership and control of industry, see the articles by R. Selucky and H. H. Ticktin in *Critique* (Autumn, 1974). Marx's actual comments on this subject make it difficult to come out strongly for either view. Typical is his claim that to say workers own their own means of production is to say "these belong to the united workers and that they produce as such, and that their own output is controled jointly by them." *Theories of Surplus Value III*, p. 525.
53. *Poverty of Philosophy*, p. 161.
54. "Gotha Critique," *Selected Writings II*, p. 23.
55. Marx, *Economic and Philosophic Manuscripts of 1844*, III, trans. M. Milligan (Moscow, 1959).
56. *German Ideology*, p. 22.
57. In communism, work is "not only a means of life, but life's prime want." "Gotha Critique," *Selected Writings II*, p. 23.
58. Marx and Engels, *Deutsche Ideologie* in *Werke III* (Berlin, 1961), p. 378.
59. Marx approvingly quotes Hegel that, "By well educated men we understand in the first instance, those who can do everything others can do." *Capital I*, p. 363. I hasten to add that for Marx this includes much more than it does for Hegel. This statement was not quoted by Marx for the purpose to which it is being used here, but I consider the inference to communist education a legitimate one.
60. *Deutsche Ideologie* in *Werke III*, p. 378.
61. *German Ideology*, p. 189; "Gotha Critique," *Selected Writings II*, p. 22.
62. This marvelous versatility of communist "man" is generally taken for granted by Marx; he never presents us with a brief. In his works, however, he gives several instances from his own time which are meant to indicate the festival of talents to come. Marx tells us that "the workers, in their communist propaganda, affirm that it is the vocation, the destination of each man to develop himself in many ways, to realize all his dispositions, including the

ability to think." *Deutsche Ideologie* in *Werke III*, p. 273. Marx opposes this claim to Stirner's view that to strive for such multifaceted development is foreign to man's nature. And even in capitalist society, when extraordinary conditions allow it, individuals surprise themselves and contemporaries with their capacity for varied work. Marx quotes a French worker of his day who writes, after returning from a stay in the New World, "I never could have believed, that I was capable of working at the various occupations I was employed on in California. I was firmly convinced that I was fit for nothing but letter press printing...Once in the midst of this world of adventurers, who change their occupation as often as they do their shirt, egad, I did as the others. As mining did not turn out remunerative enough, I left it for the town, where in succession I became typographer, slater, plumber, etc. In consequence of thus finding out that I am fit for any sort of work, I feel less of a mollusk and more of a man." *Capital I*, p. 487. In the ideal conditions of communism, this sense of accomplishment would be far greater and would apply to everybody.

63. *1844 Manuscripts*, p. 104.

64. *Ibid.*

65. *German Ideology*, p. 27.

66. It is in this sense, that Marx declares, "Society...is man himself in his social relations," and "Not until man has recognized his own capacities as social capacities...will human emancipation be achieved." Marx, *Grundrisse der Kritik des Politischen Okonomie* (Berlin, 1953), p. 600; *Werke I*, p. 370.

67. Marx claims that in production, "the labor power of all the different individuals is consciously applied as the combined labor power of the community." *Capital I*, p. 78.

68. On one occasion, this recognition is expressed as follows: "You are placed in a human relation with my product, you have need of my product. This exists for you then as an object of your desire and of your will." Marx and Engels, *Gesamtausgabe* I: 3, ed. V. Adoratsky (Berlin, 1932), p. 544.

69. *Ibid.*, pp. 546-47. Marx continues, "I would also have the job of having been the mediator between you and the human species, therefore of being recognized and experienced by you yourself as a complement of your own nature and as a necessary part of your being, therefore of knowing myself affirmed in your thoughts as in your love. Finally, the joy of having produced in the individual manifestation of my life the direct manifestation of your life, therefore of having affirmed and realized in my individual activity my true nature, my human nature, my social being." And, again, "In so far as man, and hence also his feelings, etc., are human, the affirmation of the object by another is likewise his own enjoyment." *1844 Manuscripts*, p. 136. This idea is also expressed in the claim that, "Need or enjoyment have consequently lost their egotistical nature." *Ibid.*, p. 107.

70. *Gesamtausgabe* I:3, p. 547.

71. Marx gives us some indication of what this is like in a passage where he describes socialist workers of his own time and the new need they have acquired for "society:" "what appears as a means becomes an end. You can observe this practical process in its most splendid results wherever you can see French socialist workers together. Such things as smoking, drinking, eating, etc., are no longer means of contact or means that bring together. Company, association, conversation, which again has society as its end, are enough for them." *1844 Manuscripts*, p. 124. The tendencies of an advanced section of workers in

capitalism are firmly and fully established among everyone in communism.
72. *Communist Manifesto*, p. 36.
73. *1844 Manuscripts*, p. 102.
74. *Ibid.* p. 107.
75. *Capital III*, p. 757.
76. *Ibid.* p. 854.
77. "Gotha Critique," *Selected Writings II*, p. 23. A typical criticism of this principle which shows how far most commentators are from grasping the people and conditions of communism is O.D. Skelton's claim that the individual's desire is limited, and if he himself decides his needs, "The socialist treasury would be bankrupt in a week." Yet, he claims, if there is an official estimate, the opportunities for tyranny and graft are enormous. O.D. Skelton, *Socialism* (Boston, 1911), p. 203.
78. *Deutsche Ideologie* in *Werke III*, p. 424.
79. *German Ideology*, p. 68.
80. *Capital I*, p. 75. Marx is quoting here from Engels' early essay, "Outlines of a Critique of Political Economy."
81. *1844 Manuscripts*, *III*.
82. *Grundrisse*, p. 440.
83. *German Ideology*, p. 70.
84. *Ibid.*
85. *1844 Manuscripts*, p. 104. Thus, too, Marx can declare that "communism as fully developed naturalism equals humanism," and that "it is the genuine resolution of the conflict between man and nature." *Ibid.* p. 102.
86. *Deutsche Ideologie* in *Werke III*, p. 411.
87. *German Ideology*, p. 18.
88. *Ibid.*, p. 75.
89. *Capital III*, p. 76.
90. *Communist Manifesto*, p. 36.
91. "Gotha Critique," *Selected Writings, II*, p. 23.
92. *Capital III*, p. 83.
93. *Grundrisse*, p. 505.
94. *Capital III*, pp. 799-800.
95. Marx and Engels, *The Holy Family*, trans. R. Dixon (Moscow, 1956), p. 176.
96. *Grundrisse*, p. 505. Marx also says, "Really free labor...gives up its purely natural, primitive aspects and becomes the activity of a subject controlling all the forces of nature in the productive process." *Ibid.*
97. Marx and Engels, *On Colonialism* (Moscow, n.d.), p. 52.
98. *Capital III*, p. 799.
99. *Holy Family*, p. 238.
100. *Ibid.* p. 239.
101. *Communist Manifesto*, p. 43. *Associerten Individuen* has been seriously mistranslated in most English editions of the *Manifesto* as a "vast association of the whole *nation*" (as opposed to "of associated *individuals*") lending a statist tone to this popular quotation which it does not have. I am thankful to Peter Bergman for pointing this out to me.
102. "Gotha Critique," *Selected Writings II*, p. 30.
103. *Colonialism*, p. 126.

104. Meyer, *Etudes de Marxologie*, p. 112.

105. *Communist Manifesto*, p. 39.

106. *Deutsche Ideologie* in *Werke II*, p. 378.

107. *Ibid.*, p. 411.

108. *German Ideology*, p. 27.

109. "Gotha Critique," *Selected Writings II*, p. 22.

110. *German Ideology*, p. 44.

111. "Gotha Critique," *Selected Writings II*, p. 22.

112. Meyer, *Etudes de Marxologie*, p. 108.

113. For a fuller treatment of class, see my article, "Marx's Use of 'Class'," which appears in chapter 2 of this book.

114. *Deutsche Ideologie* in *Werke III*, p. 410.

115. "Theses on Feuerbach," *German Ideology*, p. 198.

116. *Communist Manifesto*, pp. 37-39.

117. *Ibid.*, p. 37.

118. He says, "The setting up of a communal domestic economy presupposes the development of machinery, of the use of natural forces and of many other productive forces, for example, of water, of gas lighting, steam heating, etc., the removal of the antagonism of town and country. Without these conditions a communal economy would not in itself form a new productive force: lacking any material basis and resting on a purely theoretical foundation, it would be a mere freak and would end in nothing more than a monastic economy. What was possible can be seen in the formation of towns and the erection of communal buildings for various definite purposes (prisons, barracks, etc.). That the abolition of individual economy is inseparable from the abolition of the family is self-evident." *German Ideology*, pp. 17-18.

119. *Communist Manifesto*, pp. 38-39.

120. *1844 Manuscripts*, pp. 99-100.

121. *Ibid.*, p. 141.

122. See *Holy Family*, pp. 88-89, 91, 93, 102. Cecily, Rigollette, and Fleur de Marie are the positive characters in the novel for Marx.

123. *1844 Manuscripts*, pp. 100-101.

124. The tempting though dangerous comparison between the communist version of the family and the Israeli *kibutz* may have crossed the minds of some readers. Though the people living in *kibutzim* exercise considerable primary democracy, eat in communal dining halls, share some household tasks, and raise their children in common, I find the comparison dangerously misleading for the following reasons: 1) The *kibutz* operates in an economy of scarcity, which necessitates that women work, that people eat in a communal dining hall, that children are raised in common, etc. This gives a Spartan character to all these activities which is decidedly non-communist. 2) The *kibutz* is set in the countryside, which setting and its accompanying mode of existence is glorified in a sort of Tolstoyan agrarian mystique; as a result, its inhabitants have too little contact with city work, technology, and culture, all of which reflect on family relationships. 3) The *kibutz* exists in a specific state, Israel, and must abide by the laws of that state on all matters relating to marriage, divorce, children, etc. This is a straitjacket communist people do not wear. 4) The *kibutz* has too many restrictive rules for family life as for all else, especially when

compared to a society which has none. 5) Finally, people living on the *kibutz,* like all other groups in the world today, are of another *genre* than the people of communism. The same activity or form of organization becomes something else when the people involved act from widely varying motives, achieve other kinds of satisfaction, understand their actions differently, and so on.

125. Marx says that in communism the evolution of species man finally coincides with the evolution of each particular individual. Marx, *Theorien uber Mehrwert* II, ed. K. Kautsky (Stuttgart, 1921), p. 309.

126. *1844 Manuscripts,* pp. 101, 105, 151.

127. For an account of capitalism which stresses the internal relations between all its components, see my book, *Alienation: Marx's Conception of Man in Capitalist Society* (Cambridge, 1976).

128. *Ibid.,* Parts II and III.

129. A final word on the sources of Marx's vision of communism: having as my main purpose to reconstruct this vision and believing that it is internally related to Marx's analysis of capitalism. I have purposely omitted all mention of the Utopian socialists. Yet, there is no question but that Fourier, Saint-Simon, and Owen in particular exercised an important influence on Marx. They have been left out of this paper because I distinguish between those ideas which brought Marx to that analysis of capitalism and history we call "Marxism" and the somewhat similar views which exist as a part of this analysis. The Utopians' vision of the future, operating as some kind of ethical ideal because it stands outside of what is understood of man and society, contributed to Marx's early political stance and clearly influenced the direction of his studies. Once Marx's analysis reached the point where he could project the real possibilities inherent in capitalist society, however, the logical status of such views changed from being the independent principle or ideal in an ethical system to being an integral (if still to be realized) part of the real world. The same analysis resulted in a sifting and refocussing of whatever notions Marx inherited on communism in line with newly discovered possibilities. Lacking such an analysis, the Utopians could only serve up a mixture of dreams, intuitions and fond hopes. If it is necessary to study Utopians, therefore, in order to understand how Marx came to Marxism, including its vision of the future, the same study may actually distort what these ideas are and confuse rather than help our efforts to judge them.

Other useful discussions of Marx's vison of communism can be found in Ralf Dahrendorf, *Marx in Perspective* (Hanover, 1952), particularly pp. 72-117; Ramm, Thilo, "Die Kunstige Gesellschaftsordnung nach der Theorie von Marx und Engels," *Marxismusstudien,* ed. Irving Fetscher (Tubingen, 1957), pp. 77-119; J.Y. Calvex, *La Pensee de Karl Marx* (Paris, 1956), pp. 504-554; K. Axelos, *Marx, penseur de la technique* (Paris, 1970), Part V; and the various articles in *Etudes de Marxologie* (November, 1970). For the fullest selection of Marx's comments on communism, see M. Rubel, ed., *Pages choisies pour une ethique socialiste* (Paris, 1948). The extent to which Russian Marxists and their Western followers have pared down Marx's vision can be seen from the articles in *Recherches internationales a la lumiere du Marxisme,* vol. 18 (Paris, 1960).

4.

Marxism and Political Science: Prolegomenon to a Debate on Marx's Method

I

The debates between Marxists and non-Marxists that have been raging for a half century and more in the disciplines of sociology, history, economics, and philosophy are strikingly absent in political science. This is true not only in Anglo-Saxon countries, where Marxists particularly in academia have always been a rare breed, but even on the continent where Marxists and Marxist ideas play an important role in every sector of social life.

What makes this absence especially difficult to explain is that a growing number of political scientists accept such essentials of the Marxist critique of their discipline as that it deals with superficialities and is generally biased on behalf of the status quo. A recent survey of political scientists, for example, showed that two out of three "agreed" or "strongly agreed" that much scholarship in the profession is "superficial and trivial" and that concept formation and development is "little more than hair splitting and jargon."[1] The belief that most studies in political science are more useful to those who have power than to those who are trying to attain it is not as widespread, but it, too, is gaining ground. These biases are present not only in the theories which are offered to explain empirical findings, but in the choice of problems to research, and in the very concepts (themselves rooted in theory) by which the project and its product are thought about and communicated. The distortions introduced into political science, for example, by the standard assumption of the legitimacy and longevity of the present political system have yet to be adequately explored. In many ways, the least important biases (or parts of bias, since they always belong to a system of thought) are the values which an increasing number of scholars admit to at the start of their studies. This is the part of the iceberg that shows, and at least here readers stand warned.

Charges of bias, as is well known, are easier to voice than to argue, and when laid to bad faith are generally unconvincing. Few of our colleagues actually take themselves for civil servants. The same political scientists who perceive the pervading bias in the field often feel uneasy about their inability to analyze it. Similarly, political scientists (whether the same ones or not) who condemn the profession for triviality are reduced to contributing more of the same, since they do not know what else to study or how (with what theories, concepts, techniques) to study it. What is missing is a theory that would provide the necessary perspective to study and explain, to research and criticize both political life and accepted modes of describing it, i.e., political science. Marxism is that theory.

The reasons why a Marxist school of political scientists has not yet emerged, despite what appear to be favorable conditions, are rooted chiefly in the historical peculiarities of both Marxism and political science. Marx concentrated most of his mature efforts on the capitalist economy, but—even aside from essays on French and English politics and the early critique of Hegel— there is a lot more on the state in his writings than is generally recognized. In particular, *Capital* contains a theory of the state which, unlike Marx's related economic theories, is never fully worked out. This is a subject Marx hoped to develop if and when his work in economics permitted. An outline of his overall project gives the state a much more important role in his explanation of capitalism than would appear to be the case from a glance at his finished work. After Marx died, most of his followers erroneously attributed an influence to the different social spheres in proportion to the treatment accorded them in his published writings. This error was facilitated by the standard interpretation of Marx's well-known claims on the relationship between the economic base and the social-political-cultural superstructure. If the economic life of society is solely and wholly responsible for the character and development of other spheres, the activities which go on in the latter can be safely ignored or, if need be, deduced. Engels' end of life correspondence is full of warnings against this interpretation, but they seem to have had little effect. Among Marx's more prominent followers, only Lukacs, Korsch, and Gramsci wholly reject economic determinism (reductionism) as the framework in which to understand the state. The ever more active role of the state in directing the capitalist economy has led a new generation of Marxists to make the state a prime object of study. The first important fruits of this effort are Ralph Miliband's *The State in Capitalist Society* (1969), Nicos Poulantzas' *Pouvoir politique et classes sociales* (1968), James O'Connor's *The Fiscal Crisis of the State* (1973), and (though he might deny it) Gabriel Kolko's *The Triumph of Conservatism* (1963).

Given the insignificant role of the state in Marxism, as interpreted by most Marxists, it is little wonder that academics who chose to study politics were not attracted to this theory. The history of political science as a distinct discipline, however, has also contributed to this disinterest. Unlike economics and sociology, which began as attempts to understand whole societies, the origins of political science lay in jurisprudence and statescraft. Instead of investigating the workings of the political process in its connection with other social processes, political science's emphasis has been on a segment of the whole, on the political process as such. Aims have generally revolved around making existing political institutions more efficient. There is no radical tradition, no group of major radical thinkers, no body of consistent radical thought in political science such as one finds— at least to some degree—in sociology, economics, and history. From Machiavelli to Kissinger, political science has been the domain of those who—believing they understood the realities of power—have sought their reforms and advancement within the system, and has habitually attracted equally practical-minded students. The turmoil in American life, however, has taken its toll here as elsewhere. The recent flood of critical remarks (if not yet studies), the publication of *Politics and Society* and *Kapitalistate* and the organization of the Caucus for a New Political Science are signs of a change in political science that has gotten under way.*

Projecting such trends into the future—if we exclude the usual cataclysms—leads to the expectation that radical protest in political science will increasingly take on a Marxist character. What exactly this will look like, how penetrating the analyses will be, how meaningful the dialogue with non-Marxists, etc., remains to be seen. I believe it is necessary, particularly in the first stages of this development, that Marxists give priority to questions of method over questions of theory, insofar, of course, as the two can be distinguished. For it is only upon grasping the assumptions and means, forms and techniques with which Marx constructed his explanations of capitalism that we can effectively use, develop, amend, and even evaluate them. And perhaps as important for Marxists teaching in universities, only by making this method explicit can we communicate with non- (and not yet) Marxist colleagues and students whose shared language masks the real distance which separates our two approaches.

In keeping with this conception of priorities, the present paper will focus on Marx's method. It may be useful, however, to review briefly those elements in Marx's theory of the state whose comprehension requires this approach. Whether dealing with politics or any other social sector, it must be stressed that Marx is concerned with all of capitalism—with its birth, development, and decay as a social system. More specifically, he wants to understand (and explain) where the present state of affairs comes from, how it coheres, what are the forces producing change, how these facts are dissimulated, where the present is tending (including possible alternatives), and how we can affect this process. Marx's theory of the state seeks to answer these questions for the political arena, but in such a way as to illuminate the character and development of capitalism as a

---

* The developments mentioned above have all continued apace in the five years since these lines were written, but they have not proceeded so far as to require qualifications to what has been said.

whole (which is no different than what could be said of his theories dealing with other aspects of capitalist life).

The main subjects treated in Marx's theory of the state, taken in the above manner, are as follows: 1) the character of the state as a social power, rooted in the conditions of cooperation coming out of the division of labor, that has become independent of the individual producers; 2) the effect of social-economic relations established in the division of labor on state forms and activities, and the state's function in stabilizing these relations; 3) the effect of state forms and activities on the production of value and on the reproduction of the conditions underlying the production of value; 4) the control, both direct and indirect, exercised over the state by the dominant economic class; 5) the conditions in which the state acquires a degree of autonomy from the dominant economic class; 6) the ways in which politics is ordinarily understood in society, the social origins of such understanding (including both ideas and categories), and the role this perception plays in helping the state perform its stabilizing function; and 7) the possibility inherent in the foregoing relations, taken as historical trends, for the emergence of a form of state whose aim is to establish communal control over social power, or to abolish the basis of the state itself.

What Marx has to say on each of these subjects (the actual contents of his theory of the state) cannot be given at this time; but even listing what these subjects are should indicate some of the problems involved. In every instance, Marx's theory of the state is concerned with relations inside a given system, with trying to reestablish this system in an account of these relations. This makes it absolutely necessary that we grasp the logical character of such relations and of the system in which they reside. Otherwise, many of his particular claims will appear confused and contradictory. The apparent contradiction between statements which treat the state as an "effect" of economic "causes" and those which speak of "reciprocal interaction" between all social factors offers one such difficulty. Another is the way Marx treats past and possible future developments as somehow part of the present. A third, suggested by the first two, is that the concepts which express such ties have at least partly different meanings from those in ordinary speech. Only resort to Marx's method can clear up these and related problems.

II.

Most discussions of Marx's method have focused either on his philosophy, particularly on the laws of the dialectic as outlined by Engels, or on the techniques of expositions utilized in *Capital*. Such accounts, even when accurate, are very lopsided and, what is worse, useless for the scholar interested in adopting this method for his work. Numerous assumptions and procedures are left out, and their order in the construction and elaboration of Marx's theories is never made explicit. In attempting to make up for this oversight, I may have fallen victim to the opposite error of overschematization, and this is a danger readers of the following pages should bear in mind.

Two further qualifications are required before I begin. First, I don't accord much importance to the different periods in Marx's career. This is not because there were no changes in his method, but because such changes as did occur between 1844, the year he wrote *The Economic and Philosophic Manuscripts,* and the end of his life are relatively minor. I have chosen, nevertheless, to emphasize his later so-called "mature" writings, and the few examples drawn from early works involve aspects of his method which remained the same throughout his career. Second, the method outlined below is that used in Marx's systematic study of capitalism. Consequently, most of its elements can be found in *Capital*, that is, in the work he did for *Capital* and in the finished product; but many fewer are found in the shorter, more occasional pieces. How many of these elements appear in different works is chiefly a matter of Marx's skill in using his method, and neither his skill nor his style (another subject frequently confused with method) enter into our discussion.

What, then, is Marx's method? Broadly speaking, it is his way of grasping reality and of explaining it, and includes all that he does in organizing and manipulating reality for purposes of inquiry and exposition. This method exists on five levels, representing successive stages in its practice: 1) ontology; 2) epistemology; 3) inquiry; 4) intellectual reconstruction; and 5) exposition. Other social science methods could probably be broken down in the same way. What is distinctive about Marx's method, then, is not that it has such stages but the peculiar character of each one.

Ontology is the study of "being." As answer to the question "What is reality?", it involves Marx's most fundamental assumptions regarding the nature and organization of the world. The twin pillars of Marx's ontology are his conception of reality as a totality composed of internally related parts, and his conception of these parts as expandable relations, such that each one in its fullness can represent the totality. Few people would deny that everything in the world is related as causes, conditions, or results; and many insist that the world is unintelligible except in terms of such relations. Marx goes a step further in conceptually interiorizing this interdependence within each thing, so that the conditions of its existence are taken to be part of what it is. Capital, for example, is not simply the physical means of production, but includes potentially the whole pattern of social relations which enables these means to function as they do. While Durkheim, standing at the other extreme, asks that we grasp social facts as things, Marx grasps things as social facts or relations, and is capable of mentally expanding these relations through necessary conditions and results to the point of totality. This is really a version of what historically has been called the *philosophy of internal relations*.

There are basically three different notions of totality in philosophy:

1. The atomistic conception, which goes from Descartes to Wittgenstein, that views the whole as the sum of simple facts.

2. The formalist conception, apparent in Schelling, *probably* Hegel and most modern structuralists, that attributes an identity to the whole independent of its parts and asserts the absolute predominance of this whole over the parts. The real historical subjects in this case are the pre-existing, autonomous tendencies and structures of the whole. Research is undertaken mainly to provide illustrations, and facts which don't "fit" are either ignored or treated as unimportant residue.

3. The dialectical and materialist conception of Marx (often confused with the formalist notion) that views the whole as the structured interdependence of its relational parts—the interacting events, processes, and conditions of the real world—as observed from any major part.[2]

Through the constant interaction and development of these

parts, the whole also changes, realizing possibilities that were inherent in earlier stages. Flux and interaction, projected back into the origins of the present and forward into its possible futures, are the chief distinguishing characteristics of the world in this latter view. They are essential parts of what the world is like, and are taken for granted in any inquiry. Since this interdependence is structured—that is, rooted in relatively stable connections—the same interaction accords the whole a *relative* autonomy, enabling it to have relations as a whole with the parts whose order and unity it represents. These relations are of four sorts: 1) the whole shapes the parts to make them more functional within this particular whole (so it is that capitalism, for example, gets the laws it requires); 2) the whole gives meaning and relative importance to each part in terms of this function (laws in capitalism are only comprehensible as elements in a structure that maintains capitalist society, and are as important as the contribution they make); 3) the whole expresses itself through the part, so that the part can be seen as a form of the whole. Given internal relations, one gets a view of the whole, albeit a one-sided view, when examining any of its parts. It is like looking out at a courtyard from one of the many windows that surround it (study of any major capitalist law which includes its necessary conditions and results will be a study of capitalism); and 4) the relations of the parts with each other, as suggested above, forge the contours and meaning of the whole, transform it into an ongoing system with a history, a goal, and an impact. It is the existence of the last two relationships which distinguish the first two from the formalist conception of the totality that they so closely resemble, and which enables Marx to maintain that just as history makes people so do people make history.

Also deserving mention are the relations Marx sees between two or more parts within the whole and the relations between a part and itself (a form of itself in the past or in the future). What are called laws of the dialectic are meant to indicate the more important of these relations. Engels includes among these laws, "the transformation of quantity to quality—mutual penetration of polar opposites and the transformation into each other when carried to extremes—development through contradiction or negation—spiral form of development."[3] Explaining these laws now would prove too long a detour. For the present, it is sufficient to note their character as generalizations about the interaction and change which occur in a world conceived of in terms of internal relations. These generalizations are particularly important for the lines of inquiry which they suggest, and will be discussed later in connection with that stage in Marx's method.

III

Based on Marx's ontology is his epistemology, or how he comes to know and organize what is known. If Marx's ontology provides him with a prism through which to view reality, his epistemology is how he learns about a reality viewed through this prism. This stage of the method is in turn composed of four interlocking processes (or aspects of a single process): perception; abstraction (how Marx separates what is perceived into distinct units); conception (the translation of what it abstracted into concepts with which to think and communicate); and orientation (the effects abstractions have on his beliefs, attitudes, and action—including future perceptions and abstractions).

Perception, for Marx, covers all the ways in which people become aware of the world. It goes beyond the activity of the five senses to include a variety of mental and emotional states that bring us into contact with qualities (chiefly feelings and ideas) that would otherwise elude us.

In actual fact, we always perceive somewhat more and differently from what is seen or heard directly, having to do with our knowledge, experience, mood, the problem at hand, etc. This difference is attributable to the process of abstraction (sometimes called individuation) which transforms the innumerable qualities present to our senses into meaningful particulars. Abstraction sets boundaries not only for problems but for the very units in which they are studied, determining how far into their interdependence with other qualities they extend. If everything is interrelated, as I have said, such that each is a part of what everything else is, it is necessary to decide where one thing ends and another begins. Given Marx's ontology, the abstracted unit remains a relation in the sense described above. Its relative autonomy and distinctness result from his having made it so—for the present, in order to serve certain ends. A change in ends often leads to individuating a somewhat different unit out of the same totality. Capital, for example, can be grasped as the means of production used to produce surplus-value; the relations between capitalists and workers are sometimes added; and sometimes this abstraction is enlarged to include various conditions and results of these core activities and relations—all in keeping with Marx's concern of the moment.

Marx's main criticism of bourgeois ideologists is that they deal with abstractions, and are neither aware nor concerned with the relations which link these abstractions to the whole, making them both relative and historically specific. So "freedom," for example, is separated from the conditions which make it possible for some people to do what they want and others not. However, Marx, too, deals with abstraction—of necessity. All thought and study of the totality begins by breaking it down into manageable parts. But as Lukacs points out, "What is decisive is whether this process of isolation is a means towards understanding the whole and whether it is integrated within the context it presupposes and requires, or whether the abstract knowledge of an isolated fragment retains its 'autonomy' and becomes an end in itself."[4] Marx, unlike the bourgeois ideologists he criticizes, is fully conscious that he abstracts the units he then proceeds to study (rather than finding them ready-made), and is also aware of their necessary links with the whole.

The advantages of Marx's procedure are, first, he can manipulate—as we saw above—the size of any unit in keeping with his particular problem (though the many common experiences and problems of anyone living in capitalist society means there is greater similarity between Marx's and other people's abstractions than this point would suggest); second, he can more easily abstract different qualities or groups of qualities, providing himself in this way with a "new" subject for research and study (surplus-value and relations of production are examples of this); and, third, because the abstractions people carve out are the result of real historical conditions, particularly of their knowledge and interests as members of social classes, the study of abstractions becomes for Marx an important means of learning about society.

The process of conception which comes next is more than simply labeling the units which are abstracted. It is providing names which incorporate a particular understanding of what each unit is, of its function in the system examined, of the structure in the facts. The boundaries which have been imposed upon the world in abstraction are linked by this process to all the other boundaries (establishing potential as well as limits) that constitute a mode of thought. In conception, abstractions acquire a meaning which can not only be understood but communicated. Every society's understanding of itself is reflected in its categories, in what they are and mean. Like the abstractions on which they are based, categories are products of society; they both express social conditions and, through their influence on thought and action, help to reproduce them. As such, categories—their meaning and form—change in direct proportion to the evolution of society itself. A frequent criticism Marx and Engels make of other thinkers is that, by accepting traditional categories, they are limited in what they can understand to what is most apparent in the society to which these categories belong.

Marx's own achievement is sometimes characterized in terms of the fuller understanding made possible through the introduction of new concepts, such as "surplus-value." Engels compares Marx's contribution in economics, for example, to Lavoisier's in chemistry. Priestly and Scheele had already produced oxygen but didn't know that it was a new element. Calling it "dephlogisticated air" and "fire air" respectively, they remained bound within the categories of phlogistic chemistry, a chemistry which understood fire as something leaving the burning body. Lavoisier gave the name "oxygen" to the new kind of air, which enabled him to grasp combustion as oxygen combining with the burning body. Conceptualized as something outside the burning body and distinct from fire, it could join with the body during fire. In much the same way, Marx was not the first one, according to Engels, to recognize the existence of that part of the product which is now called "surplus-value." Others saw that profit, rent, and interest came from labor. Classical political economy investigated the proportions of the product which went to workers and capitalists. Socialists condemned this uneven distribution as unjust; but "all remained prisoners of the economic categories as they have come down to them."[5] The statement of fact which was widely regarded as the solution,

Marx took as the problem, and he solved this problem essentially by reconceptualizing its main elements as "surplus-value." In giving a name to the origins and ongoing relations to workers of profit, rent, and interest, "surplus-value" focused on the common thread that runs through apparently distinct economic forms. With this new concept he was able to explain the interaction of all the main categories in political economy, just as Lavoisier, proceeding from the new concept of "oxygen," had with the categories of phlogistic chemistry.

The tie between the process of conception and the process of abstraction makes it clear that the elasticity which characterizes Marx's abstractions will apply equally to the meanings of his concepts. Thus, "capital" in Marx's writings means more or less along a continuum representing its necessary conditions and results depending on the size and composition of the unit, capital, in Marx's understanding. The flexibility of definitions that critics have noted in Marx's works can only be grasped by returning to his process of abstraction and the ontology which underlies it.

Inextricably linked with perception, abstraction, and conception as a part of Marx's epistemology is the process of orientation. Marx believes that judgments, attitudes, and action cannot be severed from the social context in which they occur (including the categories in which this context is understood) and the real alternatives it allows. It is not simply a matter of what is taken as true and false, but of the structure of explanation inherent in the categories themselves. Given its social origins and practical purposes, this structure is extended by Marx into the very lives of the people involved. Consequently, his analysis of any group's values and the actions based on it deals with what they take to be true, the categories in which they organize this truth, and the social conditions and interests which structure both—all grasped as a social relation within the given and developing system. Marx's own judgments and efforts as a revolutionary are likewise part of how he understands capitalism, an understanding also reflected in his categories. Aware of this, Marx—unlike utopian socialists past and present—never engages in moral exhortation, but tries to win people to socialism by getting them to accept the structure of his explanation.[6]

IV

After ontology and epistemology, the next stage in Marx's method is that of inquiry. What Marx is looking for and how he understands what he finds exercise a decisive influence over his inquiry. And what he is looking for is essentially the internal structure and coherence of the capitalist system, its existence as a historically specific totality. No matter what Marx's immediate subject, his greater subject is capitalist society, and, whenever and however he proceeds in his research, this society is always kept in mind.

Marx's method as inquiry is his attempt to trace out relations between units themselves conceived of as social relations in order to uncover the broad contours of their interdependence. Given their logical character as internal relations, these ties may be sought in each social relation in turn or between them, conceived now as separate wholes within some larger unit. In practice, this means that Marx frequently changes both the perspective from which he sets out and the breadth of the units (together with the meaning of their covering concepts) that come into his analysis. Thus, for example, capital (generally the core notion of "capital") serves as one vantage point from which to investigate the intricacies of capitalism; labor serves as another, value as another, and so on. In each case, while the interaction studied is the same, the angle and approach to it (and with it the emphasis in definitions) differ.

More directly of concern to political scientists, and wholly in keeping with Marx's example, Gramsci in *The Prison Notebooks* investigates the intersecting social relations, class, civil society, political party, bureaucracy and state to uncover as many one-sided versions of the totality of his time. The chief advantage of Marx's approach is that it enables him (and Gramsci) to discover major influences without losing sight of interaction and change throughout the complex as tends to happen when looking for relations between narrowly defined static factors. Likewise, the transformation of one social form into another (indicated by a change in the operative concept) is best captured when tracing development within each social relation. Note Gramsci's sensitivity to how social classes and bureaucracies become political parties and how political parties can become a state.[7]

Marx assumed that the patterns of interaction and change embodied in the laws of the dialectic are universal, and they served him as the broad framework in which to look for particular developments. The law of the transformation of quantity to quality made him sensitive to how a social factor changes its appearance and/or function through the growth or diminution of one or more of its elements. Thus, money, for example, is said to function as capital only when it reaches a certain amount. The law of the interpenetration of polar opposites encouraged him to examine each social relation for its opposite, and, when faced with apparent opposites, to look for what unites them. In this way, wealth and poverty in capitalism are found to be opposite though mutually dependent aspects of the same relation.

The law of development through contradictions is undoubtedly the most important of these dialectical laws. The processes which compose any complex organism change at different speeds and often in incompatible ways. Viewed as internally related tendencies (i.e., as elements in each other and in a common whole) whose forward progress require that one or the other give way, they become contradictions. The resolution of these contradictions can significantly alter the totality. Examining tendencies for their contradictions is a way of looking for the sources of conflict, sources which may be apparent even before the conflict materializes. Contradictions frequently come in clusters, and their unity and order of importance are equally subjects of Marx's research.

Research of any kind, Marx's included, is a matter of seeking enough pieces to make sense of a puzzle which is destined to remain incomplete. In trying to trace the inner working of capitalist society, Marx adopted a strategy and set of priorities to aid him in this task. He began, for example, by investigating social relations—like capital, commodity, and value—which are rich in evident connections with the concrete totality. He also chose to concentrate on England, using the most advanced capitalist society of his time as the laboratory in which to study capitalism as a system.

According to Marxist theory, it is material production which reproduces the conditions of existence of the totality, and in the mutual interaction between all social factors, it is economic factors which exercise the greatest influence. Consequently,

Marx generally begins his study of any problem or period by examining economic conditions and practices, particularly in production. The economic interests and motives of the classes and individuals involved are also taken into account, and the contradictions he takes most care to uncover are economic ones. If we originally abstracted Marx's method from his theories in order to focus on certain aspects of this method, it is necessary to return to these theories again and again to see how he uses this method and for what.

Special attention is also given to the interaction between real processes and the ways in which they are understood. On one occasion, Marx describes *Capital* as a "critique of economic categories or, if you like, the system of bourgeois economics exposed in a critical manner."[8] *Capital*, then, is equally a work about capitalist practice and accepted ideas about capitalist practice. As indicated, Marx's main criticism of bourgeois ideology in any field is that bourgeois thinkers are unaware of the totality that surrounds and is expressed in their particular descriptions and explanations. Generally they err in taking immediate appearances for the whole truth, treating what is directly perceptible as logically independent of the structured interdependence of elements which give it meaning. In tracing the internal connections of this interdependence, Marx is uncovering the essence of these ideas, an essence which frequently contradicts the truth reflected in appearances. In bourgeois political economy, for example, the fact that workers get paid by the hour is taken to mean that wages based on the sum of hours worked represents full payment for labor. By uncovering the relations between labor and the social conditions in which it occurs, including notions like wages in which these conditions are ordinarily understood, Marx is able to show that the worker receives back only part of the wealth that he/she has produced.

Marx's reputation as a scholar has seldom been questioned, even by his foes. He believed that in order to criticize any subject one should know it and what others have written about it in some detail. He went so far as to learn Russian in the last years of his life in order to read what had been written in Russian on ground rent. All sources of information and techniques for gathering information available in his day were respected and made use of—e.g., government reports, surveys, questionnaires, fiction, newspapers, etc., and there is no reason to believe that he would be less open to the many advances in these areas made by modern social science. Once this is admitted, however, it must be added that Marx is mainly concerned with what kind of information is worth collecting, the assumptions underlying various techniques of gathering it, how studying a subject can affect it, and particularly with the influence of the concepts used (explanatory structures) on the range of possible solutions. Presented with the typical attitude survey, for example, Marx would undoubtedly focus on the biases found in what is asked, how it is asked, the sample to whom it is asked (the indifference generally shown to social class divisions), and the conditions reflected in the favored response (such that changes in these conditions ordinarily bring another response). He would probably specify, too, that no amount of questioning, given prevailing false consciousness as well as the subjective bias present in any individual account, can fully uncover social and economic structures. It does not follow that Marx would ignore the information gathered in attitude surveys—as so many of his followers unfortunately do— but that his use of it would be highly qualified and critical.

V

Marx's ontology declares the world a totality; his epistemology breaks down this totality into relational units whose structured interdependence is reflected in concepts; his inquiry, by tracing the links between these units, fleshes in the details of this totality; intellectual reconstruction, the fourth stage in Marx's method, comes with the completion of these processes. In intellectual reconstruction, the totality with which Marx began, real but featureless because unknown, is transformed into the rich, concrete totality of his understanding.

If Marx had studied the American Congress, for example, he would not have been satisfied—as most professional political scientists are—with knowing "how laws are made." Marx's intellectual reconstruction would necessarily include the history of Congress as a social-political phenomenon interacting with other institutions and practices in society, responding to them all but to none more than to the economic structure, its role in the

class struggle and in working through capitalism's major contradictions, its internal contradictions and relations to alienation,
and the ways in which these functions and relations are disguised
from the people whose daily activity as citizens reproduce them.
For orthodox political scientists who understand Congress
independently of the totality (or place it in the somewhat larger
abstraction, politics) the role of this law-making body in securing
capitalist interests and its character in light of this role can never be
adequately appreciated. In the Marxian intellectual reconstuc-
tion, on the other hand, Congress is understood as capitalism
incarnated within the legislative body, as the political rule-making
form of capitalist society, and the presence of other aspects of this
totality within this form is never lost sight of.

Within Marx's reconstruction of the totality, as much
"superstructure" as "base," as much people's activities as their
products, the central place is held by contradictions. The over-
arching contradiction which Marx sees in capitalism, the contradiction which includes in its folds all other capitalist contradictions in their peculiar interaction, is that between social production and private appropriation. This has been reformulated by
some as the contradiction between "capitalism's ever more social
character and its enduringly private purpose," or between how
production is organized and how it could be organized given
existing technology and culture; but each of these restatements
only brings out part of its meaning.[9] As the contradiction
embodying the unity of all major contradictions, the relation
between social production and private appropriation registers
Marx's complex understanding of capitalism as a concrete
system. It is the most general as well as the most sophisticated
result of his research, capitalism understood in its inner workings, and is present in one form or another at each level of his
intellectual reconstruction.

A first approximation of the intellectual reconstruction
achieved by Marx occurs whenever anyone observes that there is
a pattern in the facts of capitalist life. What is the connection
between sending people to jail for years for petty thefts while
permitting major thefts in the form of oil depletion allowances,
burning potatoes at a time when people are going hungry,
allowing apartments to remain vacant in the midst of a housing
shortage, letting machines rust while growing numbers of

workers are unemployed, forcing city dwellers to die from suffocation and to drink from sewers when technology does not require it, etc. The decisive distinction between "radicals" and "liberals" is that the latter understand social problems as relatively independent and haphazard happenings, and try to solve them one at a time. Not aware of their internal connection as parts of the capitalist system, they cannot deal with these ills at the only level on which a successful solution is possible, that is on the level of the whole society, and are reduced in the last analysis to alternating between the extremes of condemnation and despair.

Those who accept the label "radical," on the other hand, generally recognize that what liberals take to be the loose ends of a hundred unconnected ropes are knotted together as so many necessary (or at least highly probable) parts of capitalist life. Too often missing in their understanding, however, are the structures (essences, laws, contradictions) that mediate the particular events and the capitalist system as a whole. To grasp how capitalism is responsible for a given fact, one must know the interrelated functions that bring the requirements of the system to bear on the people and processes involved. Otherwise, capitalism, as an answer to our dilemma, is itself an abstraction that brings little enlightenment. Learning these mediations necessarily takes place in a spiral fashion: each success in intellectual reconstruction advances the processes that occur in ontology, epistemology, and inquiry, which in turn permit a fuller concretization of the totality, and so on. The interaction between the different parts of Marx's method which is suggested here, their progress as an integral approach, should also put readers on guard against possible distortions introduced by the schematization of well-ordered stages in the present account.

VI

The problem posed for Marx's exposition—fifth and last stage in his method—is how to explain capitalism as a system of structured interdependence relationally contained in each of its parts. If the questions which guide Marx's inquiry deal with how particular capitalist practices come about and how their very forms are expressive of the capitalist system, the answers which guide his exposition seek to re-establish this system (now incorporated in his intellectual reconstruction) in an account of these forms. Though often confused, and never more so than in works on Marxism, comprehension and explanation are distinct functions and involve different techniques. From Marx's intellectual reconstruction of capitalism, it is clear he would reject explanations that concentrate on prior conditions, or that reduce reality to instances of a few empirical generalizations, or that establish ideal models, or that are satisfied to simply classify the facts. In each of these cases, the explanation takes the form of relating two or more abstractions; the fuller context remains untouched. For Marx, capitalism is the only adequate explanation for whatever goes on inside it, but this is capitalism understood as a concrete totality.

The metaphor Marx uses to refer to his goal in exposition is a "mirrored" version of reality. He believes success is achieved if "the life of the subject matter is ideally reflected as in a mirror," and adds that when this happens "it may appear as if we had before us a mere *a priori* construction."[10] Marx's goal then is to bring together the elements of his explanation as they are related in the real world and in such a manner that they seem to belong to a deductive system. From the comments by Engels and Paul Lafargue, and from his frequent revisions of *Capital* (each draft and each edition contained major changes), it would appear that Marx's mirrored presentation of reality remained a goal that continually eluded him. Just before his death, Marx was again planning to revise *Capital*.

Marx sought to reproduce the concrete totality present in his understanding essentially in two ways, by drawing the interaction of social relations in the present and by displaying their historical development as parts of a system through various forms. In drawing their interaction, Marx frequently changes vantage points, making the ties he uncovers appear as part of each relation in turn. The dulling effects of repetition are partly offset by the changes in vocabulary which accompany shifts in perspective. The predominant role of economic factors is brought out by presenting this interaction as part of economic relations more often than not, and in greater detail than is used for other relations. Likewise, the unique role accorded contradictions in structuring the totality is reflected in the amount of attention given them in the account of social interaction.

Contradictions and economic factors also occupy privileged positions in Marx's account of the development of social relations through their different forms. With many others, Marx believes that explaining anything is, in large measure, explaining how it came to be. Where Marx stands apart is in believing that how it came to be is also part of what it is. This underlies his use of history to present current events and institutions as manifestations of a process: development is growth through internally related forms, and tendencies—which emerge from the past and arch toward the future—are considered as much a part of social relations as their appearances.

Given the internal relations Marx sees between practice and ideas, the development that occurs in the one will—through their interaction—be reflected in the other. Marx's account, therefore, of the history of capitalism deals with changes in capitalist ideology as well as in the forms of capitalist life. The numerous quotations from the history of political economy found in *Capital* are offered as a running commentary to his critique of these ideas grasped as a developing part of a developing whole. This also enables Marx to present his own understanding of capitalism, which emerges from this same totality, as the critical culmination—however imperfect and unfinished—of this development.

Marx's exposition of social interaction and development—like the inquiry through which he uncovered it and the intellectual reconstruction which constitutes his understanding—proceeds through a combination of analysis and synthesis. The central, most distinctive social relations of capitalism are analyzed, shown to contain within themselves the structured interdependence and movement of the concrete totality. Marx insisted that the importance of a relation for the functioning of the capitalist system and not its historical appearance determines the order of exposition. The analysis of capital, for example, should precede that of rent. This advice was easier given than followed, for Marx's outlines and many revisions of *Capital* begin with different social relations—capital, money, value and finally commodity (which may show only that these four social relations share top billing in his understanding of capitalism).

While Marx tries to unravel capitalism from each major social relation, he simultaneously reconstructs the system by synthesizing the one-sided views of the whole obtainable from these different vantage points. The inner workings of capitalism which emerge from the social relation, capital, have another emphasis and appearance than the same interdependence which emerges as part of value, and so on. In presenting each of these one-sided views of the whole, Marx also makes certain assumptions regarding the functioning of aspects at their periphery, which assumptions are later made good when these same aspects emerge as central features of other relations. The role of the market, for example, is assumed in the treatment of value in *Capital I,* but surfaces in the discussion of circulation in *Capital II,* and is integrated into the value relation in *Capital III.* The structured interdependence of capitalism, therefore, an interdependence present in his understanding of each major social relation, is approached by "successive approximations" in his exposition.[11] The explanation of capitalism offered in any one work (even when that work is the three volumes of *Capital*) is incomplete to the extent that major social relations remain unanalyzed. Studies of capitalist politics, culture, ethics, etc., as well as of capitalist economics, are required to bring the work of synthesis to a conclusion, and—as I noted earlier—Marx did have such ambitious projects, but *Capital* simply grew to occupy all his time.

The process of synthesis can also be seen in the manner in which Marx's concepts acquire their fuller meanings. Given the requirements of communicability, terms used at the start of a work convey everyday notions, or something very close. The more general abstractions, concepts focused on the more evident qualities of the human condition, what Marx calls "simple categories" play this role best and are used to help explain the more historically concrete abstractions, the "complex categories" whose meanings involve us directly and immediately in capitalist structures. In this way, the concept "labor," for example, is used to help explain concepts like "commodity," "value," and "capital."

In general, and particularly at the start of a work, the social relations analyzed are the more historically concrete abstractions, and the work of unraveling them proceeds with the aid of the more general abstractions. But in the course of exposition, what began as simple categories with evident meanings will begin to look like concrete categories themselves, their meanings developing as the conditions in which they are embedded are uncovered. Labor, which appears as a general abstraction at the start of *Capital*, is gradually shown to be an historically specific form of productive activity, i.e., wholly abstract, alienated productive activity. The concept "labor," Marx says, comes into existence at the time when people pass easily from one kind of work to another and are generally indifferent to what they do. This presupposes a host of historical circumstances which are in turn reproduced by the rapid spread of this form of productive activity. Thus, while simple categories make possible the analysis of complex ones, they are themselves being synthesized into complex categories (capable of undergoing their own analysis, of serving in their turn as windows through which to view the concrete totality).

Unable to provide definitions for the complex categories whose meanings stretch to the limits of the system or for the simple categories which will soon grow into complex categories, Marx can only provide "indications" (or one-sided descriptions) and images which expand a relation beyond the qualities explicitly delineated with the aid of the reader's own imagination, making Marx's striking metaphors part of his method as well as of his style of writing. Treating what I've called indications as definitions is a serious error, since the introduction of new indications will often appear contradictory. Does "capital," for example, mean "that kind of property which exploits wage-labor," "the means of production monopolized by a certain section of society" or "the products of laborers turned into independent power?"[12] The answer, of course, is that the meaning of "capital" (its full meaning) incorporates all of these indications together with the dozen more found in *Capital* grasped in their peculiar interrelations. In such cases, striving for precision too soon can only be self-defeating.

Of all the stages of Marx's method, it is the dialectic as exposition that stands most in need of rethinking by modern-day Marxists. The problems involved in communicating Marx's intellectual reconstruction of the capitalist totality were never more than partially solved. The misunderstanding about which

Marx complained and which he tried to combat with successive revisions of his major work has, if anything, grown worse. Without beginning a new subject, it is worth pointing out that many well-known distortions of Marxism—such as economic determinism and various structuralist interpretations—may be valuable first and second approximations to a full explanation of Marxism to positivist-minded audiences (meaning most educated people in Western societies). Making the transition between factoral and process thinking, between operating with external and internal relations, while learning about the special effect of the capitalist mode of production on social and political institutions and events may indeed require explanatory devices of this type. The error is to allow such misshapen and/or one-sided versions of Marxism to stand in for the full cloth in exposition or to pose as the truth of Marx's intellectual reconstruction.

VII

Once we understand that Marx is trying to present us with a mirror image of capitalism as a concrete totality and the logical character of this totality, the techniques he adopted in exposition (including the use of language) become less opaque. We are also ready to take as much from Marx's theoretical statements as he puts into them. Regarding his theory of the state, which is where we began, we can now grasp the logical character of the relations Marx posits between the forms of political institutions and practices and the dominant economic class, between the state and the mode of production, between the actual operations of the state and the ideology in which it is explained, etc.; we are also in a position to grasp the connection between the sum of these relations taken as ongoing processes and the capitalist system in which they are found. A detailed restatement of the theory of the state which brings out the role played by Marx's methodology must be left for another time. Here, I have limited myself to outlining this method and simply and boldly stating this role.

From what has been said, it should also be evident that Marx's method is not only a means of understanding his theoretical statements but of amending them to take account of the developments in the real world that have occurred since his time.

The functions of the different institutions, processes, and social sectors in capitalist life must be reassessed, and whatever changes found incorporated in the meanings of the covering concepts. What is required (and has been for some time) is a new intellectual reconstruction of the concrete totality, one which balances its respect for Marx's writings with an equally healthy respect for the research of modern scholars, including non-Marxists. Because of the complexity of this task, it can only be undertaken collectively. It may be useful to signal here that with the publication of the journal "Kapitalistate" such an effort by an international group of Marxist scholars working on the capitalist state has already begun. As with Marx's own writings, its practical effects will depend chiefly on how well the structured interdependence of capitalism is captured. Marx said he wanted to force "the frozen circumstances to dance by singing to them their own melody."[13] We do not aim for anything less.[14]

Notes

1. A. Sommit and J. Tannenhouse, *American Political Science, Profile of a Discipline* (New York, 1964), p. 14.

2. This schema for distinguishing different notions of totality was first suggested by Karel Kosik in *Dialectic of the Concrete*. There are important differences, however, in what Kosik and I understand of the second and third notions of totality presented here.

3. Friedrich Engels, *Anti-Duhring,* trans. E. Burns (London, n.d.), pp. 26-27. For an account of these laws, see my book, *Alienation: Marx's Conception of Man in Capitalist Society* (Cambridge, 1976), chap. 5.

4. Georg Lukacs, *History and Class Consciousness,* trans. R. Livingston (Cambridge, Mass., 1971), p. 28.

5. Friedrich Engels, *Preface* to *Capital II,* (Moscow, 1957), pp. 14-16.

6. For further discussion of this process of orientation see chap. 4 of *Alienation.*

7. Antonio Gramsci, *Prison Notebooks* ed. and trans. Q. Hoare and G. N. Smith (New York, 1971), pp. 146-149, 151, 155, 157-158, 191, 227-228, 264.

8. Quoted in M. Rubel, "Fragments sociologiques dans les inedits de Marx," *Cahiers internationaux de sociologie* 22, (1957), p. 129.

9. Ralph Miliband, *The State in Capitalist Society* (London, 1969), p. 34; Williams Appleman Williams, *The Great Evasion* (Chicago, 1968).

10. Marx, *Capital I,* trans. S. Moore and E. Aveling (Moscow, 1958), p. 19. 19.

11. Paul Sweezy, *The Theory of Capitalist Development* (New York, 1964), p. 11.

12. Marx and Engels, *The Communist Manifesto* trans. S. Moore (Chicago, 1945), p. 33; *Capital I,* p. 10; *Pre-Capitalist Economic Formations* ed. E. J. Hobsbawn and trans. J. Cohen (New York, 1965), pp. 84-85.

13. Karl Marx, "Toward the Critique of Hegel's Philosophy of Law: Introduction," *Writings of the Young Marx on Philosophy and Society,* ed. and trans. L. D. Easton and K. H. Guddat. (New York, 1967), p. 253.

14. It may be useful to list other major topics I intend to cover in the book of which this essay is a first "approximation," in order to forestall some of the obvious criticisms over what has been left out here. Still to be treated are 1) why Marx's method is to be preferred over other methods currently in use in the social sciences in terms of their actual results (this requires both a Marxist critique of these other methods and a comparison of their treatment of similar topics); 2) how verification is achieved; 3) how our training as social scientists (our habits as well as our beliefs, our organization into separate disciplines as well as our social function as teachers and intellectuals) inhibits adopting and effectively using Marx's method; 4) why most of Marx's followers have distorted and/or neglected his method; 5) to what extent this method is tied down to the study of capitalist society; 6) in what ways it is already present in the thinking of the "ordinary person" as opposed to the thinking of those philosophers who claim to speak in his or her name; and 7) what is the relation of Marx's method, of understanding it and using it, to political practice. To the extent that these topics bear on the meaning and value of Marx's method, what I have managed to reconstruct in this outline must be deemed incomplete.

5.

On Teaching Marxism

At many American universities, Marxism G2010 or Communist Theory V1106 or Socialist Thought A2242 are no longer "know your enemy" kinds of exercises, and the number of serious courses on these subjects is constantly increasing. Unfortunately, the opportunity they offer for promoting a true understanding of Marxism is frequently lost, either wholly or partially, under the weight of problems inherent in the university context. Having taught both undergraduate and graduate courses on Marxism for almost a decade—mainly at New York University, but also at Columbia University, Union College, and the old Free University of New York—I would like to share with other Marxist teachers my experiences in dealing with these problems.

There are three main problems facing any university teacher of Marxism: the bourgeois ideology of most students, the social and ideological restraints that are part of the university setting, and the absence of a vital socialist movement. To be sure, the same difficulties confront any radical teacher no matter what the subject matter, but the forms in which they are expressed and their disorienting effect vary considerably, and so too must the strategies for dealing with them.

The absence of a vital socialist movement makes most students approach Marxism too much in the spirit of another academic exercise, just as it confirms them in the belief—before study begins—that Marx's analysis cannot be correct. The classroom situation, whatever one does to humanize social relations, remains locked inside a university structure that is itself forced to play a certain preparatory role within society at large. Students take Marxism for four credits; for some it counts toward their "major"; for all it is a step toward their degree. Given a society with restricted privileges, some kind of grading is necessary at each stage of the education process, as in life generally. All of this affects how students prepare for a course, any course, so that all but the most committed treat the acquisition of knowledge (and often understand it) as the means to a good grade.

There are also ideological elements in the classroom situation which continually gnaw away at the foundations of a Marxist analysis. The very presence of a Marxist teacher who is allowed to teach Marxism is conclusive evidence to some that bourgeois freedom works—just as students from modest backgrounds often take their own presence in class and in the university as proof that extensive social mobility and equality of opportunity really exist under capitalism. Even the fact that the course is offered by a particular department reinforces the alienated notion of the division of knowledge into disciplines and predisposes students to view Marx as essentially an economic or a political or a philosophical thinker.

But undoubtedly the major hurdle in presenting Marxism to American students is the bourgeois ideology, the systematic biases and blind spots, which even the most radical bring with them. This ideology reflects their own class background, whatever that may be, but also their position in capitalism as young people and students. There is nothing in bourgeois ideas and ways of thinking that doesn't interfere with the reception of Marx's message, but the scrambling effect of some ideas is clearly greater than that of others. In my experience, the most trouble-some notions have been students' egotistical and ahistorical conception of human nature; their conception of society as the sum of separate individuals, and with this the tendency to reduce social problems to problems of individual psychology (the whole "blaming the victim" syndrome); their identification of Marxism with Soviet and Chinese practice; and of course the ultimate rationale that radical change is impossible in any case. Much less destructive and also easier to dislodge are the intrinsically feeble notions that we are all middle class, that there is a harmony of interests under capitalism, that the government belongs to and represents everybody equally, and that history is the product of the interaction of great people and ideas. Underpinning and providing a framework for all these views—whether in the form of conclusions or assumptions, and whether held consciously or unconsciously—is an undialectical, factoral mode of thinking that separates events from their conditions, people from their real alternatives and human potential, social problems from one another, and the present from the past and the future. The organizing and predisposing power of this mode of thought is such that any attempt to teach Marxism, or indeed to present a Marxist analysis of any event, is doomed to distortion and failure unless accompanied by an equally strenuous effort to impart the dialectical mode of reasoning.

I originally thought that students who *chose* to take my course on Marxism—the department doesn't exist where this is a required course—would be relatively free of the worst effects of bourgeois ideology, and it just may be that a survey of the whole university would show a tilt in critical consciousness in their favor. I certainly attract most of the self-consciously radical students, but it has become clear that the great majority of my students—whatever the sense of adventure or morbid curiosity that brings them to class—suffer from most of the distortions mentioned above. And even the radical students, as I have indicated, have not escaped the ideological effects of their bourgeois conditioning and education.

The problems one faces in teaching Marxism that come from the absence of a socialist movement, the university context, and the students' own bourgeois ideology permit neither easy nor complete solutions. Still, how one approaches and organizes the subject matter, where one begins and concludes, the kind of examples used, and especially what one emphasizes have considerable influence on the *degree* of success (or failure). My own courses on Marxism on both the undergraduate and graduate levels lay heaviest stress on the dialectic, the theory of class struggle, and Marx's critique of bourgeois ideology. These three theories are explained, illustrated, questioned, and elaborated in a variety of contexts throughout the term.

The dialectic is the only adequate means of thinking (and therefore, too, of examining and presenting) the changes and interactions that make up so large a part of the real world. Incorporating the dialectic, Marxism is essentially the attempt to exhibit the complexities of capitalist processes, their origins, and the possibilities for their transcendence (all of which is conceived of in terms of relations, where the conditions of existence of any process—like its potential for development—are taken to be part of what it is). Unlike bourgeois social scientists, who try to relate and put into motion what they conceive of as logically independent and essentially static factors, Marx *assumes* movement and interconnectedness and sets out to examine why some social forms appear to be fixed and independent. The problem of bourgeois social science is similar to that of Humpty Dumpty after the fall, when all the king's horses and all the king's men could not put Humpty Dumpty together again. Once reality is broken up epistemologically into externally related objects, all ties between them—just as their own changes of form and function—become artificial and of secondary importance in determining their essential character. In fixing them in time and space, the ever changing boundaries between things in the real world are systematically wrenched out of shape. My emphasis on the dialectic, therefore, can be seen as a recognition of the fact that one must understand the sense of "interconnection," "reciprocal effect," "movement," and "transformation" in order to grasp correctly whatever it is to which Marx applies these expressions.

Aside from its obvious importance in Marxism, the need I feel to give special emphasis to Marx's theory of class struggle derives from the absolute inability of most students to think in these terms. Like most Americans, they slide in their thinking from the individual to "everybody" without passing through the mediation of particular groups. Thus, for example, when responsibility for an act goes beyond its actual perpetrator, everyone is said to

be guilty. This is the logic (if not the politics) behind Billy
Graham's request that we all pray to be forgiven for the sins of
My Lai and Watergate, a request that most people can deny only
by upholding the equally absurd position that Calley and Nixon
are solely responsible. The middle terms are missing. Marxism is
an analysis of capitalism that is organized around such middle
terms (groups), the most important of which is class. Without a
notion of class, which enables us to consider human interaction
on the basis of interests that come out of people's differing
relations to the prevailing mode of production, none of Marx's
theories can be understood.

The theory of class struggle also contains the apparently
contradictory ideas that individuals have been made what they
are (that along with their class they are the product of social
conditioning), but they don't have to stay made (that along with
their class they can transform existing social relations). Paradoxically, it is when one understands the degree to which an
individual is a social product, and how and why this has
occurred, that he or she can transcend the conditions and become
the potential creator of a new and better future. To set this
dialectic of necessity and freedom into motion is another reason I
emphasize the theory of class struggle.

Capitalism differs from all other oppressive systems in
the amount and insidious character of its mystification, in the
thoroughness with which this mystification is integrated into all
its life processes, and in the degree to which it requires
mystification in order to survive (all other oppressive systems
relying far more on direct force). The importance of bourgeois
ideology is reflected in the space given it in Marx's writings,
which are throughout critiques of capitalist practices and of the
ways these practices are ordinarily understood. Our own accounts of Marxism, therefore, must at every point combine a
description of how capitalism works with a description of how
these workings are dissembled in both common sense and
"learned discourse." In universities, where bourgeois ideology is
dispensed in every classroom, the need for such a two-level
critique is greater than it would be in other settings—in factories
or neighborhood centers, for example. Furthermore, the longer
exposure of graduate students to the more refined forms of
bourgeois ideology calls for a correspondingly greater stress on

the criticisms of such ideas in graduate courses.

In preparing my own critique, I start from an awareness that bourgeois ideology is both an expression of the real situation and a product of conscious efforts to manipulate people's understanding, for the same conditions that are reflected in bourgeois ideology give rise—however confusingly and haltingly—to a correct understanding of capitalist processes. The fact is that while bourgeois ideology is systematic, it is also unfinished, inconsistent, contradictory, and constantly fighting for its life against a science of society whose most complete expression is Marxism. In class, my main contribution to this ongoing struggle is to insist at every turn that bourgeois ideology is made up of partial truths—ideas that are not so much false as severely limited by conditions of which the speaker or writer is unaware—and that these partial truths serve the interests of the capitalist class. In this manner, bourgeois ideology is transcended rather than denied outright. Focusing on immediate appearances, most bourgeois accounts of capitalism succeed in reversing the actual dynamics of what is taking place. Marx summarizes the net effect of such practices when, referring to Luther's description of the Roman mythological figure Cacus, who steals oxen by dragging them backward into his den to make it appear they have gone out, he comments, "An excellent picture, it fits the capitalist in general, who pretends that what he has taken from others and brought into his den emanates from him, and by causing it to go backwards he gives it a semblance of having come from his den."[1] My critique of bourgeois ideology, like Marx's, has the double goal of unmasking it as a defense of capitalist interests and reappropriating the evidence of immediate appearances into an account that captures the true dynamics of capitalist society.

The actual division of Marxism into lecture topics, and the ordering of these topics, is determined by the requirements of effective exposition, given the peculiar problems mentioned above. I begin with a discussion of the current crisis in our society, illustrated with stories and statistics from the capitalist press, in an effort to reach general agreement on what needs to be explained. Then, I devote at least one session to each of the following: an overview of Marx's analysis to clarify its systemic character and to provide a rough map of the areas into which the course will take us; the dialectic; Marx's treatment of the fact/value distinction; his conception of human nature and theory of alienation; the labor theory of value; the materialist conception of history; the theory of the state; the critique of bourgeois ideology; Marx's vision of communism; his theories of class consciousness and revolution; and finally—if time allows—his method, with special emphasis on its utility for our own research. I cannot hope to repeat my lectures in this space, or even to mention all the subjects that come up, but it may be useful to go through these topics one at a time to provide concrete illustrations of my pedagogical strategy. Readers of the following should keep in mind that my intention is not the ordinary one of using a scaffolding to construct a building but of using the building to display its scaffolding.

Lecture 1. I begin the first class by asking students to take out a piece of paper and write for fifteen minutes on why they are or are not Marxists. Rather than collecting these papers, I ask students to keep them until the end of term when I want them to answer the same question (either as part of a take-home final or as an addendum to their term papers), in light of their work in the course and what they have said at the start. My aim is to involve students personally in the subject, to jolt them into a recognition that Marxism belongs to their lives a well as to the curriculum, and consequently that they are as much a part of the subject as they are people studying it. I also want to make them conscious as soon as possible of their main objections to Marxism, so they can reflect on them and test them in their readings and in our discussions. Finally, I want to provide them and myself with a benchmark by which to judge some of the effects of the course.

The substantive part of this first session is devoted to parading, with the aid of appropriate newspaper stories, the worst problems of our society—poverty, unemployment, malnutrition, social and economic inequality, racism, sexism, etc. The message is that there is a lot that is wrong, but that we have to understand it better before we can hope to change it. Paradoxes are used to highlight the apparent absurdity of poverty in the midst of so much wealth and to indicate the presence of underlying contradictions. If contradictions are incompatible trends rooted in the structure and organization of society, paradoxes are the flotsam and jetsam that float on the surface of these trends, and as such they offer good clues to the existence of contradictions. My favorite paradox is found in the exchange between former Secretary of Agriculture Butz and a reporter who asked him if he thought it would help resolve the world's food shortage if we all ate one hamburger a week less. Butz responded that he intended to eat one hamburger a week more to help deal with the more serious problem of low cattle prices.

Students, particularly beginning students, need to hear in clear, simple language exactly how Marxism differs from what they already know and believe. Toward this end I distinguish between liberals, radicals, and Marxists in the following manner: liberals—which I say includes most students present—view capitalism's problems one at a time. Each problem has an independent existence and can be understood and even solved in a way that does not bring in other problems, or does so only incidentally. Thus the slogans, "one thing at a time," "first things first," etc. Radicals, on the other hand, recognize a pattern in these problems. For them, these problems are linked together as part of the necessary life processes of the capitalist system. They are correct in holding capitalism responsible, but if they are only radicals, and not yet Marxists, they don't really understand how this system gives rise to these problems: the mediations between the parts and the whole are missing. Marxists analyze the workings of capitalism to make sense of the patterns that radicals only see and liberals still have to learn about (Marxism is obviously much more than this, but for present purposes this will do). At the end of the session I try to make explicit—with the help of students—some of the patterns that emerge from the problems listed earlier. These patterns generally have to do with the power of money in capitalist society, the fact that people are willing to do almost anything for money, the great gap between the rich and the poor, the tie between being rich and powerful and being poor and powerless, and the class-biased character of our laws and their administration.

An attempt is made here, as in all later sessions, to involve students in discussion, and questions and comments are taken at any time, but I am very careful not to let the discussion overflow in all directions. The organic ties between all the elements of Marxism and the different levels of difficulty involved require a more ordered presentation. There are many ways to present Marxism, but following wherever the free association of students leads is not one of them. When necessary—and it happens quite often—I explain why I can't go into a particular topic at the moment it is raised and tell students in what session it will be dealt with.

It is also during this first class that I make it clear that I am a Marxist and that this will affect my choice of materials, the emphasis I give them, and, of course, my interpretation, but that it will not affect my honest examination of the facts or my willingness to hear other opinions. Every social science professor has a point of view. The fact that I announce mine and other teachers do not is possibly a more important difference between us than the fact that I am a Marxist and they are not. I have been open and have warned students what to expect, while they have hidden behind a specious neutrality (misnamed objectivity) from which they sally forth to surprise students at every opportunity. After this admission, I am often asked why the university allows a Marxist to teach. If a radical student asks the question, he or she is usually saying "What kind of a Marxist can you be?" I defend myself from this implied criticism by explaining how unusual, personally and politically difficult, and historically overdue this event is. The nonradical student uses this same question to proclaim his or her belief that academic freedom and complete freedom of speech really exist in America. I answer that the opportunity for such courses emerges from the contradictions in the university's functions (preparatory, humanist, and scholarly), and its need for legitimation in a world where Marxism is taken ever more seriously.

Lecture 2. The second session is devoted to trying to give students some sense of the systemic character of Marx's analysis, i.e., what it means to have capitalism as the object of study, as a reflection of the complex interdependence and developments found there. It may be that in Marx's day, or even in Europe today, one would not have to insist on this point; but most Americans don't know what it is to have a total view of any epoch, in part because they don't have a total or systematic view of anything, and in part because they don't know what constitutes an epoch. Grasping the relevant time framework is especially difficult for people who oscillate in their thinking between this minute and forever as easily and automatically as they move between the individual and everybody. Before offering the specifics of Marx's analysis, I think it is important to make students aware that its holistic quality derives in large part from the choice of a spatial and temporal object that is different from any they have ever contemplated.

To claim that Marxism is systemic, that it is a complex, organic whole whose parts cannot be grasped separately, is not to say that it is a closed and finished system with definite answers to the problems of the past, present, or future. It was such a misinterpretation of his views by some French followers that led a frustrated Marx to proclaim, "All I know is that I am not a Marxist."[2] Marxism is unfinished and, like reality itself, is open to all the revisions and corrections made necessary by new empirical research. But if Marxism is not a closed system, it remains a system of such interlocking parts that a full study of any single part implies a study of them all.

In providing an overview of Marxism I make use of the techniques described in *The Ragged Trousered Philanthropists* by Robert Tressell.[3] I ask five or six students to take the part of workers, I play the capitalist, and we reenact the primal exploitation scene that goes on daily in every capitalist factory (my only revision is that where Tressell uses bread, I use scraps of paper). In depicting the relations between workers and capitalists, I find it useful—here as later—to compare them both objectively and in the consciousness of the participants with the relations of oppression in other systems, particularly in feudal and slave societies. The charade goes on to show how surplus value gets distributed and does so in a way which makes very clear the ties of function and interest that link the different sectors of capitalist life. I avoid using Marxian concepts until the broad outlines of the situations to which they apply have been established. When the terms "exploitation," "class struggle," "value," and "surplus value" are finally used, I take special care to point out that they refer to complex sets of relations and not to things. Students are prepared in this way for what will be a major topic in the next class—the dialectic.

I consider this game from *The Ragged Trousered Philanthropists,* which I've used in dozens of classes, the most successful teaching device I have ever used. It really gives students a sense of the broad scope and systemic character of Marx's analysis, its central concern, and the way important theories are connected—all in a painless and even amusing manner. It is crude, oversimplified, and leaves out some essential elements of social life—all this I readily admit—but it does help to bring Marxist theory and the objects it studies into focus. In the future, particularly in undergraduate courses, I intend to use my board game, "Class Struggle," to achieve many of these same ends.

In this session I also discuss why so much of the debate over Marx's ideas goes on at cross purposes. Marxists believe that most bourgeois social scientists assume precisely that which needs to be explained, chiefly the unequal distribution of wealth and power and the character of social relations which result from this, and then set out with great fanfare to explain what may justifiably be assumed, the lowest common denominator features that characterize any social grouping. Social scientists, on the other hand, often criticize Marx and Marxists for drawing conclusions about the relationship between economic and non-economic factors in history on the basis of too little evidence, and for not taking account of the exceptions. Marx's hypotheses, they claim, have yet to be proven. But Marx was not concerned with collecting evidence to prove a set of hypotheses that apply to all societies. He is faulted for what he did not do, did not think could be done, or could be done with only trivial results. His project was to reconstruct the workings of an historically specific social system—capitalism—whose workings are taken for granted and treated as natural and unchanging by most social scientists engaged in the building and testing of ahistorical hypotheses.

Finally, it is in this session that I deal with such preliminary matters as problems in translating Marx, the recent availability of certain key works, and the role of Engels in Marxism. With minor qualifications, I regard Engels as coequal spokesman with Marx on the doctrines of Marxism and treat him as such for the remainder of the course.

Lecture 3. The dialectic (though it has been operating all along) is introduced under its proper name only when students begin to feel the need for it. How does one come to understand a social system composed of a multitude of constantly changing and interacting parts that has a real history and a limited number of possible futures? How does one study it to capture both its essential character, the way of working which makes it different from other social systems, and that dynamic which has brought it to its present state and will carry it to whatever future awaits it?

How does one think of the results of such a study and through what steps and forms does one proceed in presenting these results to others? The dialectic is the only adequate means for thinking and dealing with such a subject matter.

My account of the dialectic stresses its roots in the philosophy of internal relations which holds that the irreducible unit of reality is the relation and not the thing. The relations that people ordinarily assume to exist *between* things are viewed here as existing *within* (as a necessary part of) each thing in turn, now conceived of as a Relation (likewise, the changes which any "thing" undergoes). This peculiar notion of relation is the key to understanding the entire dialectic, and is used to unlock the otherwise mysterious notions of totality, abstraction, identity, law, and contradiction. In the interests of clarity, these notions are examined in Hegel as well as Marx and contrasted with their equivalents in Aristotelian logic and its watered-down version—common sense.

The philosophy of internal relations also accounts for Marx's understanding of language as a social relation, his use of what appear to be elastic meanings, and the total lack of definitions in his works. On the basis of this conception, words are taken to mean what they describe, with the result that Marx's major concepts mean—at their limit—the analysis made with them. Marx seldom uses a concept in this full sense, but neither does he stick to the core notion meanings that are carried by tradition and clearly understood by non-Marxists. What he does ranges between the two, with actual usage depending on the context. This practice makes it very difficult to know what Marx is saying on any occasion without an understanding of the dialectic (which supplies the framework and the possibilities), his analysis (which supplies the actual content), and the context (which determines how much of this content is relevant). Students are warned that they can have only a superficial understanding of Marx's theories until they learn the fuller meanings of his concepts, which in turn hinges on their progress in understanding his theories. In the sessions to follow, I explain, I will be concerned with developing both Marx's analysis of capitalism and, beginning with core notion meanings, the fuller definitions of the major concepts with which he makes this analysis.

In the philosophy of internal relations, truth is linked to the notion of system: statements are more or less true depending on how much they reflect in extent and detail the actual complexity of the real world. The criteria for judging whether Marxism is true, therefore, go beyond its correspondence to capitalist reality to its completeness and coherence as a total interpretation. Hence the irrelevance and/or insignificance of those rebuttals of Marx which focus on the odd exception. Marxists, as is well known, generally stress practice as the test of the truth of Marxism, and there is a sense (which I cannot develop here) in which this is so. Unfortunately, for non-Marxists—which means for most of my students—the "test of practice" can only be understood as the fact that revolutions occurred in Russia and China, the policies currently followed by these regimes, or the feeble efforts by workers and working-class parties to make a revolution in the West. As practices go, none of these do very much to convince people that Marx's analysis of capitalism is correct. On the other hand, people do begin to gravitate to Marxism insofar as it provides a more complete and coherent understanding of their lives and their society than they had before. I urge students to use these criteria in judging Marx's theories.

If I begin to discuss the dialectic by opposing it to common sense in order to establish its distinctive character, in my conclusion I try to point out that common sense also contains elements of the dialectic. Children, and less educated people in general, often operate with a rough, unconscious dialectic, while those who have benefited from an education that is constantly breaking down processes and wholes without putting them together again do so much less or not at all. It is important that students see that formal education in America is in large part training in how to think undialectically.[4]

What of Marx's materialism? In most treatments of Marx's philosophy, his dialectic and his materialism are coupled. I believe this practice has led to a serious confusion over the various senses in which Marx can be said to be a materialist, because—unlike the dialectic—his materialism cannot be abstracted very easily from its real content. Marx's materialism *is* the particular relations he sees between people, nature, and society, including ideas. (I treat Marx's conception of human nature in the fifth lecture, and his materialist conception of history again in the seventh lecture.) When this content is abstracted, all that remains of Marx's materialism is his opposition to various idealist positions which view the world as the effect and/or expression of disembodied ideas, and the methodological imperative (one, however, which admits exceptions) that we should begin our analysis of problems with their material aspects. What is to be avoided at all costs is the presentation of Marx's materialism as the belief that only matter is real, or that matter comes before ideas (since the concept "matter" is already an idea), or that ideas never affect matter, or that one should *never* begin an analysis from the vantage point of ideas. In every instance, such claims are undialectical, and the last two prejudge—incorrectly, as it turns out—the results of empirical research. Since the prevailing ethos is no longer idealist in the sense mentioned above, and given the dangers of misinterpretation at this early stage, my own presentation of Marx integrates his materialist philosophy with its real content, except in the treatment of method at the very end of the course, where materialism reemerges as a methodological principle regarding priorities.

Lecture 4. A major constituent of bourgeois ideology is the belief that the facts we know are logically independent of the values we hold. It is what permits people who disagree on facts, if these are viewed broadly, to treat their disagreement as one of values, while holding that the latter are beyond rational examination, i.e., one that takes account of the conditions and interests in which values emerge and flourish. To maintain that Marx himself subscribed to this logical distinction makes it possible to agree with him on his description of capitalism while disagreeing with his socialist solution simply because one believes in other values. It also makes whatever is labeled Marx's values appear as arbitrary and as ultimately unconvincing as the values of anyone else.

Marx does not accept a logical separation between facts and values, and, on the basis of his philosophy of internal relations, could not. On this conception, judgments cannot be severed from the people who make them and the conditions (including real alternatives) in which they are pronounced. In this session I work out the meaning of the dialectic for the entire sphere of ethics, other people's ethics and what are said to be Marx's. It should be clear that what is at stake here is the status of Marx's whole critique and with it the grounds on which one can reasonably accept or reject it. Marx does not condemn capitalism on moral grounds but analyzes it (and the views of those who praise or condemn it) in a way that confronts present conditions with their real alternatives. Rather than an external ideal, communism—or what is usually taken to be the basis of Marx's value judgments—is the extension of patterns and trends found in the present that Marx has projected into the future, given the new priorities that would be established by a socialist government. The content of this projection is treated in the session on Marx's vision of communism, but its logical status as part of the world of fact is clarified at this time. The great majority of students operate with the fact/value distinction, however, and it is a very difficult task to get them to see how Marx could have done otherwise.

Finally, to help bring out the ideological dimensions of the fact/value distinction, I make a special effort to recount its history from the time of Hume, along with its uses and ramifications in modern social science.

Lecture 5. From Marx's philosophy I proceed to his theory of alienation rather than to any of his other theories. I do this in order to force an early confrontation of Marx's conception of human nature with the individualistic conception held by most students, and also because of the connections this enables me to make between Marx's analysis and the students' own life situation. As Marx's conception of human beings in capitalist society, the theory of alienation is a cross between Marx's conception of human nature in general and the special conditions of capitalism. In explaining such concepts as "powers," "needs," "appropriation," "activity," "natural," "social," "species," and "freedom," with which Marx integrates both society and nature into humanity, as part of his conception of human nature, I am careful to stress the reliance of this conception on his dialectic. Later I show how the theory of alienation, which focuses on the separation and dissembling of these elements, cannot be conceived of outside of the foregoing conception of human nature and its underlying dialectic. The language of separation in which so much of the discussion of alienation is couched only makes sense in a context where a unified whole of some sort is already assumed to exist.

In displaying the four basic relations of alienation—between the individual and his or her activity, product, other people, and the species—I make the point that most students will soon be workers and that whatever their status and material rewards, the relations Marx describes will apply to them. Studying, I remind them, is usually but a temporary respite in the life of a worker. We then examine what forms these four basic relations of alienation take in politics, religion, and finally—with special emphasis—in education. Applying this framework to general feelings of student malaise invariably strikes a responsive chord. It is here, too, that the limitations on learning anything, especially a radical critique of society, within the alienated context of a capitalist university receives the attention it deserves.

In discussing Marx's conception of human nature and his theory of alienation, it becomes clear that he is concerned with the typical rather than with the unique individual, or with the unique individual insofar as he is typical. The social types of greatest interest to him are classes, which are presented both as products of alienated social relations, and as co-instigators of the dynamic that gives rise to these relations. Classes in struggle over their interests are the human subjects of Marx's analysis. Given his conception of human nature, no other subdivision of mankind carries the same influence. Given his broader subject matter—the real history of the capitalist mode of production— no other subdivision of the human species is as relevant. It is important that American students, for whom this mode of thinking is so foreign, see the necessity as well as the advantages and limitations in Marx's choice of class as his human subject. As for limitations, I point out that interests do not translate easily into motives, a quality possessed by unique individuals, and that the attempt to reduce one to the other has led to some of the more serious, vulgar distortions of Marx's analysis.

Lecture 6. There is still another advantage in treating Marx's theory of alienation before the labor theory of value. This is that it enables me to bring out better the social relations inherent in the latter theory, because the labor Marx has in mind in discussing value is alienated labor, with all that entails in the way of relations between the producer and his or her activity, product, fellow human beings, and the species. Likewise, value can now be seen as that which happens to and can be done with the products of alienated labor just because of its alienation, or, alternatively, as the form this alienation takes when viewed from the vantage point of its products. Both use- and exchange-value exhibit these effects. After clarifying the social content of labor and value, most of this session is devoted to the metamorphosis of value, the fetishism of commodities, and the theory of crisis, understood not only as a crisis in accumulation and consumption but also as a social crisis. Facts from our present crisis are used as illustrations. At a time when the standard of living of the working class throughout the capitalist world is going down, Marxists bear a heavy responsibility to present clearly—and frequently—the only explanation of this social disaster that makes any sense.

Lenin said that it is necessary to read Hegel's *Logic* before one can truly understand *Capital,* and I am very much in sympathy with this view. But it is not a recipe for how to teach the labor theory of value to beginners. Hegel is even more difficult to understand than Marx, and it seems perverse to prepare students for Marxism with something that is even more difficult, even easier to distort. In this course, Hegel is dealt with directly only in the session on the dialectic, but his presence is felt throughout. The central position accorded the philosophy of internal relations in the dialectic, and the use of internal relations as the framework in which to set Marx's other theories, gives my interpretation of Marx a very Hegelian cast. This is never more evident than in my presentation of the labor theory of value.

At the very start, I try to get students to see that Marx's labor theory of value is not an economic theory, narrowly understood, but a theory about the workings of capitalism viewed from the vantage point of the production and exchange of commodities. The question to which Marx addresses himself in the first volume of *Capital* is, "Why is labor represented by the value of its product and labor-time by the magnitude of that value?"[5] This is not a question about how much things cost or even why they cost what they do. Following Smith and Ricardo, Marx can assume that labor is responsible for the bulk of these costs. What he sets out to study are the historical conditions in which prices come about in the first place, in which all the things that people produce are available for exchange—indeed, are produced with such exchange in mind. In unraveling the social conditions which make this process both possible and necessary, Marx also shows how, in the very act of reproducing these conditions, contradictions emerge that point to the demise of the system. The main tendencies that lie at the core of these contradictions—the concentration of capital in fewer economic units, the expansion of capital throughout the globe, the falling rate of profit, the disappearance of the middle class, and the pauperization of the working class—are sometimes called Marx's predictive economic theories. It is the failure of these predictions to come unambiguously and permanently true that is all that many know (or care to know) about Marxism. It is important to make clear to students that these predictions are really projections of tendencies Marx found in his research, and since they are often countered by other tendencies (the tendency of the rate of profit to fall, for example, by the tendency of capital to expand), what actually transpires and when requires continual study.

The widespread acceptance of the economistic interpretation of Marx's labor theory of value shows how essential it is to recover Marx's actual questions, which make all his theories (his answers to these questions) accounts of the workings of an entire social system. These theories differ in the sector and problems from which they take off, and each is organized around a distinctive set of concepts, but the systemic pretension of each theory is the same. The labor theory of value, the theory of alienation, the materialist conception of history, the theory of class struggle, the theory of the state, and the theory of ideology do not, in the final analysis, deal with different subjects, but with the same subject differently. Rather than a series of externally related sectoral analyses, Marx offers overlapping analyses—some more, some less worked out—of the same capitalist reality. In presenting each of these theories I try to bring out the special contribution to our understanding that comes from approaching capitalism from this vantage point (chiefly the privileged access it gives us to certain kinds of information and the insights that come from ordering reality in this manner), and the ways it sustains and qualifies the analyses undertaken from other vantage points.

By this point in the course most students are able to grasp the uniqueness of Marx's project and something of the manner in which he sets out to achieve it, but as yet only a few really understand or accept his analysis. Taking the theory of exploitation found in the labor theory of value, it is useful to address this hiatus directly and, in the process, to examine our own class positions in the light of Lukacs' observation that of all classes the proletariat is best placed to grasp the Marxian totality.

Lecture 7. Unlike most Marxists, I take the materialist conception of history to be mainly a theory about capitalism, where the history referred to is the origins of capitalism, and not a theory about history in general, where capitalism is but the major illustration. Consequently, most of this session is devoted to an account of the real history of the capitalist mode of production and especially to the transition from feudalism to capitalism in western Europe. The story revolves around contradictions that arose in the reproduction of then existing conditions of production which, at a certain point, burst asunder the social and political forms in which production was taking place, and how the reproduction of the conditions of capitalist existence, now under new forms, have given rise to its own peculiar contradictions. Coming after discussions of alienation, class struggle, and value, an effort is made to discuss the unfolding of these contradictions on these different levels. From the facts of this historically specific evolution it is possible to draw (and Marx does draw) certain conclusions regarding the role and influence of forces and relations of production, economic processes generally, and class struggle that have a wider applicability. In every case, however, these conclusions admit the kind of exceptions that Marx himself often introduces when examining specific social formations.

Most students come into the course holding a caricature of the materialist conception of history in which "economics" is supposed to be the cause of everything people do and think and of all that happens in history. To counter this crude economic determinism, it is important to distinguish the determinism expressed in special conditioning and limited alternatives from the metaphysical determinism that denies choice altogether, and to illustrate this difference in Marx's treatment of real historical personalities. The influence Marx often attributes—because this is what his studies reveal—to political, scientific, cultural, religious, geographical, and still other factors must also be brought out.

In combating economic determinism, however, there is a serious danger—and one that I myself have often succumbed to—of overreaction, in which case students are left with a picture of Marx as an eclectic thinker not that different from other eclectic thinkers they know. We are operating in an academic environment where people readily admit that, along with everything else, "economics" is important (hence, the absurd claim that "we are all Marxists now"). For most, however, such eclecticism is merely an excuse for not studying any area in depth, so it is not surprising that the organic connections between areas are likewise neglected. Marx made these connections his subject matter, but his explanation accords a special role to the mode and relations of production, and it is this special role that our account must try to capture. If most students caricature Marxism as economic determinism, they also have little understanding of economic processes or their importance, and I have come to believe that in explaining the materialist conception of history the latter is our immediate problem. Consequently, I now begin my presentation with a heavy stress on economic processes and gradually qualify it in the manner and direction suggested above. The opposite distortions of economic determinism and eclecticism are avoided by leaning first in one direction and then in the other. This holds both for the account of the real history of capitalism and the conclusions Marx draws from this account for the rest of history (really history organized in other ways).

Lecture 8. The state has already come into earlier discussions of alienation, class struggle, the labor theory of value, and especially the materialist conception of history, although the picture we got of the state's function and history differed somewhat with each theory. Approaching the state directly permits a fuller grasp of its character and a more adequate estimate of its influence, just as it casts a new, political light on alienation, classes, value, and the mode and relations of production. But just as the state, conceived of as a Relation, serves as another dimension for the examination of capitalist society, the various aspects of the state, also conceived of as Relations, serve as complementary dimensions for the examination of the state. The institutions of government, the dominant role of the ruling economic class, the objective structures which maintain the cohesion and equilibrium of the social system, political parties, political socialization, the state's function in the reproduction of value, the illusory community (the alienated social power) and the hegemonic political ideology are all aspects of the state, and interpretations which focus only on one or a couple of these aspects—as so many Marxist accounts do—are necessarily lopsided and distorting. For example, in the recent *New Left Review* debate between Ralph Miliband and Nicos Poulantzas, the real issue is not, or rather should not be, whether the state is the executive committee of the ruling class or a set of structures which maintain the cohesion and equilibrium of the social system, but how it can be both and what it means for it to be both. Without a firm grasp of the dialectic, and in particular its foundations in the philosophy of internal relations, Marxist scholars are no more immune to one-sided, ideological interpretations of Marxism than their bourgeois counterparts. Marx himself dealt relatively little with the state. He planned to do a systematic study of it but like so many of his other projects this was sacrificed to the demands of his political economy. For this reason—and also because of the important ways the capitalist state has changed in our century (particularly, in its economic role and with regard to socializing people to the status quo)— there is a great need for serious Marxist studies in this area.

In my interpretation of the Marxist theory of the state, each aspect of the state Relation is itself treated as a Relation within which to unfold the workings of the state as a dimension of capitalism. I have found this to be one of the most successful illustrations of Marx's dialectical approach which discovers change and interaction within the very units—Relations—that undergo it, and seeks to understand and explain these processes through frequent changes of perspective. It is in discussing the state, too, that the class biases in capitalist institutions and practices become clear to everyone, and that the many radical but hitherto disconnected facts and intuitions that most students have begin to connect up and make Marxist sense. All along I have told students that there is a big difference between patches of critical knowledge or occasional insights, which anyone can have and which lead to nothing in particular, and a critical analysis which integrates such facts and insights into a systemic whole. Lincoln, after all, recognized that labor produces all value; Woodrow Wilson saw that our nation's laws serve the interests of the capitalist class; and even Eisenhower could warn us of the growing influence of a military-industrial complex. But by themselves, outside of a comprehensive analysis, such insights remained barren of further understanding and politically led nowhere at all.

Lecture 9. In this session I sum up the Marxist critique of bourgeois ideology, a critique which has already appeared as aspects of other theories throughout the course. The main emphasis now is on how bourgeois ideology in its various forms functions to serve capitalist interests. Starting with pro-capitalist solutions to common problems, we examine in turn how capitalism is treated as the natural form of society, the mystification involved in mistaking appearances for essences, the substitution of concepts that don't allow an adequate comprehension of their subject matter for those that do (or could), the division of knowledge into separate and competing disciplines, the use of the abstract individual or the sum of such abstract individuals as the human subject of study, and finally the defining of fact/value, cause/effect, freedom/necessity, nature/society, and reason/feeling as absolute opposites (so that any "thing" must be one or the other). Bourgeois ideology is present in the forms that promote divisive, static, and unsystematic (i.e., undialectical) thought, as well as in its not too surprising conservative content. Throughout, I stress that bourgeois ideology not only serves capitalist interests openly, but also when it confuses people, or makes them pessimistic and resigned, or makes it difficult for them to formulate criticisms or to imagine alternative systems.

Marx's critique of bourgeois ideology is as concerned with how these ideas and concepts arise (as a result of what activities, at what juncture in the class struggle, within which groups, in connection to what other ideas and events, etc.) as it is with their role in reproducing existing conditions. Since the origin of bourgeois ideology has received most of the attention up to this point—particularly in the sessions on the theory of alienation, the labor theory of value, and the materialist conception of history—it is primarily the role of ideology in society that concerns me here. My main effort is to get students to see bourgeois ideology as a piece, and the great variety of positions in practical politics, social science, and common sense as just so many versions of the same thing. Again, I stress that what these positions have in common is not that they are completely false, but that they are partial (though not recognized as such), that they are generally limited to appearances (hence, for Marx, unscientific), that they disregard the real history and actual potential of their subject, that they confuse the real relations between their elements, and that as a function of possessing just such qualities they are biased in favor of the capitalist class.

Lecture 10. From the first day of the course, students ask, "How would a 'Marxist society' be different?" Many, if not most, believe that such societies already exist in the Soviet Union, China, and Cuba, and that it should be easy for me to respond. My answer, which I generally have to repeat again and again, is that this is a very difficult question and that I cannot approach it without some preparation. First, it is absolutely essential to grasp that, for Marx, communism was to succeed capitalism and that the seeds of communism are already present within capitalist society. It is necessary, therefore, to examine Marx's analysis of capitalism to see what he found that led him to believe in the possibility of communism. Second, the elements in Marx's vision of communism are interdependent (none of them can exist or even be conceived of correctly without the others), so that only a systematic account that ties these elements together can avoid serious distortions.

Putting off students' requests for information on communism does not mean I consider the subject unimportant. On the contrary, it is of such importance, particularly today, that great care must be taken to circumvent the many ideological traps that await its telling. As is well known, Marx never devoted an entire work to communism, but the raw materials for it are scattered throughout his writings. Among his reasons for not doing so, undoubtedly, was a fear that it would appear too much like science fiction and that many people would confuse him with the Utopian socialists for whom such accounts were the main stock in trade. Another objection Marx must have had to addressing communism directly and systematically is that it is not a very effective way—as compared to analyzing exploitation, for example—of raising workers' class consciousness. Today, however, no one is likely to confuse Marxism with other socialist schools whose very names are difficult to recall. Furthermore, given the success of bourgeois ideology in getting people to accept the Soviet and Chinese models as "ideal" Marxist societies, a return to Marx's vision of communism may be a necessary complement to the analysis of exploitation in raising the consciousness of any oppressed group in modern capitalism.

My account of Marx's vision of communism begins by making clear that we are really talking about two different societies, a first stage, socialism, also called the "dictatorship of the proletariat," which is essentially a transition period of indefinite duration, and a second stage of full communism. Most of the session is devoted to the first stage and, in particular, to showing how practical, rational, and democratic are the reforms Marx foresees. Wherever possible I try to locate these changes within the technological and organizational possibilities of modern capitalism, given the priorities that would be adopted by a new socialist government. It is here, and not before, that meaningful comparisons can be made between Marx's vision of world socialism and those isolated societies that have tried to build socialism under such trying conditions. In reconstructing the sketchy picture Marx paints of full communism, I again emphasize its logical status as part of the present grasped as a process, and clarify its role as the point of ultimate reference within the theory of alienation and as the probable future of humankind within the materialist conception of history.

Lecture 11. I present Marx's ideas on class consciousness and revolution *after* presenting his vision of communism, because I want once again to make the point that the latter—as a projection of existing patterns and trends—belongs to his analysis of capitalism. As such, Marx's vision of communism is— at least in broad outline—part of what class conscious workers understand and part of the reason that socialist revolution is desirable. To study revolution without paying attention to its real causes and attainable goals (such as occurs in most bourgeois courses on revolution) is to get lost in a maze of practical politics, where there is no more reason to favor one side than the other.

Marx had no specific theory of revolution, of the steps and mechanisms by which capitalist society is to be overturned, unless we choose to view the whole of Marxism in this light. He was not committed, in other words, to any one strategy or form of organization as the means to make the revolution. Both his comments and his practical political activities show an enormous flexibility in response to the specific conditions of time and place. Despite what bourgeois scholars would have us believe, Marx—like every other socialist revolutionary—was opposed to violence, but he objected far more to the violence done daily to the working-class majority by a minuscule capitalist minority than to the violence that might be required to right this situation. According to Marx, the actual degree of violence in a revolution is, in any case, determined by the way the supporters of the status quo choose to defend it. Where revolutions have led to blood-baths, this was generally the work of the counterrevolution—France in 1848 and 1871 (in our century, China in 1927, Germany after 1933, Spain after 1939, Indonesia in 1965, and Chile in 1972). Given the position that so many students take of being against violence in the abstract, it is important that they realize that greater violence is done by capitalists and, indirectly, by those, like themselves, who permit the capitalists to continue their oppression.

The one constant in Marx's approach to revolution is the belief he had that in one crisis or another the working class would come to see its class interests and would act upon them in a massive, organized, and effective way—which brings us to the theory of class consciousness. Marx always focused on the conditions in which this consciousness would emerge—indeed was already emerging—and hardly at all on the character of the people who were being called upon to respond. His masterly analysis of alienation was never integrated into his theory of class consciousness, so that the continued refusal of the mass of workers to become class conscious in conditions which should have made this possible remained a mystery that only drove him back (as it has most of his followers) to reexamine underlying conditions. It is in this area that I feel Marxism is in most need of revision. My own contribution here is an attempt to expand Marx's theory of alienation to include some of the findings of modern psychology (particularly in the early work of Wilhelm Reich) and to integrate this expanded conception of alienation with the theory of class consciousness. As part of this revision, I also argue that Marxists must pay greater attention to the "politics of everyday life," both in our analyses of how capitalism works and in our strategies for changing it.

In this session I also introduce for the first time some of the

Marxist political parties, their strategies and political activities, and briefly analyze why they have been so unsuccessful (the relative material well-being of American workers, the greater social mobility in the United States as compared to other capitalist countries, political repression, racism, the Cold War, etc.). I am neither very favorable toward, nor particularly critical of, these parties. Not having a comprehensive strategy for achieving socialism, I urge interested students to explore the various alternatives for themselves.

Delaying the discussion of revolution to the end of the course means that students do not have to come to a decision on whether a revolution is possible until—with the aid of Marx's analysis—they understand the forces which make it both likely and desirable. Approaching the subject of what workers are or want or are capable of directly, as happens in so many discussions of revolution, usually leads to pessimism and its concomitant, political apathy ("Why bother?"), and undermines whatever interest exists in learning Marx's analysis. Studying Marx's analysis first, approaching workers' class consciousness as a problem within this analysis, permits a view of the possibilities and limitations inherent in our situation that is at once realistic and challenging. Understanding how capitalism works permits people to contribute more effectively to the struggle for socialism, knowing all the while that to do any less is to aid the other side.

Lecture 12. In graduate courses I try to leave a session at the end to summarize my remarks on Marx's method—to do for the dialectic, in other words, what Lecture 9 does for Marx's critique of bourgeois ideology. If the theory of alienation, the labor theory of value (particularly the discussion of exploitation), and the materialist conception of history are of most interest and have the greatest impact on undergraduates, it is Marx's philosophy, the critique of bourgeois ideology, the theory of the state, and his method that graduate students seem to find most relevant to their special concerns. Already committed to teaching and/or to some kind of serious research, they want to know how Marxism can help them in these tasks. It is very difficult for them—as it was for most of us—to make the necessary transition between the subjects treated early in the course and their practice as teachers and scholars. I consider this transition of such importance that it is the subject of a term-long seminar; in my lecture course on Marxism it occupies only the final session.

I divide Marx's method into four interlocking phases or moments: 1) philosophy, which can also be divided into ontology and epistemology (stressing the process of abstraction by which Marx establishes the units of reality); 2) inquiry, or how Marx proceeds from doubting everything (the skeptical stance he takes before the world of appearances) to studying it in just these units, whose changes and interactions as parts (expressions) of the capitalist system are his real subject; 3) intellectual reconstruction, or how Marx pieces together and clarifies for himself the results of this inquiry; and 4) exposition, or how he presents this understanding to others. Viewing the forces that produce change and the possible changes produced as a part of what anything is, the dialectic encourages us to expect change and to look for it, just as it helps us eventually to find it. It is this which makes the dialectic "in its essence critical and revolutionary," and underlies my course-long concern to have students think dialectically.[6] Most discussions of Marx's method focus on his philosophy or on his exposition, especially in *Capital*. I try to rectify this imbalance and particularly the neglect of the moment of inquiry, which is the aspect of method that is most discussed in non-Marxist works on method. In treating this moment, I consider it very important that students see both the possibilities in and the limitations of standard social science techniques in gathering information for a Marxist analysis.

Exposition is a social relation between a writer (or speaker) and a chosen audience, whose mode of thought, interests, knowledge, and biases must be carefully considered before determining the order and form of presentation. I illustrate this point with Marx's occasional essays as well as with *Capital* and—if time permits—with my own presentation of Marxism in this course. Ideally, the session and the course then concludes with student criticism of the strategy I used in teaching them Marxism.

On re-reading what I have written I am forced to admit that this outline includes not only what I have done, but what I have tried to do and what, on reflection, I believe I should have done and will try to do in future courses. Readers will also have noticed that some major aspects of our subject—such as the origins of

Marxism, nineteenth-century social and political history, Marx's own life, the various schools of Marxist interpretation, and the standard criticisms of Marxism—are not treated in separate sessions. To some extent, they are integrated into discussions throughout the course—with undergraduates getting more history and biography and graduates a greater variety of interpretations and criticisms—but it is also true that I have chosen to underplay these topics. My main goal is to have students understand Marxism not as intellectual history, political biography, or partisan rhetoric, but as the only adequate analysis of capitalism today; and given this end—and the limitations on time—it is simply that other topics have been given a higher priority.

What are the practical results of my course on Marxism? How can one judge them? Most students who answer the question, "Why are you or aren't you a Marxist?" indicate at the end of the course that they now accept Marx's analysis, though the majority are still wary of the label "Marxist." Where this happens, these students know better than most comrades with whom I have talked when and how they adopted a Marxist outlook. I have always been amazed at how little socialists, who are forever trying to effect a change of consciousness in others, have reflected on the circumstances surrounding their own change of consciousness. For most, the break with bourgeois ideology seems to have taken place behind their backs, so that at one moment they considered themselves liberals (or worse) and then a little later—without quite noticing the transition—they considered themselves socialists.

If non-Marxists see my concern with such questions as an admission that the purpose of my course is to convert students to socialism, I can only answer that in my view—a view that denies the fact/value distinction—a correct understanding of Marxism (or any body of scientific truths) leads automatically to its acceptance. I hasten to add that this is not reflected in my grading practices where non-Marxist students (i.e., students who don't yet understand Marxism) do at least as well as the rest of the class (would that so much could be said of Marxist students in classes given by bourgeois professors). Furthermore, I do not consider that I introduce more "politics" into my course than do other social science professors, or that I am more interested in convincing students of the correctness of my interpretations than they are of theirs. If my concern with a teaching strategy suggests manipulation (whereas, supposedly, their concern with pedagogy is morally neutral), I can only reply that the truth being what it is, I have no interest in lying, or in hiding any facts or in misleading students in any way.

Along with a growing number of socialist teachers, however, I have become very concerned with pedagogy because we have learned (usually the hard way) that truth doesn't always win out in the struggle with half-truths and lies, that it doesn't always forge its own means of expression, and that the very complexity of a Marxist analysis invites confusion and easy caricaturing. In addition, our own personalities and shortcomings often come between what we have to say and our audiences, while these audiences have undergone an ideological preparation that all but immunizes them against our message. The need so many socialist teachers feel to work out ways of presenting Marxism effectively implies, of course, an equal interest in the process by which students learn and understand Marxism, which is but the other side of the coin. And given the identity that I and most Marxists see between understanding Marxism and accepting it, this means, too, a concern with the process by which one becomes a socialist.

Becoming a socialist is obviously a process that varies with each person, but judging from my own frequent but highly informal inquiries there are certain experiences and insights that have a disproportionate influence in triggering or speeding up this transformation. Among these experiences are the following: undergoing a particularly brutal example of capitalist exploitation (or seeing it happen to one's parents or other loved ones); becoming involved in radical political activity, even of a minor sort, and being treated as a socialist by others (it is surprising how many comrades told me that they only knew they were socialists or were becoming socialists when people who disagreed with them said as much); living socialist relationships and finding them humanly more satisfying; having socialist friends and coming to take their assumptions for granted; knowing a socialist whose wisdom or kindness or courage one admires. Among the intellectual events that constitute major breakthroughs in the process of becoming a socialist there are the realizations that one has been consistently lied to; that the personal oppression from which one suffers is shared by others and is socially determined; that the path on which society is traveling leads to economic and social disaster; that the problems of capitalism are inter-related and cannot be solved individually; that classes exist and the class struggle is real; and that the socialist ideal represents a morally superior way of life. This last shows that even though ethics has no place in Marxism (see Lecture 4), people may come to Marxism by an ethical route.

A course on Marxism, such as the one I have outlined, provides the occasion for many of these insights but for only a few, if any, of these experiences. Nowhere else do Marxists have so much freedom and time to present their case to non-Marxists. Still, I have come to believe that unless a course on Marxism is coupled with experiences at work or in some kind of political struggle, benefiting from the emotional jolt that such experiences bring, its effect on most students is likely to be minimal and probably short-term. But the fact is that the daily life of most people, including my students, contains many examples of oppression and struggle, and occasionally of cooperation. For them, it is the opportunity to study Marx's analysis of capitalism that has until now been missing. Where the most painful of these experiences are still to be lived, however, as is the case with students who have never looked for or held a job or raised a family, Marx's analysis may take years to bear political fruit. With such people, it is through experiences to come that the Marxism they study now will have its full impact, an impact that these experiences alone would probably not produce. This delayed-action effect makes it impossible to estimate with any accuracy the influence of socialist teachers, and has led many, among both friends and foes, to seriously underestimate it.

Still another impediment to acquiring a socialist conscious-ness in the classroom is the irrational tie that exists between the ideology of most people and whatever emotional equilibrium they have attained, so that an attack on one is felt as a threat to the other. The struggle to make sense of the world within bourgeois categories is experienced by them as a need as well as a choice. One of the reasons they cling to their ideology, therefore, is because it is "comfortable," and when studying Marxism makes what they believe increasingly untenable, many students experience real anxiety. For even as its rationalizations begin to falter, bourgeois ideology offers its adherents the acceptance and respect of their own families and of society's leaders, and, perhaps more important, the emotional security of having been right all along. No one finds it easy to admit that what he or she has been thinking and doing for many years is mistaken (this becomes harder with age, as there is more to justify and less time to make amends). Against this, what do we have to offer? In the absence of a socialist movement and without a circle of socialist friends, the transition to adopting a Marxist outlook—for all its intellectual excitement—can be a cold and lonely affair. To be sure, students differ in how much they need comradely support in making this transition and in how much support they are already getting. And if time permitted, the need itself could be analyzed within the framework of Marx's theory of alienation, expanded to include Reich's theory of character structure. The point remains, however, that the classroom in which their bourgeois ideology is being dismantled does not provide the continuity of contact and emotional security that many students need to extend their critical thinking to its logical conclusions and embrace Marxism. In the years to come, a change in their personal situations or in the political climate might produce different results.

Consequently, though many students write at the end of my course that they are now Marxists, I consider—for the reasons given—that the real effect of the course both on them and on their more resistant peers will not be known for some time.

Appendix

Readings. There are two major problems here: students, particularly in graduate classes, vary a great deal in how much Marxism they have read; and there are few writings by Marx and Engels that deal with only one or a few theories at a time. I am not wholly satisfied with my solutions to either of these problems, but this is what I have done. First, I ask beginners to read either the Mehring, Berlin, or McLellan biographies of Marx, "The Communist Manifesto," and Engels' *Socialism: Utopian and Scientific* before doing any other reading for the course. They simply need to get some feeling for the range and tone of Marxism before setting out to understand it in a systematic fashion. The two sessions at the beginning of the term in which we prepare to study Marxism give them the time to do most of this reading. Second, the reading for each lecture is broken down into works for beginners and works for advanced students. Many works, of course, are so important that I ask beginners— especially as the course progresses—to try to read them, though I warn them of the difficulty. I tell the advanced students to read the works on the beginners' list first, if they haven't already done so (except in the case of selections), and then to go on to other works. I also suggest that they use the course as an opportunity to read/finish *Capital* I and III, and urge them to investigate at least one other interpretation of Marx besides my own for each of the topics covered. Everybody is asked to read my book, *Alienation*, so that I can devote most of the lecture time to elaborating on its content and to other matters.

Log. The problem is how to get students to focus on the more important and provocative questions arising out of what they read and to try to answer them, not in some hectic and distant final exam, but leisurely, while they are doing the readings. I have recently begun to ask students in this course to keep a critical log of what they read, responding to what they consider the most significant arguments and generally giving their reasons for agreeing or disagreeing with each author. I provide several study guide questions for each topic. To encourage students to take their log seriously, I've made it the only requirement for the course—there are no exams or term papers. The result, I am convinced, is that students do more reading than they otherwise would, and critically consider fundamental questions ranging over the entire term's work.

Taking Notes: I have found it very helpful in my own reading of Marx to devote separate pages in my notebooks to his key concepts. Marx never supplies us with definitions, but we can more or less reconstruct them by collecting examples of what he says about these concepts and of how he uses them in his various works. As Relations, as aspects of the whole which offer different vantage points for its examination and comprehension, each successful reconstruction will also be a version of Marx's analysis. Consequently, I urge students at the very start of the course to put aside separate pages in their notebooks for such concepts as "labor," "capital," "value," "commodity," "class," "mode of production," "relations of production," "alienation," "ideology," "private property," and "freedom." It is not a matter of writing down everything that is said about these concepts, but the effort to record what seems most important or unusual will prove very rewarding as the patterns both within and between each group of comments begin to emerge.

Notes

1. Karl Marx, *Theories of Surplus Value,* (Moscow, 1971), p. 536.
2. Karl Marx and Friedrich Engels, *Selected Correspondences,* ed. and trans. by Dona Torr (London, 1941), p. 472.
3. Robert Tressell, *The Ragged Trousered Philanthropists*, (London, 1965), pp. 209-214; to be published in paperback by Monthly Review Press, (New York, 1978).
4. Marx's philosophy has proven the most difficult subject to summarize in this outline. For a more detailed account see my book, *Alienation: Marx's Conception of Man in Capitalist Society* (New York, 1971), particularly chapters 2 and 3 and Appendix I; in the second edition (New York, 1976), see "In Defense of Internal Relations," Appendix II. This subject is treated from another vantage point in my article, "Marxism and Political Science: Prolegomenon to a Debate on Karl Marx's Method," reprinted as chapter four of this book.
5. Karl Marx, *Capital I* (Moscow, 1958), p. 80.
6. *Ibid.* p. 20.

II. Reich

6.

Social and Sexual Revolution

Marx claimed that from the sexual relationship "one can...judge man's whole level of development...the relationship of man to woman is the most natural relation of human being to human being. It therefore reveals the extent to which man's natural behavior has become human."[1] The women's liberation movement has provided ample evidence to show that in our society this relationship is one of inequality, one in which the woman is used as an object, and one which does not bring much satisfaction to either party. As predicted, these same qualities can be observed throughout capitalist life. Inequality, people treating each other as objects, as instances of a kind (not taking another's unique, personalizing characteristics into account), and the general frustration that results are major features in the alienation described by Marx.

Yet Marx himself never tried to explain what we may now call "sexual alienation." Pointing to the fact of exploitation and indicating that this is typical of what goes on throughout capitalist society is clearly insufficient. We also want to know how the capitalist system operates on the sexual lives and attitudes of people, and conversely, what role such practices and thinking plays in promoting the ends of the system. What is missing from this dialectical equation is the psychological dimension which, given the state of knowledge in his time, Marx was ill equipped to provide.

Half a century after Marx's death, the task of accounting for sexual alienation was taken up by Wilhelm Reich. Born in Austrian Galicia in 1897, Reich came to Vienna after World War I to study medicine, and in 1920, while still a student, became a practicing psychoanalyst. By 1924, he was director of the Viennese Psychoanalytic Society's prestigious seminar in psychoanalytic technique and highly regarded for his contribution in this field. Almost from the start of his career as an analyst, however, Reich was troubled by Freud's neglect of social factors. His work in the free psychoanalytic clinic of Vienna (1922-30) showed him how often poverty and its concomitants—inadequate housing, lack of time, ignorance, etc.—contribute to neuroses. He soon became convinced that the problems treated by psychoanalysis are at their roots social problems demanding a social cure. Further investigation brought him to Marxism and eventually, in 1927, to membership in the Austrian Social Democratic Party.

Reich's voluminous writings in his Marxist period (roughly 1927-1936) sought, on the one hand, to integrate basic psychoanalytic findings with Marxist theory, and, on the other, to develop a revolutionary strategy for the working class based on this expansion of Marxism. The chief of these writings are "Dialectical Materialism and Psychoanalysis," 1929 (in opposition to the Communist-inspired caricature, Reich argues that Freud's psychology is both dialectical and materialist); *Sexual Maturity, Abstinence and Conjugal Morality,* 1930 (a critique of bourgeois sexual morality); *The Imposition of Sexual Morality,* 1932 (a study of the origins of sexual repression); *The Sexual Struggle of Youth,* 1932 (a popular attempt to link the sexual interests of young people with the need for a socialist revolution); *The Mass Psychology of Fascism,* 1933 (an investigation of the character mechanisms that underlie the appeal of fascism); *What is Class Consciousness?,* 1934 (a redefinition of class consciousness that emphasizes the importance of everyday life); and *The Sexual Revolution,* 1936 (along with a revised edition of *Sexual*

Maturity, Abstinence and Conjugal Morality, a history of the sexual reforms and subsequent reaction in the Soviet Union).

The social revolution is only a prerequisite (and not a sufficient condition) for the sexual revolution, but Reich believed that recognition of their close relationship, particularly among the young, helped to develop consciousness of the need for both revolutions. With the exception of *Character Analysis* (1934), which psychoanalysts still regard as a classic in their field, and a few related articles, Reich's early work was devoted almost entirely to the attainment of such a consciousness.

Not content to debate his ideas, in 1929 Reich organized the Socialist Society of Sexual Advice and Sexual Research. A half dozen clinics were set up in poor sections of Vienna, where working-class people were not only helped with their emotional problems but urged to draw the political lessons which come from recognizing the social roots of these problems. Moving to Berlin in 1930, Reich joined the German Communist Party and persuaded its leadership to unite several sexual-reform movements into a sex-political organization under the aegis of the party. With Reich, the chief spokesperson on sexual questions, lecturing to working-class and student audiences throughout the country, membership in the new organization grew quickly to about forty thousand.

By the end of 1932, however, the Communist Party decided —whether to placate potential allies against fascism or because of the general reaction that was then overtaking the Soviet Union— that Reich's attempt to link sexual and political revolution was a political liability. Interpretations which were previously considered "sufficiently" Marxist were now declared un-Marxist, and party organs were prohibited from distributing Reich's books. In February 1933, despite the support of his co-workers in Sex-Pol, Reich was formally expelled from the party.

If the Communist leaders found Reich's stress on sexuality intolerable, his psychoanalytic colleagues were no more appreciative of his Communist politics. Badly frightened by the import of Reich's *Mass Psychology of Fascism* (1933)—and, as difficult as it is to believe today, still hoping to make their peace with fascism—the International Psychoanalytic Association expelled Reich the following year.

First from Denmark, then from Sweden and Norway, Reich

continued his efforts to influence the course of working-class protest against fascism. Most of his writings of this time appear in the *Zeitschrift für politische Psychologie und Sexualökonomie,* a journal he edited from 1934 to 1938. From about 1935 on, however, Reich's interest in politics was gradually giving way to a growing interest in biology, spurred by the belief that he had discovered the physical basis of sexual energy (libido). From being a psychoanalyst and Marxist social philosopher, Reich became a natural scientist, a metamorphosis that was to have drastic effects on both his psychoanalysis and social philosophy. Reich emigrated to America in 1939. Each year added to his spiritual distance from Marx and Freud. After a new round of persecution by the authorities, this time in connection with his scientific research, he died in an American prison in 1957.[2]

Reich's later work, as fascinating and controversial as it is, lies outside the bounds of this essay which is concerned solely with his Marxist period. What does concern us is that the break with his Marxist past led him to dilute much of the class analysis and politically radical content of whatever works of this period he chose to republish. Consequently, *The Sexual Revolution* (1945) and *The Mass Psychology of Fascism* (1946), until recently the only "Marxist" works available in English, give a very misleading picture of Reich's Marxism. Two recent pirate editions of *The Mass Psychology of Fascism,* both taken from the 1946 English version, and a new translation of the third German edition, exhibit the same fault, as does *The Invasion of Compulsory Sex Morality* (Farrar, Straus & Giroux, 1971), which takes account of textual revisions Reich undertook in 1952. Only "Dialectical Materialism and Psychoanalysis" (*Studies on the Left,* July-August 1966) and "What is Class Consciousness?" (*Liberation,* October 1971) are exempt from this criticism, but besides being difficult to obtain, these essays in themselves are hardly adequate as an introduction to Reich's Marxism. *Sex-Pol: Essays 1929-1934,* then, offers the English-speaking reader his or her first real opportunity to become acquainted with Reich's contribution to Marxist theory.

As indicated above, I believe Reich's main efforts as a Marxist were directed to filling in the theory of alienation as it applies to the sexual realm. Reich himself would have been surprised by such a judgment, since he was only partially familiar with this theory and seldom employed the vocabulary associated with it. *The German Ideology* and *1844 Manuscripts,* which contain Marx's clearest treatment of alienation, became available only in 1928 and 1931 respectively, and it seems as if Reich never read the latter work. Still, fitting rather neatly into this Marxian matrix is his discussion of the split between the individual and his natural sexual activity, reflected in part by the split beween spiritual and physical love (likewise between tenderness and eroticism); the fact that sexuality comes under the control of another (repression and manipulation); of its objectification in repressive structures (symptoms as well as social forms); of the reification (neurotic attachment) connected with each; of people's treatment of one another as sexual objects and the dissatisfaction this breeds; of the role money plays in purchasing sexual favors (which is only possible because they are no longer an integral part of the personality); and of the incipient conflict between repressors and repressed. Moreover, by using the theory of alienation Marx tried to show—in keeping with his dialectical conception—that people were not only prisoners of their conditions but of themselves, of what they had been made by their conditions. It is perhaps in marking the toll of sexual repression on people's ability to come to grips with their life situation (and, in particular, on the working class' ability to recognize its interests and become class-conscious) that Reich makes his most important contribution to Marx's theory of alienation.[3]

In his investigation of sexual alienation, Reich was greatly aided by Freud's four major discoveries: 1) human psychic life is largely under the control of the unconscious (this shows itself in dreams, slips of the tongue, forgetting and misplacing things—all have a "meaning"); 2) small children have a lively sexuality (sex and procreation are not identical); 3) when repressed, infantile sexuality is forgotten but doesn't lose its strength, its energy (this only gets diverted into various psychic disturbances which are beyond conscious control); 4) human morality is not of supernatural origins but is the result of repressive measures taken against children, particularly against expressions of natural sexuality.

To these basic discoveries, Reich soon added two of his own.

Psychoanalysis of the time was puzzled by the fact that many severely disturbed people had a "healthy" sex life, i.e., in the case of men, had erections and experienced orgasm. On investigation, Reich found that none of these people enjoyed sex very much or experienced a full release of tension in orgasm. He concluded that the notion of potency should not be restricted to the ability to have erections and ejaculations but should be expanded to include "orgastic potency," which he defined as "the capacity for complete surrender to the flow of biological energy without any inhibition, the capacity for complete discharge of all dammed-up sexual excitation."[4] Without orgastic potency, a lot of the sexual energy built up through the natural functioning of the body is blocked and made available for neuroses and other kinds of irrational behavior.

Reich also noted that orgastic impotence in his patients was always coupled with distinctive ways—including both beliefs and bodily attitudes—of warding off instinctual impulses. He labeled these defensive behavior patterns "character structure." The origins of character structure lay in the ways an individual protected himself or herself from the repressive force and techniques used in early socialization, particularly in the area of sexuality. If at the start, character structure develops in response to real or imagined threats in one's environment, once it gets established its main function is to control impulses coming from within the individual that threaten the emotional equilibrium that has been established.

Such instinctual control is not without its price. According to Reich, it makes "an orderly sexual life and full sexual experience impossible."[5] All the inhibitions, fears, awkward mannerisms and stiffness associated with character structure interfere with the capacity to surrender oneself in the sexual act, and in this way reduce the pleasure and discharge of tension achieved in orgasm. The same dulling effect makes it possible for people to do the repetitive and boring work which is the lot of most people in capitalist society, while reducing the impact on them, on their beliefs and feelings, of later life experiences.

Drawing upon his clinical experience, Freud had already pointed out a number of disturbing personality traits and problems that result from sexual repression. Specifically mentioned are the "actual" neuroses, tension and anxiety ("modern nervousness"), attenuated curiousity, increased guilt and hypo-crisy, and reduced sexual pleasure and potency. On one occasion, he goes so far as to claim that repressed people are "good weaklings who later become lost in the crowd that tends to follow painfully the initiative of strong characters."[6] Though Freud never took this observation any further, it served Reich as the basis for much of his later work. For Reich, the most important effects of sexual repression are submissiveness and irrationality: it "paralyzes the rebellious forces because any rebellion is laden with anxiety" and "produces by inhibiting sexual curiousity and thinking in the child, a general inhibition of thinking and critical faculties."[7]

But if the human cost of repression is so great, the question arises: Why does society repress sexuality? Freud's answer is that it is the *sine qua non* of civilized life. Reich replies that sexual repression's chief social function is to secure the *existing* class structure. The criticism which is curtailed by such repression is criticism of *today's* society, just as the rebellion which is inhibited is rebellion against the status quo.

Closely following Marx, Reich declares, "every social order creates those character forms which it needs for its preservation. In class society, the ruling class secures its position with the aid of education and the institution of the family, by making its ideology the ruling ideology of all members of the society." To this Reich adds the following: "it is not merely a matter of imposing ideologies, attitudes and concepts...Rather it is a matter of a deep-reaching process in each new generation, of the formation of a psychic structure which corresponds to the existing social order in all strata of the poplulation."[8]

In short, life in capitalism is not only responsible for our beliefs, the ideas of which we are conscious, but also for related unconscious attitudes, for all those spontaneous reactions which proceed from our character structure. Reich can be viewed as adding a psychological dimension to Marx's notion of ideology: emotions as well as ideas are socially determined. By helping to consolidate the economic situation responsible for their forma-tion, each serves equally the interests of the ruling class.

Within the theory of alienation, character structure stands forth as the major product of alienated sexual activity. It is an objectification of human existence that has acquired power over the individual through its formation in inhuman conditions. Its various forms, the precise attitudes taken, are reified as moral sense, strength of character, sense of duty, etc., further disguising its true nature. Under the control of the ruling class and its agents in the family, church and school who use the fears created to manipulate the individual, character structure provides the necessary psychological support within the oppressed for those very external practices and institutions (themselves products of alienated activity in other spheres) which daily oppress them. In light of the socially reactionary role of character structure, Reich's political strategy aims at weakening its influence in adults and obstructing its formation in the young, where the contradiction between self-assertiveness and social restraint is most volatile. The repressive features of family, church and school join economic exploitation as major targets of his criticism.

To avoid the kind of misunderstanding that has bedeviled most discussion of Reich's ideas, I would like to emphasize that Reich's strategy is not a matter of "advocating" sexual intercourse. Rather, by exhibiting the devastating effects of sexual repression on the personality and on society generally, he wants people to overturn those conditions which make a satisfactory love life (and—through its connection to character structure—happiness and fulfillment) impossible. In a similar vein, Reich never held that a full orgasm is the *summum bonum* of human existence. Rather, because of the psychological ills associated with orgastic impotence, the full orgasm serves as an important criterion by which emotional well-being can be judged. Furthermore, with the relaxation of repression, Reich does not expect everybody to be "screwing" everybody all the time (a fear Freud shares with the Pope), though such relaxation would undoubtedly lead—as it already has in part—to people making love more frequently with others whom they find attractive.

Many of Reich's critics make it a point of honor never to engage him in intelligent debate, simply assuming that any position which is so "extreme"must be erroneous. Among those from whom we deserve better are Herbert Marcuse, who remarks, "sexual liberation *per se* becomes for Reich a panacea for individual and social ills," and Norman Brown who says of Reich "This appearance of finding the solution to the world's problems in the genitals has done much to discredit psychoanalysis; mankind, from history and from personal experience, knows better."[9] Reich's masterly analysis of the social function of sexual repression is duly lost sight of behind these unsupported caricatures.

Another related misinterpretation, which is widespread among Marxists and must be taken more seriously, holds that Reich replaces "economic determinism" with "sexual determinism." At the time of his expulsion from the Communist Party, a spokesperson for the party declared, "You begin with consumption, we with production; you are no Marxist."[10] It is only fitting that special attention be given to an objection which calls into question his entire enterprise.

Marxist theory offers Reich two complementary ways of responding: either the notion of production can be differently defined to include sexuality (which his Communist Party critic restricted to a form of consumption), or the interaction between the "base" and such elements of the "superstructure" as sexuality can be emphasized to bring out the hitherto neglected importance of the latter. Reich's strategy, as found in several of his works, takes advantage of both possibilities. On the one hand, he points out that Marx's materialism logically precedes his stress on economic factors, such as production, and that sex is a "material want." On the other hand, while willingly declaring even for sexual practices the primacy "in the last instance" of economic factors (work, housing, leisure, etc.), he argues that the social effects of sexual repression are far greater than have previously been recognized.

Marx's materialism is first and foremost a matter of beginning his study of society with the "real individual," who may be viewed strictly as a producer but is just as often seen as both producer and consumer.[11] In his only methodological essay, Marx is at pains to show that production and consumption are internally related as aspects of the individual's material existence and that information which generally appears under one heading may be shifted—in order to satisfy some requirement of inquiry or exposition—to the other with no loss of meaning.[12] Likewise, the "real individual" has both subjective and objective aspects— he feels as well as does—and again, because of this interrelatedness his life situation can be brought into focus by emphasizing either feelings or actions. Based essentially on methodological considerations, this choice simply subsumes those aspects not directly named under those which are.

Perfectly in keeping with this broader notion of materialism is Reich's claim that "Mankind exists with two basic psychological needs, the need for nourishment and the sexual need, which, for purposes of gratification, exist in a state of mutual interaction."[13] Stressing the active component, Engels had said as much: "According to the materialist conception, the determining factor in history is, in the final instance, the production and reproduction of the immediate essentials of life. This, again, is of a two-fold character. On the one side, the production of the means of existence...on the other side, the production of human beings themselves, the propagation of the species."[14] The social organization of each epoch, according to Engels, is determined by both kinds of "production."

So little is this dual basis of Marx's conception of history appreciated—not least by Marx's followers—that the editor of the Moscow edition of *Origins of the Family, Private Property and the State*, where this remark appears, accuses Engels of "inexactitude," a serious admission for any Communist editor to make in 1948.[15]

Reich, too, is not altogether satisfied with Engels' formulation. The parallel Engels draws between production and procreation as determining forces in history requires some emendation. For if people produce in order to satisfy the need for food, shelter, etc., they do not engage in sex in order to propagate the species. Goods are not only the result of production but its aim. Sex, however, is almost always engaged in for pleasure or to relieve bodily tension. For the greater part of human history the link between sexual intercourse and paternity was not even known. Beyond this, sexual desire, which makes its appearance in early childhood, precedes the possibility of procreation in the life of everyone. Consequently, as a material need, as a subjective aspect of the "real individual," sex is essentially the drive for sexual pleasure. It is, therefore, how society responds to the individual's attempt to satisfy his hunger and obtain sexual pleasure that determines the social organization of each epoch.[16]

Besides accepting Marx's notion of "material forces" (however extended), Reich, as I have indicated, also accepted the primacy "in the last instance" of economic factors (narrowly understood). To grasp the latter admission in the proper perspective one must replace the causal model into which it is often forced with a dialectical one. On the basis of the dialectic, mutual interaction (or reciprocal effect) exists between all elements in reality. This basic assumption does not rule out the possibility that some elements exert a proportionately greater effect on others or on the whole as such. As Marx discovered, this was generally the case for economic factors. His claim regarding the primacy of economic factors is an empirical generalization based on a study of real societies, and not an *a priori* truth about the world. Consequently, Marx himself could call attention to the predominant role that war and conquest seem to have played in the development of ancient societies, and Engels could say that before the division of labor reached a certain point, kinship groups bore the chief responsibility for determining social forms.[17] Reich, who made a special study of primitive societies, concurs with Engels' judgement, though his qualification shows him to be even more of an "economic determinist" in this matter than Engels. Basing himself primarily on the anthropology of Malinowski, Reich emphasizes the importance of the marriage dowry (arranged as a form of tribute between previously warring primal hordes) in establishing both clan exogamy and the incest taboo; whereas Engels, under the influence of Morgan and Darwin, attributes both developments to natural selection.[18]

If Reich's research into the social origins of neuroses, beginning with his work in the free psychoanalytic clinic of Vienna, led him to accept the primacy in the last instance of economic factors, the same research made him want to alter the weight Marx attached to at least one of the elements in this interaction. Marx had mentioned sex as a natural and human power, as a way of relating to nature, along with eating, seeing, working and many other human conditions and functions. He did declare, as we saw, that the quality of the sexual relationship offers the clearest insight into the degee to which man the animal has become a human being. Yet, the only power whose influence is examined in any detail is work.

Reich does not by any means seek to belittle the importance Marx attributes to work, but he does wish to accord greater importance to sexuality, particularly in affecting people's capacity for rational action. For very different reasons, Marx and

Freud had underestimated the influence on character and social development of the area of life investigated by the other. The result was that "In Marx's system, the sexual process led a Cinderella existence under the misnomer 'development of the family.' The work process, on the other hand, suffered the same fate in Freud's psychology under such misnomers as 'sublimation,' 'hunger instinct' or 'ego instincts.' "[19] For Reich, synthesizing Marx and Freud meant breaking out of the prison imposed by such categories to redistribute causal influence in line with the basic discoveries of both men.

Sartre has recently remarked that most Marxists treat people as if they were born at the time of applying for their first job.[20] Writing as a Marxist psychoanalyst, it is chiefly this distortion that Reich sought to correct.

The attack on Reich as a sexual determinist has led most Marxist critics to overlook the real differences that exist between Marx's materialist conception of history and Reich's. The chief of these has to do with the different time periods brought into focus. Whereas Marx concentrated on the social-economic forms that have come into existence in the West in the last two to three thousand years (slavery, feudalism, capitalism), Reich—while accepting Marx's divisions—generally operates with a periodization based on social-sexual developments, whose three main stages are matriarchy, patriarchy (covering the whole of recorded history) and communism. Though they overlap, these two ways of dividing time are not fully integrated, either conceptually—so that one is forced to think of one or the other—or practically—so that followers of Marx and Reich often dismiss economic or psychological factors (depending on the school) in accounting for social change.

This contrast between the two thinkers is nowhere so clearly drawn as in their treatment of contradictions. At the core of Marx's materialist conception of history, insofar as it passes beyond methodology (how best to study social change) to a set of generalizations on how changes occur, is his stress on the reproduction of the conditions of social existence which at a certain point begins to transform the old order into a qualitatively new one. For Marx, the content of contradictions is always provided by the particular society in which their resolution takes place.

As a kindred thinker to Marx, Reich, too, is particularly attuned to contradictory tendencies in the material he examines. Yet, with few exceptions, the contradictions he believes will be resolved in capitalism possess a content that is derived from patriarchal society as such. This is the case with the contradiction between repression strengthening marriage and family and, by virtue of the sexual misery caused, undermining them; and likewise of the contradiction he sees between repression producing a character structure which inclines youth to accept parental authority (and by extension all forms of authority) and simultaneously provoking sexual rebellion against parents (and by extension all forms of authority).

Without roots in the particular society in which they are found (capitalism), it is not altogether clear how these contradictions contribute to the demise of this society, nor why its demise will necessarily lead to the resolution of these contradictions. And adding that repression is greater in the capitalist era does not solve the problem. Even sexual alienation is affected, for to the extent that its peculiarly capitalist features are overshadowed by patriarchal ones it becomes, for the time span with which Marx is concerned, an ahistorical phenomenon. Thus, a form of sexual alienation, as Reich was forced to admit, could exist even in the Soviet Union, still a patriarchal society.[21]

Reich's error—for all the use he made of Marx's analysis—lies in conceptualizing his findings apart from the findings of Marxist sociology, rather than integrating the two within the same social contradictions. He himself offers a good example of the alternative when he speaks of the captalist economy fostering family ideology while simultaneously undermining it through inner family tensions caused by unemployment and forcing women to go to work. In this way, that is, through the operation of typical capitalist trends, the family whose ideological function is necessary to capitalism is rendered increasingly dysfunctional.[22] Such examples in Reich's work, however, remain the exception.

Marxists have always managed better to explain the transition from slavery to feudalism and from feudalism to capitalism than to explain the onset of class society and, as events show, its eventual replacement by communism. It is just such developments, however, that Reich's work does most to illuminate. Yet, while Reich's contradictions occur in patriarchal times and the main contradictions Marx uncovered take place in capitalism, Reich's contribution to Marx's analysis can only be peripheral and suggestive. If Reich's "sexual economy" is ever to become an integral part of Marxism, the peculiarly capitalist qualities of sexual repression, including its distinctive forms and results within each social class (making allowances for racial, national and religious differences), must be brought out in greater detail. And, conceptually, from a patriarchal social relation, sexual repression must be broken down into slave, feudal, capitalist and even "socialist" social relations, in order to capture its special contribution to each period as well as the opportunities available in each period for its transcendence. Most of this research and work of reformulation is still to be done.[23]

Aside from the accusation that Reich's theory is of sexual determinism, another potentially telling criticism raised by many radicals today has to do with the relevance of his ideas in light of all the changes in sexual behavior that have occurred since he wrote. Have Reich's teachings missed their revolutionary moment? Reimut Reiche, in his book *Sexuality and the Class Struggle,* argues that the spread of sexual education, the availability of birth control pills and abortions, the easy access to cars (if not rooms) in which to make love, etc., have made it impossible to link the denial of a satisfactory sex life with the requirements of the capitalist system. The market has been able to absorb even these needs, turning their satisfaction into a profitable business venture for some section of the capitalist class. For him, the focus of interest has changed from finding out why sexuality is being denied to discovering how in the very means of its satisfaction it is being manipulated to serve the ends of the capitalist system.[24]

Neither Reimut Reiche's optimism regarding the extent to which repression has diminished nor his pessimism as to the extent capitalism is able to exploit whatever new freedom exists seems fully justified. A recent poll of eighteen-year-old college students in the United States, for example, shows that 44 percent of the women and 23 percent of the men are still virgins, and one expects that a far greater percentage have known only one or a few encounters.[25] Radicals tend to believe that on sexual matters, at least, their generally liberated attitudes and practices are shared by most of their age peers. This is a serious mistake.

As for capitalist reforms blunting the revolutionary edge of sexual protest, it must be admitted that this can happen. What remains to be seen, however, is whether the new contradictions embodied in these reforms simply make the old situation more explosive. How long can the pill be easily obtainable, venereal diseases curable, etc., and youth still frightened by the dangers of sexual intercourse? At what point in making marriage unnecessary for sex will young people stop getting married in order to have sex? When will the rebellion that has known some success in sexual matters be directed against intolerable conditions elsewhere? Put in Reichian terms, how long could capitalism survive with a working class whose authoritarian character structures have been eroded through modifications in their sexual lives?

The revolutionary potential of Reich's teachings is as great as ever—perhaps greater, now that sex is accepted as a subject for serious discussion and complaint virtually everywhere. The origins of the March Twenty-second Movement in France illustrate this point well. In February 1967, the French Trotskyist, Boris Frankel, spoke on Reich and the social function of sexual repression to a crowd of several hundred students at the Nanterre branch of the University of Paris. I can personally attest to the enthusiastic response of the audience, for I was there. In the week following the talk, Reich's booklet, *The Sexual Struggle of Youth,* was sold door to door in all the residence halls. This led to a widespread sex-educational campaign based—as Danny Cohn-Bendit tells us—on Reich's revolutionary ideas, and resulted in the occupation by men and women students of the women's dorms to protest against their restrictive rules.[26] Other struggles over other issues followed, but the consciousness which culminated in the events of May 1968 was first awakened in a great number of Nanterre students in the struggle against their sexual repression.

The same struggle is being repeated with local variations at universities and even high schools throughout the capitalist world. Generally lacking, however, is the clear consciousness of the link between restrictions on sexual liberty and the capitalist order that one found at Nanterre. Reich's teachings, whatever their shortcomings, are the indispensable critical arm in forging these links.

Notes

1. Karl Marx, *Economic and Philosophic Manuscripts of 1844,* trans. by Martin Milligan (Moscow, 1959), p. 101.

2. There is no good biography of Reich available. The only English-language account of Reich's life to which I can in good conscience refer readers is Paul Edward's brief essay, "Wilhelm Reich," in *The Encyclopedia of Philosophy,* VII, Paul Edwards, ed. (New York, 1676), pp. 104-15. A more detailed study by Constantine Sinelnikoff *L'Oeuvre de Wilhelm Reich,* which also contains a good bibliography of Reich's Marxist writings, will soon be brought out in English.

3. For a fuller treatment of the theory of alienation, see my book, *Alienation: Marx's Conception of Man in Capitalist Society* (Cambridge, 1971).

4. Wilhelm Reich, *The Function of the Orgasm,* trans. by T. P. Wolfe (New York, 1961), p. 79. First published in 1948, this book contains a very useful account of the development of Reich's psychology and particularly of his changing relationship to Freud.

5. Wilhelm Reich, *Character Analysis,* trans. by T. P. Wolfe (New York, 1970), pp. 148-149.

6. Sigmund Freud, "'Civilized' Sexual Morality and Modern Nervousness," *Collected Papers,* II, trans. by J. Riviere (London, 1948), p. 92.

7. Wilhelm Reich, *Mass Psychology of Fascism,* trans. by T. P. Wolfe, (New York, 1946), p. 25.

8. *Character Analysis,* XXLL.

9. Herbert Marcuse, *Eros and Civilization,* (New York, 1962), p. 218; Norman O. Brown, *Life Against Death,* (New York, 1961), p. 29.

10. Wilhelm Reich, "What Is Class Consciousness," *Sex-Pol Essays 1929-1934,* ed. by Lee Baxendall and trans. by A. Bostock (New York, 1971), p. 350.

11. Karl Marx and Friedrich Engels, *The German Ideology,* trans. by R. Pascal (London, 1942), p. 7.

12. Karl Marx, *A Contribution to the Critique of Political Economy,* trans. by N. I. Stone (Chicago, 1904), pp. 274-292. Marx also says that the forces of production have their subjective side, which is the "qualities of individuals," and refers to the "communal domestic economy" which replaces the family in communist society as a "new productive force." Karl Marx, *Pre-Capitalist Economic Formations,* ed. by E. J. Hobsbawm and trans. by Jack Cohen (New York, 1965), p. 95; and *German Ideology,* p. 18.

13. Wilhelm Reich, "The Imposition of Sexual Morality," *Sex-Pol,* p. 232.

14. Friedrich Engels, "Origins of the Family, Private Property, and the State," *Marx/Engels Selected Writings,* II (Moscow, 1951), pp. 155-56.

15. *Ibid.* p. 156.

16. "The Imposition of Sexual Morality," *Sex-Pol,* pp. 231-33.

17. Marx, *Pre-Capitalist Economic Formations,* p. 83; Engels, *Selected Writings,* II, p. 156.

18. "The Imposition of Sexual Morality," *Sex-Pol,* pp. 183-225.

19. Wilhelm Reich, *People in Trouble,* (Rangely, Maine, 1953), p. 45.

20. Jean Paul Sartre, *Critique de la raison dialectique* (Paris, 1960), p. 47.

21. For Reich's account of the sexual reforms and subsequent reaction in the Soviet Union, see his book *The Sexual Revolution,* trans. by T. P. Wolfe (New York, 1951).

22. Wilhelm Reich, *La lutte sexuelle des jeune,* (Paris, 1966) trans. from the German, p. 121.

23. For further discussions of the conceptual difficulties involved in integrating Reich's theories into Marxism, see my article, "The Marxism of Wilhelm Reich: or the Social Function of Sexual Repression," particularly the final section, republished as chapter seven of this book.

24. Reimut Reiche, *Sexualite' et lutte de classes,* trans. by C. Parrenin and R. J. Rutten (Paris, 1971).

25. Quoted in "The International Herald Tribune" (Paris, Aug. 13, 1971).

26. Daniel Cohn Bendit, *Obsolete Communism and the Left Wing Alternative,* trans. A Pomerans (London, 1969), p. 29. Reich's *Sexual Struggle of Youth* is now banned in some French high schools.

7.

The Marxism of Wilhelm Reich: Or the Social Function of Sexual Repression

I

"Just as Marxism was sociologically the expression of man's becoming conscious of the laws of economics and the exploitation of a majority by a minority, so psychoanalysis is the expression of man becoming conscious of the social repression of sex."[1] How does sexual repression occur? What forms does it take? What are its effects on the individual? And, above all, what is its social function? Freud deserves credit for first raising these questions, but it is Wilhelm Reich who went furthest in supplying answers. In so doing, he not only developed Freud's own insights but immeasurably enriched both the theory and practice of Marxism.

Reich's writings fall into three main categories: 1) that of an analyst and co-worker of Freud's, 2) that of a Marxist, and 3) that of a natural scientist. In this essay I am only concerned with Reich the Marxist, though excursions into these other fields will occasionally be necessary since the division between them is often uncertain both in time and conception. Reich's Marxist period runs roughly from 1927, when he joined the Austrian Social Democratic Party, to 1936, when he finally despaired of affecting the strategy of working-class movements. From 1930 to 1933 he was a member of the German Communist Party.

Marx had said, "It is not the consciousness of men that determines their existence, but on the contrary, their social existence determines their consciousness."[2] This formula has been hotly attacked and defended, but seldom explored. Marxists have generally been content to elaborate on aspects of social existence and to assume a sooner or later, somehow or other, connection of such developments with the mental life of the people involved. Reich is one of the few who took this formula as an invitation to research. How does everyday life become transformed into ideology, into types and degrees of consciousness? What works for such transformation and what against? Where do these negative influences come from, and how do they exert their effect?

Reich believed that psychoanalysis has a role to play in answering these questions. Marxists, however, have always had a particularly strong aversion to Freud's science. On the practical level, psychoanalysis is carried on by rich doctors on richer patients. Conceptually, it starts out from the individual's problems and tends to play down social conditions and constraints. It seems to say that early traumatic experiences, especially of a sexual nature, are responsible for unhappiness, and that individual solutions to such problems are possible. It also appears to view the individual's conscious state as being in some sense dependent on his or her unconscious mental life, making all rational explanation—including Marxism—so much rationalization. In short, in both its analysis and attempts at cure, psychoanalysis takes capitalist society for granted. As if this weren't enough to condemn it in the eyes of Marxists, psychoanalysis adds what seems to be a gratuitous insult in suggesting that Marxists in their great desire for radical change are neurotic.

Reich is not interested in defending psychoanalysis, particularly psychoanalysis as practiced, from such charges, and even adds to them by carefully restricting what Freud's science can and cannot do. As an investigation of individual mental processes, it cannot draw conclusions about social processes, either as to how they do or should operate; psychoanalysis is neither a sociology nor a system of ethics. To use psychoanalysis to explain social phenomena—as when S. Laforgue accounts for the existence of the police by reference to people's need for punishment—is an idealist deviation when it isn't simply nonsense.[3] Similarly, Reich declares, the belief widespread among analysts that the way to social betterment is through a "rational adjustment of human relations and by education toward a conscious control of instinctual life" is not logically derived from Freud's findings.[4]

Yet, for Reich, this list of shortcomings does not exhaust the possibilities of psychoanalysis. It is particularly in the effect of social phenomena on individuals that he believes psychoanalysis has something to teach Marxists. In concentrating on what it is about social conditions that produces ideas and attitudes, Marxists have ignored the process by which one gives rise to the other, by which the external situation is transformed into ideology. They also ignore the role played by irrational forces in keeping people from recognizing their interests. According to Reich, Freud's theories offer the means to correct such oversights.

II

Freud's science of psychoanalysis rests on three foundations: the libido theory, the theory of the unconscious, and the theory of the defense mechanisms of the conscious (each understood in light of existing repression). The different schools of psychoanalysis and, indeed, the different periods in Freud's own life are most readily distinguished by the degree of attention given to each of these foundations.

Of all Freud's followers, Reich is probably the foremost exponent of the libido theory, which holds that sexual excitement and fantasy are functions of a quantifiable sexual energy. Reich claims: "The basic structure of psychoanalytic theory is the theory of the instincts. Of this, the most solidly founded part is the theory of the libido—the doctine of the dynamics of the sexual instinct."[5] Even the theory of the unconscious, he believes, is a consequence of the libido theory.[6]

Paradoxically, Freud's great "discovery" was known to everybody but was never taken seriously on that account. Who hasn't experienced a buildup of sexual excitement? Who hasn't felt a sense of release of sexual tension? Who hasn't used "more" and "less" in connection with both? People have always dicussed sex as if a type of energy were involved. Freud said there is, and, more significantly, gave it a name and function in his broader theory of the personality.

Freud's conception of instinctual activity focuses on libido but takes in the aim, source, and object of such activity as well. The aim is to increase pleasure and avoid or reduce pain. The source is that part of the body where the tension or irritation is felt, and the object is that which is desired or whatever will relieve this tension. Before Freud, Reich says, instinct theory was in disarray, with as many instincts recognized as there are actions.[7] However, the degree of order Freud brought to this situation is somewhat exaggerated. For example, Freud uses "sexual instinct" and "sexual instincts" interchangeably. The former is generally a synonym for libido, while the latter treats each source of libido (mouth, anus, genitals) and, on occasion, each class of objects as indicative of a separate instinct.[8]

Though Freud spoke of non-sexual instincts, such as the self-preservation or ego instincts, and, later, the death instinct, only sexuality was explored in any detail. In this area, his main achievement lay in expanding the notion of sexuality to include all pleasure functions that are erotic in character and charting their progress from pregenital to genital forms. Reich, who accepted Freud's developmental map, was more consistent in linking such views to a single sexual instinct.

Marxists, as a rule, have been very uncomfortable with any theory of the instincts, because talk of instincts is often used to oppose sociological explanations of social phenomena and as a justification for leaving human nature as one finds it. The concept of instinct has also been attacked as but another name for the activities from which it is derived (since it is only in these activities that we observe it), and because what is said to be instinctual behavior differs so much from society to society.[9] Such criticisms make a good case for caution, but they do not abolish the need for an instinct theory to explain the universality of the sexual drive. Admittedly, without the assumption of an existing sexual energy, instinct is just another name for observed sexual activity. This is the trap into which Freud, with his occasional talk of sexual instincts, and those of his followers who reject the libido theory fall. With the assumption of libido, on the other hand, different sexual activities become manifestations of one instinct that is something other than the forms it takes.

The chief importance of libido theory is that it serves as the central organizing principle in Freud's treatment of sexual repression and the resulting neuroses. The given is sexual energy that is forever pressing for release. Sometimes the pressure is great, sometimes meager. Relations with parents, siblings, friends, teachers and others provide the objects and opportunities for gratification. They are also the instruments of social repression. Repression takes place in all the ways human beings fashion and enforce the command "don't." The immediate effects are a blocked libido and the creation of a repressive force, or conscience, within the individual him or herself. As pressure from the libido builds up, alternative means of gratification make their appearance. Generally these are permitted by the individual and society only insofar as their real sexual character is disguised. When these alternative means of gratification make it difficult for the individual to function effectively or comfortably in the given surroundings, they become symptoms of neurosis.

Freud distinguished between two kinds of neurosis, actual neurosis and psychoneurosis. The former includes anxiety neurosis and neurosthenia, and is attributed to current disturbances in one's sexual life. These are simply the immediate results of dammed-up sexuality. Psychoneuroses, on the other hand, such as hysteria and compulsion neurosis, have a psychic content, primarily the patient's fantasies and fears. To be sure, these ideas generally revolve around real or imagined sexual experiences, but their relation to the patient's present sexuality is unclear. Freud, whose clinical practice was almost entirely restricted to cases of psychoneurosis, suggested that every psychoneurosis has an "actual neurotic core," but he never made explicit what it is.

Reich does. He claims that the actual neurotic core Freud spoke of is dammed-up sexual energy, and that it provides the motor force in every psychoneurosis. The psychoneurosis retains its psychic content, but these ideas become troublesome only in the presence of sexual blockage or stasis. It follows that the inner conflict loses its strength when the sexual block is eliminated.[10]

The criticism most frequently leveled at Reich's account of neurosis is that many people who suffer from one or another psychoneurosis have a "healthy" sex life. Indeed, it was this observation that kept Freud from following up his own suggestion in the manner of Reich. Reich, too, was perplexed over the ability of people with severe sexual blockage to have erections and experience orgasm. He began to question his patients more closely about the quality of their sexual activity, and he discovered that none of them had great pleasure in the sexual act and that none of them experienced a complete release of tension in orgasm. In none was there "as much as a trace of involuntary behavior or loss of alertness during the act."[11] Reich concluded that erective and ejaculative potency (the only types then recognized by psychoanalysis) did not necessarily lead to orgastic potency, which he defined as "the capacity to surrender to the flow of biological energy without any inhibition, the capacity for complete discharge of all dammed-up sexual excitation."[12] Only genital orgasm can discharge the full amount of sexual energy generated in the body, but without orgastic potency a lot of this energy remains blocked and available for neuroses and other kinds of irrational behavior.

The barriers to orgastic potency that Reich sees are of three sorts: psychic, physical, and social. Psychically, they lie in the patient's moralistic beliefs and neurotic fantasies and fears, in which considerable sexual energy is invested. Physically, they exist in the bodily attitudes, in the stiffness and awkwardness assumed in self-repression in order to withstand energy breakthroughs. These psychic and physical restrictions interact, and they were incorporated by Reich into the notion of character structure (of which more later). Socially, the barriers to orgastic potency are not only the repressive conditions that brought about the original stasis, but also the conditions that make it so difficult to achieve a satisfactory love life in the present. The most important of these are the institutions of monogamous marriage and the double standard applied to premarital intercourse.

Freud never accepted Reich's orgasm theory as a proper extension to his own libido theory. As odd as this may seem, it appears that this was due at least in part to sexual prudery. Reich comments, "It is unbelievable but true that an exact analysis of genital behavior beyond such vague statements as 'I have slept with a man or a woman' were strictly taboo in psychoanalysis of that time."[13] Probably more important in determining Freud's refusal was his unwillingness to openly contest the social order. His overriding concern was that the new science of psychoanalysis be accepted. This fear of consequences for his work had not always determined his behavior. In " 'Civilized' Sexual Morality and Modern Nervousness" (1908), Freud made clear society's responsibility for a wide range of neurotic ills that crossed his couch, and in 1910 he even considered joining his movement to the "International Fraternity for Ethics and Culture" to fight against the repressive influence of church and state.[14] Such decisiveness was soon replaced by more ambiguous social criticism and, eventually, in *Civilization and Its Discontents* (1930), by an equally ambiguous defense of sexual repression. The very indefiniteness of the libido theory permitted such mutations. The orgasm theory, which identifies society's role in denying the cure as well as in providing the illness, put psychoanalysis on the collision course that Freud had so far successfully avoided.

Reich's other main contribution to psychoanalysis, besides the orgasm theory, is his theory of character structure. Reich understands character structure as the internalized pattern of behavior that each person brings to his daily tasks, as organized habit; it "represents the specific way of being of an individual" and is "an expression of his total past."[15] In character structure, the typical reaction has become an automatic one. With this theoretical innovation, the transformation of the whole character replaced symptom relief as the goal of Reich's therapy.

Alfred Adler had already introduced the concept of character into the psychoanalytic lexicon, but for him it was a way of drawing attention away from the libido theory. He grasped character teleologically, in terms of the individual's will to power. Reich, on the other hand, accounts for character formation both causally, as a result of early repression, and functionally, as a requirement of the libido economy.

For Reich, character structure has its origins in the conflicts of the Oedipal period as ways of responding to external pressures and threats. Both its form and strength reflect the kind of repression which the individual was subjected to at this time. The motive for developing such a structure is conscious or unconscious fear of punishment. Consequently, Reich refers to character structure as a "narcissistic protection mechanism" and says it is composed of "attitudes of avoidance."[16] By acting as parents want, or hiding what one does, or steeling oneself for a spanking, or any combination of these, the child transforms his spontaneity into character structure. Similar responses to teachers, priests, and others as the child grows reinforce and sometimes modify the pattern.

While protection against the outside world is the chief objective in the formation of character structure, this is not its main function in the adult individual. One's intellect and muscular structure as well as various social institutions protect him/her against external dangers. After maturation, it is mainly against internal dangers, against unruly impulses, that character mechanisms guard. In this case, character structure blocks the impulse and redirects its energy, acting both as suppressing agent and controller of the resulting anxiety. The energy that goes into the formation and maintenance of character structure also reduces the degree of repression needed by reducing the force of the drives to be repressed. Again, because of the energy expended in its maintenance, character structure serves as a means of reducing the tension that has built up as a result of its own operation.

Achieving impulse control in this manner has serious side effects on a person's overall motility and sensibility. According to Reich, it makes "an orderly sexual life and a full sexual experience impossible."[17] The inhibition and fears, the tense and awkward mannerisms, the stiffness and the deadness, all the manifestations of character structure work against the capacity to surrender in the sexual act and, thus, limit the degree of discharge attained in orgasm. Character structure also deadens people sufficiently for them to do the boring, mechanical work that is the lot of most people in capitalist society.[18] The same dulling insulates people from outside stimuli, reducing the impact on them of further education and of life itself. Finally, the increased sexual stasis that results from damming up the libido is responsible for reaction formations, such as the development of an ascetic ideology, which in turn increases the stasis.

Freud had already noted several personality traits and

problems that result from sexual repression. Among these are the actual neurosis, tension and anxiety ("modern nervousness"), attenuated curiosity, increased guilt and hypocrisy, timidity, and reduced sexual potency and pleasure. Freud even refers to repressed people as "good weaklings who later become lost in the crowd that tends to follow painfully the initiative of strong characters."[19] This provocative remarks is never developed. Reich, on the other hand, emphasizes those aspects of submissiveness and irrationality that we now associate with the notion of the authoritarian personality. For him, the most important result of sexual repression is that it "paralyzes the rebellious forces because any rebellion is laden with anxiety" and "produces, by inhibiting sexual curiosity and thinking in the child, a general inhibition of thinking and critical faculties."[20] And Reich is unique in rooting these negative qualities in the very character mechanisms responsible for self-repression.

Reich further divides the characterological effects of repression into those that result from membership in a particular class and those that result from living in a class-dominated society. As influences on the instinctual apparatus differ broadly depending on a person's socio-economic position, so do certain basic personality traits: "One has only to think of well-known character types such as 'the bourgeois,' 'the official,' 'the proletarian,' etc."[21] Reich's account of these differences within capitalism is extremely meager compared to what he has to say about that part of character structure that comes from living in class society.

According to Reich, "every social order creates those character forms which it needs for its preservation. In class society, the ruling class secures its position with the aid of education and the institution of the family, by making its ideology the ruling ideology of all members of society. But it is not merely a matter of imposing ideologies, attitudes, and concepts on the members of society. Rather, it is a matter of a deep-reaching process in each new generation, of the formation of a psychic structure that corresponds to the existing social order in all strata of the population."[22] Reich's concern here is with the widespread respect for private property and established authority, and with the dullness and irrationality that make it so difficult for people in all classes to recognize and act upon their interests. The problem, as he says in one place, is not why hungry people steal, but why they don't.[23]

The two dimensions of character structure are not always easy to distinguish, and Reich himself often speaks as if the character of workers, for example, is all of a piece. Yet, the distinction between class-determined and class-society determined character must be maintained if Reich's contribution is to remain within a Marxist framework. As it stands, the notion of character structure qualifies the base-superstructure formulation of Marx by accounting for the origin and hold of ruling class ideology on people who, nonetheless, possess distinctive class traits. In this way, the theory of character structure is as much a contribution to Marxism as it is to psychoanalysis.

Reich himself believed that with the notion of character structure he "bridged the gap" between social conditions and ideology in Marx's system.[24] It was now possible to supplement Marx's explanation of why people are driven to recognize their interests with an explanation of why, even in the most favorable conditions, they generally don't do so. This paradox is represented in Marx's writings by the tension between the theory of class consciousness and the theory of alienation. The tension remains unresolved, so that Marx never accounts for the workers' inability to attain class consciousness by referring to their alienation, nor qualifies their alienation with a reference to their skill in "calculating advantages."[25] Though Reich does not seem to have been very familiar with Marx's theory of alienation (*The German Ideology* and *1844 Manuscripts* first became available in 1929 and 1932 respectively), his concept of character structure can be viewed as bringing elements of this theory into the discussion of class consciousness.[26]

III

In 1934 Reich summarized his position as follows:

Basically it contains three parts: 1) The concepts held in common with Freudian theory (the materialistic dialectic already developed by Freud). 2) Orgasm theory and character analysis as consistent extensions of Freud's natural science and simultaneously representing those theories that I opposed to the death-instinct theory and the interpretive techniques. Point two is still in the realm of psychology. 3) My own concepts of sexuality, based on the orgasm theory and transcending the spheres of psychology (sex-economy and sex-politics). Part three has merely points of contact with psycho-analysis. It forms an independent field: the basic law of the sexual process.[27]

This essay has dealt so far with Reich's psychology. Attention will now be directed to the social analysis and political strategy that Reich derives from it.

For Reich, "the basic law of sexual process" has to do with the forms taken by human sexuality, the influences under which these forms developed, their "metamorphoses," and their effect upon movements for social change. Marx had meant something very much like this in his discussion of economic laws. The question he set out to answer in *Capital* is "Why is labor represented by the value of its product and labor-time by the magnitude of that value?"[28] Reich's fundamental question may be paraphrased as follows: "Why is sex represented, on the one hand, as screwing, and on the other, as procreation?" In his answer, Marx sought to explain how capitalist forms of produc-tion, distribution, exchange, and consumption arose, and how they are dependent on one another and on the character of human activity and achievement in areas far removed from the economy proper. Though much less systematic, Reich's account of sexual life in capitalism follows the same broad pattern.

The sexual drive is universal. Reich believes that every society structures people's sexuality by its kind and degree of repression, the sexual objects permitted, the opportunities made available, and the value set upon things sexual. In our era, the limits of sexuality are prescribed, particularly for women, by the twin values of premarital chastity and marital fidelity. These values prevailed, of course, in earlier patriarchal societies, but Reich's concern is with their special forms and functions in capitalism. The problem with premarital chastity, as every good observer knows, is that even small children desire sexual intercourse. In adolescence, long before marriage becomes possible, this desire becomes overpowering. Sexual desire shows as little concern for social conventions after marriage. Sooner or later, most (all?) couples find themselves sexually attracted to other people, leading to frequent infidelity and its concommitants of hypocrisy and divorce.

The sexual life of young people in capitalism is characterized by extreme frustration and guilt: guilt, because sexual activity of one kind or another occurs despite the social prohibition, and frustration, because such experiences are a fraction of what is desired. Virtually all adolescent boys and most adolescent girls masturbate, but their pleasure in this act is frequently spoiled by notions of sin and feelings of disgust and inadequacy. Homosexual encounters, which again are widespread in adolescence (and which Reich attributes to the early repression of heterosexuality), are even more laden with guilt feelings.[29] On the rare occasions when sexual intercourse occurs, it is hidden, done in great haste and worry over being discovered. Too often, youth's sexual ignorance and the unavailability or high cost of contraceptives take their toll in venereal diseases and unwanted pregnancies.

As indicated, the demands of bourgeois morality are directed primarily against women. Boys who have an active sexual life and married men who philander meet with mild disapproval, while girls and women who act in similar ways are generally viewed as outcasts. The greater repression of women that corresponds to this double morality has the effect of removing most women as love partners for men. One result is the creation of a class of prostitutes and a general commercialization of sex outside of marriage. Another is the division that occurs in the sexuality of most men between the sentiments of tenderness and passion. The man gratifies his "brutish" sexuality with "fallen" women, who are often of a lower class, and reserves his tenderness for women of his own class whom he might marry. Reich says, it is no wonder that 90 percent of women and 50 percent of men have serious sexual problems; the essence of bourgeois morality is "sexual atrophy."[30]

Within capitalist society, the fight against extramarital relations, prostitution, venereal disease, and abortion is fought in the name of abstinence. Yet, it is this very abstinence, with its attendant ignorance, that is responsible for these ills. When asked to do what is biologically impossible, people do what they can, with their real living conditions determining the forms this will take.

Reich places the origins of sexual repression in the period of transformation from matriarchal to patriarchal society. With the development of the institution of private property, men acquired an interest in marriage because of the dowry that came with it. The sexual repression of female children developed as a necessary means of getting them to accept the restraints imposed by the marriage bond.[31] Young people who have an active love life before marriage find it difficult, if not impossible, to remain faithful to a single partner afterwards. The early rule regarding premarital chastity then was meant for women, and its application to men came later (where it came at all) and has never been as severe.

If the desire to accumulate property lies at the origins of sexual repression, its chief function today is to produce submissive beings of both sexes. In our treatment of character structure, the diminution of critical faculties, general passivity, resignation, and other negative effects of repression were identified. According to Reich, people's sexual satisfaction "is not simply satisfaction of a need, like hunger or defecation, but their spiritual development, their freshness of life, their capacity for work and their enthusiasm for struggle" are affected every bit as much by their sexual life as by their material existence.[32] More important still, "the suppression of the gratification of primitive material needs has a result different from that of the suppression of the gratification of the sexual needs. The former incites rebellion. The latter, however—by repressing the sexual needs and by becoming anchored by moralistic defense—paralyzes the rebellion against either kind of suppression."[33] It is the greater suppression of women that makes them more apolitical and generally more passive than men.

The work of sexual suppression is carried on primarily by the family. In his Marxist period Reich believed the suppression that was most decisive in determining character occurred between the ages of four to six in the ways parents respond to sexual play and questions.[34] So important is the role of the family in these early years that Reich refers to it as the "factory of submissive beings."[35] To him, it is no coincidence that "the lack of victorious spirit, the outlawry of protest, the absence of personal opinions characterizes the relations of faithful children to their parents just as they do the relations of devoted bureaucrats to the state authorities and that of non-class conscious workers to the owner of the factory."[36]

The same suppression that remakes the child's character severely limits the possibilities of his social development generally. Sexual needs, by their very nature, drive the individual (male and female) into relationships with other people. With their suppression, they find expression only in the family. This event "turns an original biological tie of the child to the mother—and of the mother to the child—into an indissoluble sexual fixation and thus creates the inability to establish new relationships. The core of the family tie is the mother fixation."[37] Thus, the Oedipus complex is not one of the causes of sexual suppression, as Freud believed, but a major result. Other results are guilt and sticky sentimentality that make any rational view of the family so difficult to achieve.

The family also plays the chief role in the character development of adolescents. The increase in libido that occurs at this time corresponds to an increased desire for independence, which in turn leads to a greater conflict with parents. Due to their early upbringing, most people, according to Reich, are more or less neurotic at the start of puberty. The neurosis and its accompanying social attitudes, however, only take on definitive form through the family conflicts of this period and, in particular, through the inhibition of a natural love life.[38]

Sexual abstinence, by making adolescents more obedient, strengthens the father's hand in any dispute. It also makes access to "social and sexual reality more difficult...when it doesn't make it altogether impossible."[39] If parents succeed in stifling this thrust for independence, the young person becomes more attached than ever to the pattern of behavior and authority relationships that prepare him or her for a life of political indifference and/or reaction. Reich notes that youth's views for and against the capitalist order correspond very closely to their views on the family—conservative youth respecting and often idealizing it, and radical youth opposing the family and, in the process, becoming quite independent of it.

The picture of family relations presented here applies throughout capitalist society, the differences between classes, according to Reich, being chiefly ones of degree. Bourgeois ideology in respect to marriage, family, premarital chastity, abortion, etc., has penetrated to all groups, though to none more than the bourgeoisie themselves. Reich believes that as a worker's income and style of life approach that of the bourgeoisie, as social respectability becomes possible, the sexual suppression of children is intensified. Minus these pretensions, working-class parents tend to be less repressive. To be sure, this is mostly due to the fact that they have less time to spend with their children, who are left to their own devices—and pleasures. Enough repression and moralizing occur even here, however, for the characters of most workers to exhibit many of the traits described above.[40]

For the most part, religion and education only reinforce the moralistic attitudes that have already been inculcated in children by their parents. The link between sexual repression and religion has long been known. Every patriarchal religion, which means every modern religion, is antisexual to one degree or another. If God is always watching, if he (!) even knows what we are thinking, what does he find out? He finds out what our confessor does—most confessions deal with masturbation and other sexual acts. Reich believes that beside serving as a brake to sexuality, religion offers an alternative outlet to the energy that has been repressed. Going beyond Marx, who said that religion functions socially as an opium, and Freud, who said that its beliefs are illusions, Reich maintains that religion is also a substitute for the very sexual feelings it helps to suppress. Praying, listening to organ or choral music, sitting in a dimly lit church, the ecstasy and mysticism of the true believer, are all, psychologically speaking, means to relieve unbearable sexual tension. They are only partially successful, but as long as the individual will not or cannot obtain full sexual gratification, they perform a necessary stop-gap function. Adolescence, the time of increased sexual desire and repression, is also the period when religious feelings are most intense.[41]

Education contributes to sexual repression not only when it is openly antisexual as in some church schools, but also when it tries to ignore children's sexuality, when it puts the effects of sexual frustration and tension under other headings, such as "hyperactivity" or "laziness," in short, when it discusses everything but what children are thinking about. The so-called "objective" approach to sex education, which reduces sex to procreation and venereal disease and leaves out all mention of desire and pleasure is equally destructive. For the result is that the sexually obsessed youngster, meaning practically all young people, considers him or herself a freak. Guilt mounts, and the qualities born in repression become exaggerated.[42]

Reich's account of the social function of sexual repression serves as the basis of his mass-psychological explanation of fascism, the social phenomenon that so baffled the intellectuals of his time. Reich does not deny the importance of the economic depression, the Versailles Treaty, or any of the other events that are generally held responsible for German developments. Nor does he disagree that fascism is objectively in the interests of big capitalists, who benefit most from Fascist economic policy, or that it is politically rooted, at least initially, in the lower middle class. However, he wants to know why fascism, this particular non-solution to German problems, appealed to people, including workers. What was there in their lives and characters that prepared the way for the nationalist, racist, and imperialist propaganda of the Nazis? What was there in Nazi symbols, slogans, uniforms, etc. that was so attractive?

Reich's answer focuses on the authoritarian character structure that is produced by strict patriarchal families and sex-negating religion. The submissive, uncritical, sexually anxious person is drawn to fascism, first, as a means of opposing what are felt as threats to his/her neurotic equilibrium. In Fascist propaganda, Jews are consistently represented as sexual perverts, and communism as the sharing of women. The widespread mother fixation (referred to above) is taken advantage of by frequent comparisons of the nation to mother, and of the enemies of the nation (Jews, Communists, etc.) to those who would abuse mother. On the positive side, freedom for the nation and race compensate for personal misery, particularly in the sexual realm. Moreover, like religion, the ceremonies and rituals of fascism offer an alternative outlet for sexual tension, a means to reduce the intolerable frustration that is the lot of most of its followers. Uncritical support for the Leader is a chance—maybe the sexually blocked person's only chance—to "let go." Sexuality, through repression, has metamorphosed into sentiments and ways of functioning that—in circumstances of capitalist decay—make fascism appealing. The rich assortment of evidence and argument that Reich brings together in support of this thesis (material I have barely touched upon) makes *The Mass Psychology of Fascism* the major achievement of his Marxist period.[43]

IV

Reich's concern with the laws of the sexual process was not an academic one. Like Marx, he wanted to learn how society works in order to change it. He knew that sexual repression cannot be completely abolished until the conditions that require and promote it—including family, religion and private property—have all disappeared. And until that time, the effects of repression will hamper all attempts at radical change. The question arises whether in these conditions radical change is possible at all.

Asking this question does not place Reich beyond the bounds of a Marxist analysis. The mode of production is still the main factor in determining the character of social conditions generally. Society is still divided into classes based primarily on people's relationship to the mode of production. Workers still have an objective interest in making a socialist revolution, a revolution that will one day do away with all repression, including sexual repression. The fact remains, however, that a successful socialist revolution requires most workers to become conscious of their interests now, under capitalism, and this has never occurred. Reich's account of the social function of sexual repression provides an important and hitherto neglected part of the explanation, but as an explanation it offers little hope for change. If sexual repression produces submissive, uncritical workers who in turn set up authoritarian families, there doesn't seem to be any place to break the circle.

Reich's own response is twofold: first, he believes it is possible to fight against the suppression of youth from outside the family, to conduct a political struggle on behalf of youth's right to love. And, second, he believes that the range of rationality of many adults can be extended by speaking to their most personal problems and showing the link between these problems and the capitalist system.

Reich tried to put his ideas into practice in Austria (1929-1930) and Germany (1930-1932). With four other radical analysts and three obstetricians, he founded the "Socialist Society for Sex

Hygiene and Sexological Research." Six clinics were set up in working-class areas of Vienna. Later, when Reich moved to Berlin, he convinced the Communist leadership to unite several sexual reform movements into one sex-political organization under the aegis of the party. Membership grew quickly to around 40,000 people. Reich was one of the organization's chief spokespersons on sexual questions until the end of 1932 when the Communist Party prohibited the further distribution of his works, charging that his emphasis on sexuality was un-Marxist.

As we saw, Reich did not deny the Marxist interpretation of social conditions or, for that matter, the existence of other natural drives, but his special interest in human irrationality led him to focus on the modes of sexuality he believed most responsible for it. Unfortunately for him, what was sufficiently Marxist for the German Communist leadership in 1930 and 1931 was not so in late 1932 in the face of growing reaction in the Soviet Union and when, it appears, the need to attract Christians (who viewed Reich as the worst of the Communists) to an anti-Fascist front was raised to a higher priority. Despite the strong support of his co-workers, Reich was ousted from the Communist Party in February 1933.[44]

During his years as a sex-political activist, Reich directed most of his efforts toward working-class youth. In talks, articles, and some personal consultation, he sought to clarify their sexual confusion. Rather than "promote sex," as he was often accused of doing, he concentrated on correcting the false notions that underlie most sexual prohibitions (sex needs no promoting), and on linking youth's sexual plight to life in capitalism. Intercourse, masturbation, sexual desire, orgasm, venereal disease, abortion, etc., were all discussed in connection with existing repression and the social prerequisites for a healthy sexual life. Reich scorned a false neutrality, and placed himself four-square on the side of young people and their physical needs. The results, he tells us, were widespread enthusiasm, more effective work on the part of youth who were already radicalized and the radicalization of many who were formerly apolitical.

To lead a healthy sexual life, what adolescents need is complete and accurate sexual information, free access to contraceptives, time to be alone with the other sex, and their own rooms. Adolescents, who want sexual happiness more than anything else, are all more or less aware of these needs. No matter what their political views, Reich believes, they can be appealed to and won over by a platform that addresses itself to these questions. Explaining their sexual suffering is the best way to make youth understand their total oppression in capitalism. This view is qualified by Reich's admission that the strongest impulse to revolutionary sentiment in the young comes from identification with class conscious parents or older siblings. However, there are very few such adults, and most youth must be won over to socialism by other means.[45]

For all but a few youth who live in nonrepressive socialist families (this is, of course, a matter of degree) the adoption of an anticapitalist perspective begins with rebellion against the father. Striving for independence is a natural phenomenon of puberty. It is always connected with intensified sexual feelings and a greater consciousness of surroundings, including social impingements of various sorts. In this context, rebellion against the father, who represents state authority in the family, carries with it a tendency to opt for left politics. To the oft-repeated criticism that young radicals are simply rebelling against their fathers, Reich seems to answer—yes and no. Yes, every adolescent growing up in a repressive family rebels against his father; no, this rebellion is not simply against father, but against authoritarian relationships and abuses throughout society. Moreover, Reich believes, it is generally the scope and success of this rebellion that foretells who will be a revolutionary and who will be apolitical.[46]

Reich's strategy for politicizing the sexual struggle of youth is clearly prefigured in his analysis of sexuality and repression under capitalism. The same cannot be said of his strategy for developing class consciousness among adults. Much of what he says about authoritarian character structure makes it appear that nothing short of therapy or revolution would have a radicalizing effect. Yet, particularly in his essay "What Is Class Consciousness?" Reich argues as if a different approach by Communist parties could convince many adults of the need for a revolution.

To begin, Reich says, it is important to recognize that the class consciousness of workers is somewhat different from that of their leaders. A class conscious worker understands his needs in every area of life, the means and possibilities of satisfying them, the difficulties in the way of doing so, his own inhibitions and anxieties, and his invincibility when acting as part of the class.

Their class conscious leaders, as Reich calls members of the Communist Party, understand all this as well as the historical process outlined by Marx. Furthermore, they are (or should be) particularly aware of the progressive ideas, wishes and emotions that come with being a worker as well as of their conservative counterparts and of the anxiety that holds the former in check.

Reich says that, for the proletariat, working in industry and belonging to a union are the most important influences in becoming class conscious. They permit each individual to see him/herself as a member of a class and to learn something of the position of this class in the economy. But this is not enough. While a worker remains ignorant of how the rest of his/her life is affected by the work roles of capitalist society, he/she will desire only limited reforms.

Unfortunately, most workers are interested in social problems only insofar as these problems enter into everyday life. The only oppression they recognize is that which involves eating, sleeping, working, making love, walking, shopping, etc. The precise form of each of these activities (meaning, too, why they are so unsatisfactory) is, to a very large extent, given by the capitalist system in which it occurs. Yet, Marxists on the whole have paid little attention to the variety of ways this system intrudes into the personal lives of its inhabitants. Reich would reverse this trend. He wants socialists to hold up the personal life as a mirror in which people can catch sight of their oppression and of the possibilities for change.

Among the practical suggestions Reich offers to realize this strategy are more public lectures on personal problems, setting up consultation and sex hygiene centers, starting radical theaters to do plays on everyday life from a socialist perspective, and devoting three-quarters of every radical newspaper to communications with readers, again, on personal problems.

Reich's insight into the irrational aspects of character is also the basis for his advice on how to improve socialist propaganda. It is wrong, for example, to constantly stress the power of the ruling class. This not only creates fear but feeds the worker's authoritarian complex. The weaknesses and stupidities of the capitalists should be stressed instead. He believes, too, that it is wrong to present the main symbol for authority in society, the police, as the enemy, for again this activates authoritarian tendencies. Reich would have socialists emphasize that the police are also workers. Indeed, he says that concentrating on the class nature of personal problems, problems which they as workers share, will bring many police over to the side of the revolution.

Reich also argues that socialist propaganda should be positive and preparatory to the new life awaiting people, as well as being critical. Workers must be helped to see how work conditions and relations would be different in socialism. Women must be given some idea of how cooperative living would deal with the problems of housework and childcare. The same applies, of course, to youth, professionals, farmers, and even the police and the army. In every case, when contrasting present dissatisfaction with the socialist alternative care must be taken to show the special responsibility of the capitalist system and what the people appealed to can do to change it.[47]

Most of what Reich advocates here, as regards both what to do and say, has been put into practice by one or another radical group in the years since he wrote. Women's liberation, anarchists, hippies, black and brown revolutionaries and, occassionally, Marxists have all sought to radicalize people by helping them draw lessons from their personal lives. Only Reich, however, has tried to systematize this approach. Only Reich recognizes that sexual concerns are at the center of most people's personal lives. And only Reich bases his strategy on a deep-going socio-psychological analysis of life in capitalist society.

V

The criticism of Reich that one hears most often today is that the situation he described has ceased to exist, that for young people the sexual revolution has already taken place. When Daniel Guerin, the French anarchist, suggested this in a talk he gave to Belgian students, he was met with a loud chorus of "no, not true!"[48] Certainly, some of the basic facts have altered. The pill did not exist forty years ago. Reich's discussion of the dangers of venereal disease was also written before the discovery of penicillin. Politically, some humanizing reforms have taken place, the most recent being the abortion laws passed by many American states. Socially, there is more sex with less guilt—or so it appears. Information and pseudo-information, sexy books, films, and advertisements (and with them sexual stimulation) are all more readily available. Psychologically, people are more open to discussions about sex, more ready to accept it as a natural and necessary function even outside marriage than ever before.

What needs to be stressed, however, is that such changes have only improved, and not by much, a very bad situation. On the basis of their own generally liberated sexual lives, young radicals tend to overestimate the degree to which the mores of their peers in out-of-the-way schools and jobs have altered. Furthermore, a lot of what passes for sexual freedom—the wife-trading of the suburbanite, the frantic consumption of pornography, the boom in homosexuality, orgies—have, if Reich is to be believed, little to do with sexual happiness. Instead, they appear to be strong indications of sexual dissatisfaction and evidence of the continued effect of sexual repression.

Most important, youth of all classes still do not receive sufficient information. Contraceptives remain a problem for many. Rooms to be alone with members of the opposite sex are generally unavailable (making love in cars is not a satisfactory substitute). Parents still suppress overt sexuality and offer indirect answers or worse to sexual questions. Religious training continues to produce guilt, and schools to frown on all manifestations of sexuality. Thus, Reich's analysis still applies and the radicalizing potential of his writings even today is enormous. If anything, our greater openness on sexual matters enhances this potential by making it easier to get Reich's ideas the wide hearing that was denied them earlier.

If Reich's analysis of the sexual repression of youth and his strategy to combat it are as useful as ever, his strategy for developing class consciousness in adults is open to the same objections now that it was earlier. I have already said that, in my opinion, Reich's analysis of authoritarian character structure makes it doubtful that the measures he advocates for modifying this structure once it has taken hold will do much good. Even if he is correct that helping adults understand the social function of sexual repression and their own sexual misery makes them better parents (a doubtful assumption), it is unlikely that their political attitudes will undergo much change. With few real possibilities to improve their love lives—with their social situation and character rigidities fixed—the enlightenment Reich offers is more likely to create anxiety and to arouse hostility and fear. Moreover, the corresponding effort to liberate youth, with its concommitant of family conflict, is bound to be taken as a threat by most parents and to influence the way they react to Reich's teachings as a whole. This is not an argument against a politics that focuses on the personal life, but is a reason for not expecting too much from it.

Reich's adult politics suffer from not making adequate distinctions between adults in different age groups and different family situations. Those who do not have teenage children and whose character structures and familial situations have not taken final shape, in short, young adults, are the only ones Reich's strategy could favorably affect. Older people are likely to react only negatively.

Reich's strategy then, is one for influencing children, adolescents, and young adults. Therefore, it is a long-term strategy. It is an attempt to assure that ten, twenty, and more years from now oppressed people will respond to the inevitable crises that occur in capitalism in a rational manner, in ways best suited to promote their interests. The upsurge of fascism and the need for an immediate response to it inclined Reich to see in his findings a way to alter adult consciousness. It was not, and, despite all recent changes, is not still.

If German political events pushed Reich to misrepresenting his long-term strategy as a short-term one, it is important to see that this error was abetted by his conceptual scheme. Reich was able to conceive of his strategy drawing psychologically crippled people into the revolutionary movement, because, for all his effort to create a Marxist psychology, he kept his psychological and sociological findings in separate compartments. Rather than combine Marx and Freud, Reich showed that the main discoveries of these two giants are complementary and argued that each needed supplementing by the other. This is what he tried to do in taking psychoanalysis, as he believed, to its logical conclusion. But the basic conceptions with which Marx and Freud circumscribe their respective subject matters are hardly tampered with. Reich's "logical" conclusion is not without its logical problems.[49] The exception is the concept of character structure that Reich introduced to capture the meeting place of Marx and Freud's teachings, but progress to and from this juncture is made within two incompatible schemes.

Freud's categories of instinct, ego, id, energy, neurosis, etc., which Reich passes on, all focus on the individual in abstraction from his social situation. Freud does not neglect society, but—except for early family training—relegates it to the background. Individuals, he believes, enter into social relationships only to satisfy needs. Marx does not neglect the individual and his needs, but for him they have no existence outside the social situation. These opposing views as to what is important are embedded in their conceptual schemes. And though both thinkers accept an interrelationship between phenomena on all levels, the concepts each uses convey a distorted, one-sided view of the phenomena studied by the other. Reich was unusual in adopting both conceptual schemes and applying, on each occasion, the one that was most appropriate to his subject matter—Freud for individuals and Marx for society. When the two led to different conclusions on a topic that spanned both systems, Reich was at liberty to choose either one. This is what happened when his study of character structure carried on within a Freudian framework indicated workers could not become class conscious, and his study of character structure carried on within a Marxist framework indicated they could.

To correct this double distortion, a set of concepts must be constructed that unites the two perspectives so that Freud's discoveries are not attached as an afterthought to Marx's, nor Marx's to Freud's, and so that attention to one oversight does not lead to getting lost in the other. What are needed are concepts to "think" people in all their concreteness, people as they are and become, and not as they have been carved up by competing disciplines.

I should like to propose the concept "relations of maturation," understood as the interaction between natural growth and the sum of the conditions in which it occurs, as a first step in uniting the Marxian and Freudian perspectives. Just as Marx in his concept "relations of production" sought to bring out the fact that production is more than the act of making something, that it includes distribution, exchange, and consumption in a complex pattern that takes us eventually into every area of life— in the same way, by "relations of maturation" I intend to highlight the fact that maturation is more than a physical process of growth, that it includes the full conditions in which human development occurs and particularly the effect upon the individual of family, church, school, and media.

Within the context of the relations of maturation, desire, for example, is seen as a structure that includes libido, the developmental stages through which an individual passes, and the objects made available by circumstance. As such, desire is rooted as much in history as in biological processes. The puberty of today's youth becomes a capitalist social relation.

The individual is no longer independent of his setting nor absorbed by it. If Freud grasps the human as a biological entity, and Marx as a social relationship, I am proposing that humans be grasped as a bio-social relationship. The dialectical character of Marx's conception is retained, but merely extended (perhaps simply explicitly extended) to cover elements whose great importance has been demonstrated by Freud. The interaction and flux of all elements within the relations of maturation are taken as given, so that one may focus on any segment without becoming one-sided.

It was the lack of concepts like relations of maturation, of adequate means to think his subject matter, that led to a contradiction between Reich's psychological analysis and his political strategy for adults. Perhaps more important, it made possible, if not likely, Reich's own drift away from radical politics. The immediate cause, of course, lay in his mistreatment at the hands of the German Communist Party and his growing disillusionment with the Soviet Union. Stalinist politics had a similar effect on many intellectuals of the period. What makes this an inadequate explanation for his turnabout is that he understood better than most of his equally tramped-on comrades why "Thermidor" happened. Moreover, Reich's analysis of capitalism is in no way faulted by the reaction he saw in the Soviet Union.[50] So it is that Reich continued to espouse a revolutionary war against capitalism for a few years after his ouster from the Communist Party.[51]

Then, the analysis underlying his political stance began to erode. It began to erode because Reich, still operating with two conceptual schemes, introduced psychological concepts to help explain social phenomena, such as the policy of the Communist Party. Marxism was clearly insufficient to account for the behavior of the largest Marxist organization. But Freud's and

Marx's concepts are incompatible; they cannot occupy the same account. With the introduction of Freud's psychology into the social realm, Marxism was pushed aside.

It is not clear when exactly Reich ceased to be a Marxist, but after *The Sexual Revolution* (1936) the class analysis that served as the social framework for his psychology gradually disappeared. The parts—Reich's Marxism and Freudianism—became disconnected because they were never conceptually welded together. With his Marxism gone, Reich eventually fell prey to the same mistake for which he had earlier condemned other psychoanalysts, to wit, generalizing from the individual to society and treating the latter as the patient. The result was the notion of the emotional plague, understood as the irrational social activity of sexually sick people, which he then, in good psychoanalytic fashion, blew up to be the determining force in history.[52]

Reich's later work, as fascinating and controversial as it is, lies outside the bounds of this essay. My interest has been to show that Reich's analysis of capitalist relations of maturation and the political strategy for youth and young adults based upon it are, for all the updating required, extremely relevant today. To determine how relevant, we must study recent developments in sexual life as well as Reich's writings, and test our conclusions in revolutionary practice.[53]

Notes

1. Wilhelm Reich, "Dialectical Materialism and Psychoanalysis," translated by A. Bostock *Studies on the Left,* 6, no. 4, 1966, p. 41.

2. Karl Marx, *Introduction to the Critique of Political Economy,* trans. by N. I. Stone (Chicago, 1904) pp. 11-12.

3. Wilhelm Reich, "Pour l'application de la psychanalyse a la recherche historique," *Materialisme dialectique, materialisme historique et psychoanalyse* (Paris, 1970), pp. 37-38.

4. Wilhelm Reich, "Dialectical Materialism and Psychoanalysis," p. 6.

5. *Ibid.* p. 12. For Freud's views see *Three Contributions to the Theory of Sex,* trans. by A. A. Brill (New York, 1962), pp. 74-76.

6. Wilhelm Reich, *Reich on Freud,* edited by M. Higgins and C. Raphael (New York, 1967), p. 15.

7. Wilhelm Reich, *The Function of the Orgasm,* trans. by T. P. Wolfe (New York, 1961), p. 9.

8. See, particularly, Freud's "Instincts and Their Vicissitudes," *Collected Papers,* vol. 4, trans. by Jean Riviere (London, 1956).

9. For a clear statement of such criticisms from a radical vantage point (the authors would not call themselves Marxists), see H. Gerth, and C. W. Mills,

Character and Social Structure (London, 1954), pp. 8-9.

10. For Reich's development of Freud's theory of the neurosis see *Function of the Orgasm,* pp. 66-72.

11. *Ibid.* p. 78.

12. *Ibid.* p. 79.

13. *Ibid.* p. 77.

14. Ernest Jones, *The Life and Work of Sigmund Freud,* vol. II (New York, 1955), p. 67.

15. Wilhelm Reich, *Character Analysis,* trans. by T. P. Wolfe (New York, 1970), p. 44.

16. *Ibid.* pp. 158, 185.

17. *Ibid.* pp. 148-149.

18. Wilhelm Reich, *People in Trouble,* (Rangely, Maine, 1953), p. 74. This highly provocative remark appears in an essay written in 1936-1937; it was never developed.

19. Sigmund Freud, "'Civilized' Sexual Morality and Modern Nervousness," *Collected Papers,* vol. II, trans. by Jean Rivierre (London, 1948). Unfortunately, this explosive essay receives little attention today.

20. Wilhelm Reich, *Mass Psychology of Fascism,* trans. by T. P. Wolfe (New York, 1946), p. 25. Other effects of sexual repression noted by Reich are "the pallor, depression, nervousness, disturbances in the ability to work, quarrelsomeness, criminal inclination and perversion." *People in Trouble,* p. 81. Reich found strong support for his and Freud's views on the characterological effects of repression in Bronislaw Malinowski's comparison of the Trobriand Islanders, who have sexual intercourse from about the age of five, with their close neighbors, the Amphlett Islanders, who share our sexual taboos. See, particularly, Malinowski's *The Sexual Life of Savages* (London, 1930). Despite such confirmation, it must be admitted that this central thesis of Reich's work is still not wholly understood or verified.

21. *Character Analysis,* p. 146.

22. *Ibid.* XXLL.

23. Wilhelm Reich (pseudonym Ernst Parell), *Was ist Klassenbewusstsein?* (Copenhagen,1934), p. 17.

24. *People in Trouble,* p. 46.

25. This useful caption for the rational qualities Marx ascribes to workers comes from Thorstein Veblen's *The Place of Science in Modern Civilization and Other Essays* (New York, 1961), p. 441.

26. For a discussion of Marx's theory of alienation, see my book, *Alienation: Marx's Conception of Man in Capitalist Society* (Cambridge, 1971). I attempt to integrate Reich's theory of character structure into Marx's theory of alienation in "Social and Sexual Revolution" republished as chapter six of this book.

27. *Reich on Freud,* pp. 197-198. Reich's fullest account of Freud's materialist dialectic appears in "Dialectical Materialism and Psychoanalysis," *Studies on the Left,* pp. 22-39.

28. Karl Marx, *Capital I,* trans. S. Moore and E. Aveling (Moscow, 1958), p. 80.

29. For Reich's views on homosexuality see his *La lutte sexuelle des jeunes* (Paris, 1966), pp. 93-100.

30. Wilhelm Reich, *La crise sexuelle* (Paris, 1965), p. 58.

31. The origins of sexual repression is the subject of an entire book: Wilhelm Reich, *Der Einbruch der Sexualmoral (Berlin, 1932).*

32. *La lutte sexuelle des jeunes,* p. 107.

33. *Mass Psychology of Fascism,* pp. 25-26.

34. *La crise sexulle,* p. 70.

35. *La lutte sexuelle des jeunes,* p. 119.

36. *Ibid.*

37. *Mass Psychology of Fascism,* pp. 47-48.

38. *People in Trouble,* . 82.

39. *La crise sexuelle,* p. 70.

40. For Reich's treatment of the family, see, particularly, *The Sexual Revolution,* trans. by T. P. Wolfe (New York, 1951), pp. 71-80; and *Mass Psychology of Fascism,* pp. 28-62, 88-96.

41. For his treatment of religion, see *Mass Psychology of Fascism*, pp. 122-142.

42. For his treatment of sex education, see, particularly, *The Sexual Revolution,* pp. 61-70.

43. Erich Fromm's better known psychological study of fascism, *Escape From Freedom* (New York, 1942), was greatly influenced by Reich's *Mass Psychology of Fascism* (1933).

44. The chief source of information on Reich's sex-political activities is the semi-autobiographical work, *People in Trouble.*

45. *La lutte sexuelle des jeunes* was written for young people in an attempt to politicize their sexual struggle.

46. *Ibid.* pp. 119-123.

47. *Was ist Klassenbewusstsein?* is rich in suggestions on how to radicalize people on the basis of their unsatisfactory personal lives.

48. Daniel Guerin, *Essai sur la revolution sexuelle* (Paris, 1969), p. 25.

49. Reich showed some awareness of this failure later in his life when he admitted that his attempt to unite Marx and Freud "failed logically." *People in Trouble,* p. 42.

50. Reich's fascinating account of the sexual changes and reforms that took place in the Soviet Union after the revolution and the subsequent reaction is found in *The Sexual Revolution,* Part II.

51. *Was ist Klassenbewusstsein?,* pp. 40-41.

52. For a discussion of the Emotional Plague, see *Character Analysis,* pp. 248-280. This chapter was added to the third edition, 1948.

53. *Sex-Pol: Essays 1929-1934,* edited by Lee Baxandal (New York, 1971) brings together Reich's most important Marxist essays, including several which have not otherwise appeared in English. Only now can English speaking readers acquire a clear understanding of Reich's Marxism. The reason is that the English editions of *Mass Psychology of Fascism* (1946) and *The Sexual Revolution* (1945), the best known works of Reich's Marxist period, underwent political adulteration at Reich's own hands. Without altering the structure of these two works, Reich made clear his new political stance and left out prefaces and numerous statements and bits of analysis which had contributed to their Marxist character.

III. Minor Pieces

8.1

Reply to
Stolzman's Critique of
'On Teaching Marxism'

How can any Marxist help but favor teaching students the history of the socialist movement? Unfortunately, in the case at hand, there is also the question of priorities, and if I wish to present a detailed account of Marx's theories I have to forego an exploration of subsequent socialist practice (as well as much else, I might add, which is relevant to a fuller appreciation of these ideas). In a theory-deprived culture such as ours—and I'm referring to the movement as much as to American society in general—there is a place for a course which permits students to concentrate on Marx's texts. This is the easy answer.

But Stolzman is also making a number of related criticisms: 1) that explaining Marxism apart from its subsequent history in the practice of the socialist movement is necessarily distorting; 2) that this approach gives up the pedagogical advantage which comes from using instances of 20th-century communist practice to illustrate Marxist theories; and 3) that the practical political effect of my one-sidedness is to bias students against the Leninist answer to the question "What is to be done?"

Must an account of Marxism be seriously distorted if it is not accompanied by a history of the socialist movement? I think not. Marx devotes the bulk of his writings to an analysis of the capitalist mode of production, and on the level of generalization to which most of it is directed most of this analysis still holds. To be sure, knowledge of what happened in the hundred years since Marx wrote, including the history of the socialist movement, enables us to revise and update this analysis. But the events of these years, and none more so than those associated with the struggle for socialism, have given rise to many contradictory interpretations, and it is only knowledge of Marx's theories which permits us to avoid the worst distortions. Thus, rather than —as Soltzman argues—the history of the socialist movement helping us to understand Marxism correctly, it is most likely (and more often) the other way around. I have been more bothered, for example, by comrades' confused interpretations of the Soviet or Chinese revolutions because of their weak understanding of Marxism, than by its converse. Admittedly, this is not a matter of either/or (or even of before and after) but of where one puts the emphasis in an interaction, and Stolzman and I simply disagree on which—Marxism or the history of the socialist movement—is more important for understanding the other.

To the criticism that my approach makes it impossible to illustrate Marx's ideas with the practice of different communist parties and regimes, I plead guilty, but is this a fault or a virtue? It's one thing to know that the Chinese, the Vietnamese, etc., have something to teach us about Marxism; it is quite another to know, without a careful analysis of our different conditions and histories, just what that is—and such an analysis is too much to attempt in a course on Marxist theory. Furthermore, given the bourgeois ideology of most students, for every useful illustration one finds in communist practice one invariably raises a half-dozen negative ideas that cannot easily be put right without again devoting considerable attention to the overall context. From the pedagogical point of view, therefore, the sparing use of such materials may be worse than no use at all. Finally, though the example of socialist countries has influenced many people to adopt socialist ideas (and I was wrong not to mention it in the article), it is my impression that the commitment of such comrades fades rather quickly when their version of events in the "socialist homeland" is upturned in the latest purge of Trotsky-ists, Titoists, Stalinists, or Maoists. The "high road" to becoming a socialist and remaining one is learning—with the aid of whatever working class experience is available—Marx's analysis of *our* conditions and the potential inherent in them.

The third and probably most damning criticism Stolzman levels at me concerns the kind of socialists which come out of a course such as mine. Without the object lessons provided by the history of the socialist movement, will those students won over by Marx's analysis simply wait for the "objective laws of capitalist development to work themselves out?" I certainly hope not. In the course, I often stress that history is made by people and that socialism will only come about through the conscious effort of the majority of workers and other oppressed people—which brings us to those perennial questions: how are the workers going to acquire such consciousness and what strategy should they use to capture state power? It is interesting to note that whereas Marx devoted most of his scholarly and political life to dealing with the first question, most of his followers have focused on the second. Marx clearly considered it more important to help to promote the kind and spread of workers' consciousness that was necessary to the success of any political strategy. In so far as he himself participated in or wrote about the seizure of state power, he can be found on the side of legal parties, illegal parties, loosely and tightly organized parties, elections, general strikes, and armed struggle, depending on the particular place and its conditions. In discussing Marx's political strategy, therefore, the beginning of wisdom would seem to be to avoid all dogmatism (i.e. formulae argued from principles rather than from conditions), whether Leninist or anti-Leninist.

If Marx had little use for the kind of political debates which, unfortunately, distinguish so many of his followers, it was not because all strategies are equally good, but because in the absence of widespread class consciousness they are all equally bad. In the United States, with perhaps 1%-2% of the people holding socialist ideas of any sort, he would probably view intense discussion of what is the best way to capture state power as not only premature and irrelevant but counter productive as it convinces many who would otherwise be open to socialist arguments—but who are only too aware of the balance of forces in capitalist society—that socialists are foolish and irresponsible people. On the other hand, should there be a significant increase in the number of class conscious workers, it just may be the case that more than one political strategy might work. Thus, while Castro says the task of every revolutionary is to make the revolution, I think that at least for the United States Marx would disagree, insisting that our prior task is to make more revolutionaries. The revolution will only occur when there are enough of us and in a way conditions then allow—and I believe this way is at least as undecided now as it was in Marx's day, when he recognized the possibility of a democratic, though not necessarily peaceful, transition to socialism in Britain, Holland and the United States.

On this interpretation, the success of the socialist cause in the United States is to be judged not by the growth of this or that socialist party or tendency with its set views on how to capture state power, but by the growing number of people, particularly workers, in and out of formal groups who recognize the mechanisms of their oppression in Marx's analysis of capitalism and favor some kind of socialist solution. The time for coalescing around a single program and political strategy will come. In the meantime, all socialist groups and individuals who help to convey this understanding are participating in a common work, whether they know it or will admit it or not. All their efforts to educate and to deepen ongoing struggles, strikes and the like, are mainly valuable in so far as they promote the growth of class consciousness (which in turn permits an increase in the scale of struggle, which in turn makes more people into socialists...which, after a series of such dialectical interchanges— and with the "aid" of still another capitalist crisis—makes a socialist revolution possible). By this standard, one can see considerable value in the activities of most socialist groups, whatever their form of organization. It also offers us a clear basis for condemning those few groups (and occasions in the life of many others) which reserve most of their invective for fellow socialists, understand organizing as jockeying for position in the next American Soviet, or engage in actions that frighten and outrage workers while providing the state with an excuse to intensify its repression of the entire left.

By this standard too, the work of socialist teachers deserves to be seriously upgraded. Nowhere else in our society is so much time and attention given to presenting socialist arguments to future workers (and, unlike the situation in Europe, most of the nine million students in our universities and colleges are future if not actual workers). In my article, I dealt briefly with the processes by which consciousness gets changed. Here, I only want to affirm that radical professors themselves—too often laden with liberal guilt for all that they are not doing and suffering—are generally unaware of either the importance or the signficant achievements of their own wing of the Movement. How many of the comrades reading this piece, for example, know that the last five or six years have witnessed the birth of over fifty socialist journals and newsletters throughout academia, and that radical caucuses are alive and well (and increasingly adopting Marxist approaches) in practically every discipline.* In political science—which always lags behind sociology, economics and history in such matters—we now have four widely used radical introductions to American Government where six years ago there were none. These are all new developments. In the late 1960s, there were many fewer radical materials available for classroom use and even fewer radical teachers to use them—I'm not including the liberals whose criticism of the system was limited to muckraking and marching in anti-Vietnam War demonstrations. Some of these liberals, of course, have become socialists, but more numerous, I think, are the former SDS members who are now socialist faculty. Consequently, it is my impression that despite the job cut-backs there are probably more socialists teaching in higher education today (whether full- or part-time) than there were five and certainly ten years ago. Has anyone bothered to estimate the number of college students who have taken one or more courses from socialists? My guess is that we would all be pleasantly surprised. For the socialist teacher, recognition of such facts should lead to renewed dedication to make the most effective use of the classroom situation, in full consciousness of its possibilities (and dangers) and without apologies to anyone else in the Movement.

*For a full bibliography of these and other socialist journals and newspapers, see the appendix in Ted Norton's and my *Studies in Socialist Pedagogy* (New York, 1978).

Earlier I maintained that Marxism can be adequately taught without introducing the history of the socialist movement, and that examples of communist practice in other lands and times are not effective in clarifying Marx's analysis of our own society. Stolzman's provocative and comradely criticism permits me to add still a third clarification—that presenting Marxism in this way, while leaving open the question of an ultimate strategy for attaining state power, both involves and promotes a political practice aimed at spreading class consciousness, which, as I've argued, was also Marx's preferred practice.

Jim Stolzman's criticism appeared in *The Insurgent Sociologist,* Summer, 1977, which is also the issue in which this reply appeared.

8.2

Reply to
Mussachia's Critique of
'Social and Sexual Revolution'

I agree with Mussachia that sexual repression is one kind of repression among many; that sexual repression is not peculiar to capitalism; that poor people put a greater value on food, clothing, and decent housing than they do on a sexual revolution; that interest in a sexual revolution has come chiefly from materially satisfied members of the middle class whose erotic fun and wisdom have not proven too difficult for capitalism to coopt; that those involved in making a socialist revolution or in building socialism in a country which has had its revolution need a lot of self-discipline and that in certain conditions this *may* require restrictions in their sexual lives. I believe that Reich the Marxist would have agreed as well.

Where Mussachia and I disagree is on the social function of sexual repression in *capitalism* and, it would appear, on whether it even pays to look for it. According to Mussachia, capitalism has inherited the authoritarian family, like religion, from "the past" and simply uses it to "support its main mechanisms of social control." But religion in capitalism is significantly different, both in character and function, from religion in feudalism (I am thinking of the reforms in Catholicism and Judaism as well as the development of Protestantism); and the same applies to the authoritarian family. Though possessing certain trans-historical qualities, family and religion do not stand already completed, somehow outside capitalism, with a simple instrumental relationship to the mode of production. Rather, they exist as interacting and overlapping dimensions of capitalist life, helping to shape the same mode of production which in the last analysis determines their particular forms and functions. In his Introduction to *The Critique of Political Economy*, Marx declares: "The conditions which generally govern production must be differentiated in order that the essential points of difference be not lost sight of, in view of the general uniformity which is due to the fact that the subject, mankind, and the object, nature, remain the same."[1] Without dismissing those aspects of human activities which different periods have in common, Marx's analysis invariably focuses on the forms of these activities that are peculiar to each period.

Reich sees sexual repression at the core of authoritarian family relations and, while recognizing its existence in pre-capitalist societies, he is most concerned to uncover its unique character and role in capitalism. In particular, he wants to know how and to what extent it contributes to the inability of the mass of the workers in advanced capitalist societies to attain class consciousness. This is the main question to which Reich addresses himself and as such provides the relevant context in which to examine and assess all his efforts during his Marxist period. In the past century, a half dozen major crises have come and gone in the capitalist world without producing the degree of proletarian class consciousness Marx had anticipated. Among his followers, three kinds of answers are generally given to account for this failure. One emphasizes some inadequacy in Marx's analysis of capitalist conditions: "Marx did not (could not) see (foresee)...." A second answer focuses on the mistakes of earlier leaders and organizations of the working class. The third answer points to some failing in the workers themselves, not in their "human nature" but in their conditioned nature. Though usually treated as mutually exclusive, there is probably some truth in each of these explanations, but the work which succeeds in weaving them together has not been written. In my opinion, Reich's is the most successful attempt to examine that part of the problem of class consciousness which lies within the workers themselves, but I don't by any means believe that what he has done is wholly adequate.[2]

Reich's special contribution to this subject derives from his (and Freud's) discovery of the importance of early conditioning and especially of sexual repression in the formation of character structure. At the start of his letter, Mussachia seems to grant that character structure is a product of early conditioning; but he then insists that it is competition in the market place for jobs and goods—in short, adult life—that gives people both their bourgeois ideology and their equally bourgeois "emotional syndrome." I certainly don't want to deny that adult life in capitalism produces such results, but the real question is, to what extent does it mainly intensify and give final form to ways of thinking and feeling that are already present in the growing child and adolescent. Having already presented family and church as ahistorical phenomena, it is not surprising that Mussachia minimizes their contribution in capitalism to the formation of character. He is obviously and unfortunately the kind of Marxist Sartre criticizes for treating people as if they are born at the time they apply for their first job.[3]

What of the special importance Reich attributes to sexual repression? As a practicing therapist, Reich found that sexual repression was at the core of most of his patients' neurotic conflicts. As a doctor interested in youth, he saw that young people spend the greater part of their time thinking about and trying to establish a sexual life (something most people tend to forget when they become adults). As a Freudian theorist, he recognized how sexual feelings could be transformed by experiences and conditioning to appear as their very opposite. It can be argued that consistently repressing any strong impulse contributes to the formation of an authoritarian character. The relatively greater strength of sexual impulses and the equally intense repression which it calls forth, the almost unique sense of guilt and morbid anxiety connected with inadequate sexuality, all led Reich—as it did Freud—to give priority to sexual repression. Moreover, Reich found that the undischarged energies resulting from sexual repression are used to control a variety of impulses, sexual as well as non-sexual, and serve in this way to underpin the whole of character structure.

Does this mean that workers who have not been sexually repressed or—more to the point—have been less repressed will necessarily become class conscious? No. If Reich is correct, all that will happen is that a major impediment which interferes with workers' rationally coming to grips with their condition will be weakened or removed. It is a matter of forestalling the development of a characterological predisposition to misconstrue and accept the conditions of their life. The crucial role of these conditions, and of socialists in educating workers about them, remains as we have always understood them. Hence, whatever sexual liberation occurs (not in talk but in practice, not on middle-class university campuses but in working-class high schools) cannot be said to *produce* class consciousness but only to *permit* it to arise in connection with later life experiences.

Finally, it may be useful to speculate on why Reich's work on the social function of sexual repression in capitalism raises so much irrelevant criticism from committed comrades, for the exchange printed here is only too typical. Without pointing to particular individuals, I believe it is mainly due to the conceptual problem of integrating mass psychology into the socio-economic framework of Marxism, the political difficulty of developing a strategy that takes account of Reich's analysis, the unacceptable long-term persective that this strategy seems to assume, the bad name given to sexual revolution by hippies, etc., and the criticism Reich's analysis implies of existing organizations and strategies for ignoring mass psychology. There is no doubt that these are, or mask, real problems. It is unfortunate, indeed tragic, that they keep so many Marxists from learning what Reich has to teach about their solutions.

Notes

1. Karl Marx, Introduction, *Critique of Political Economy,* trans. by N. I. Stone (Chicago, 1904), p. 269.
2. For a fuller discussion of the topic, see my article, "Marx and the Working Class: Toward Class Consciousness Next Time," reprinted as chapter I in this book.
3. J. P. Sartre, *Critique de la raison dialectique* (Paris, 1960), p. 47.

8.3

Comment on
Kelly's 'Alienation'

Agreed, confusion over the use of the word "alienation" has reached a point where one is tempted to scrap the term altogether (a suggestion several writers have made over the past decade). Agreed, too, a short note on alienation can only indicate a "port of embarkation" for the study of the subject. Where do we go from here? Do we try to understand what can be understood of alienation by looking at how the term has been used, particularly in ordinary language, or by examining one or more of the systems of analysis in which it appears? Kelly, who adopts the first approach, is left with very little to say after penetrating the fog surrounding the term's use. The common residue of "alienation" is found to be a wholly subjective feeling, whose cultural tone and core—as Kelly rightly argues—is captured at least as well by several much less ambiguous words.

But what can this approach teach us about alienation in Marxism—or in Hegel's or Kierkegaard's work, for that matter? Is it possible to confront a concept that is central to a particular thinker's analysis without confronting that analysis (and clearly Kelly's conclusion that we drop alienation is directed to political theorists as well as to ordinary mortals)? In fact, Kelly has ignored the basic distinction between words which belong to a particular language, and concepts (or ideas contained in words) which belong to particular systems of analysis. "Alienation" is both a word and a concept. Kelly, who uses these labels interchangeably, argues from the condition of the word "alienation" to conclusions regarding the concept.

Yet Kelly says he has struggled with the *Phenomenology* and the *1844 Manuscripts,* and I have no reason to doubt him. To judge by his conclusions, however, these works merely served as further instances in which to look for the use of the term "alienation" in the process of trying to understand alienation in general. The alternative is to see that, in the work of each of these thinkers, "alienation" is a concept whose meaning cannot be divorced from the analysis made with its help. In effect, we are dealing with many different, though related, concepts that receive expression in the same word, and it is chiefly this fact which underlies the confusing use of "alienation" in ordinary speech.

Marx's concept of alienation, for example, conveys the capitalist forms of the four basic relationships which structure his analysis of people in society. These are the relations between the individual and his activity (particularly in production), his product (particularly the commodity), other people (particularly those who control his productive activity and its product), and the species. Even the subjective feeling of alienation, the lowest common denominator on which Kelly focuses, is grossly distorted in Marx's case when viewed outside the broader conditions which produce and shape it and which it in turn helps to perpetuate.

The relation between the individual and the human species, or what it means to be a person, introduces the element of human potential into Marx's analysis of capitalism, enabling him to grasp existing ties in light of alternatives posed by other and better, though still realistic, conditions. The inadequacy of ordinary language as a tool or framework for treating Marx's chosen subject is nowhere as apparent as in its denial of this dimension. Whether it is taken as a noun, an adjective, or a verb, "alienation" can never convey more—especially with regard to human fulfillment—than the experience of the person speaking allows him to understand, without an analysis that probes the reasons for this limitation. Reflecting the false consciousness that is produced by daily life in capitalist society, ordinary language can illustrate alienation but not explain it.

It is in recognition of the place of alienation in the Marxian system that my book *Alienation* is subtitled *Marx's Conception of Man in Capitalist Society*. My main aim in this work was to present alienation as Marxism—that is, the analysis of capitalism we call Marxism—viewed from the vantage point of the acting and acted-upon individual. The value of this concept is wholly dependent on the value ascribed to this analysis. It also follows that we cannot separate this concept from the dozen or so other concepts which are central to Marx's system. The word alienation, however, can be taken from Marx—or from any other writer who uses it—and bent, as we have seen, into a variety of shapes.

The lesson to be drawn from this approach to the subject—from seeing "alienation" as composed of related concepts and not as a word—is that one cannot exorcise confusion over the use of alienation by banning the word or declaring all but one of its meanings illegitimate. Only general acceptance of one of the analyses using "alienation" could bring real order to our linguistic practice. Until that far-off day, studying the systems in which "alienation" appears may also shed light on why such varied thinkers choose to use the same term. For in asking that we focus on what is unique in the different conceptions of alienation, it has not been my intention to deny the existence of a common thread. What I have opposed is misrepresenting the search for this thread, especially insofar as it concentrates on ordinary language, as an act of evaluating the analyses in which "alienation" is found, and, indeed, as a replacement for these analyses in dealing with reality. If essays in intellectual history which emerge from a detailed understanding of particulars are always welcome, those which function as substitutes for such an understanding must be rejected.

Finally, as for Kelly's own attempt to come to grips with the human condition, it can only remain on the level of literature—good literature in Kelly's case—as long as the search is for adequate words to describe this condition and not for adequate concepts with which to understand it. Kelly says he "hates" the word alienation. As it happens, I like the word. I also like Kelly's words—"loss," "exile," and "migration." How far does any of this take us in understanding what humanity is, what it has become and can become, or how to go about finding the answers to these questions?

8.4

Review of
Miliband's Marxism and Politics

For the better part of a century, Marx's theory of the state could only be viewed through the haze of Marx's own partial and disconnected treatment of politics and the contradictory practices and concurrent rationalizations of assorted Marxist parties. Recent scholarship by Shlomo Avineri, Richard Hunt, Hal Draper, Nicos Poulantzas and Ralph Miliband have raised the discussion to a level fitting the importance of its subject matter. In his latest contribution to this literature, *Marxism and Politics,* Ralph Miliband offers a popular overview of the character and role of the state in capitalist society (generally the staple of this kind of work) and of the politics that socialists do and should practice in both capitalist and post-capitalist societies. Of the two, the discussion of socialist politics is a model of scholarly insight, critical balance and revolutionary good sense.

In particular, what Miliband says about the relation of class and party, the contradiction in the notion of party (and in the Dictatorship of the Proletariat itself) between the imperatives of democracy and efficiency, and his restatement of the revolution/reform dichotomy as one of insurrection and constitutionality deserve the attention of every serious student of this subject.

I also found Miliband's scenario of what is likely to happen if (when?) a reformist Marxist party gets into power in an advanced capitalist society (Italy? France?) the most convincing of the dozens which are now circulating. In all these matters—and more—the cool and careful gaze that Miliband brings to an area of Marxist politics that is generally dominated by sectarian squabbling merits our deep respect and thanks.

Unfortunately, Miliband's analysis of the capitalist state proper—despite insightful digressions on the role of intellectuals and on the national question—is much less successful. Miliband is aware that at the core of Marx's theory of the state is the view that the state serves capitalist class interests through 1) members of this class who occupy the more important political offices, 2) the various parties and other organizations of the capitalist class which exercise decisive influence over who holds state office, their decisions and the conditions effecting these decisions, and 3) the structural constraints of the capitalist system as such which provide the real options and preferred goals of any state action, given the system itself is never put into question. Despite criticisms of his earlier work by Poulantzas and others, however, Miliband continues to underplay (not ignore) the last of these elements. Thus, though Miliband mentions various economic functions of the capitalist state, they are never integrated into the organic processes of the capitalist mode of production. What the processes of capital accumulation and the production of value require of the state, any capitalist state, if it is to succeed in reproducing the conditions of capitalist existence is never explained. Granted that the works in which these requirements are laid out in greatest detail tend to offer an overly deterministic account of political activity, understating them is at least equally destructive of Marx's meaning. For example, one never gets from Miliband, as one does from Marx and his more dialectical followers, a sense of the workings of the whole capitalist system from the vantage point of whatever aspect or sector is being examined.

Another aspect of Marx's broad theory of politics, his view of the state as the alienated social power/illusory community, which might have served Miliband as an alternative mode of viewing capitalism within the state as well as the state within capitalism, is ignored altogether (hence, though alienated politics is often described, it is never theorized). The result is a study of politics as a sector of capitalist life (as opposed to an expression of capitalist existence), extremely competent as far as it goes, but partial, one-sided and necessarily distorting.

Miliband's attempt early in the book to define the proletariat is one such distortion. Only after the system in which classes operate has been delineated, at least in broad outline, can one hope to say who falls into which class—not only because it is the whole which gives meaning to the part but because the meaning of the part alters somewhat in function of its changing relation to the whole (a relation that changes with the development of the whole *and* with the different perspectives—themselves related to different purposes—that are adopted for viewing it). Hence the elasticity of the boundaries Marx seems to draw around different classes and the fact that he sometimes places the same group in one class and sometimes in another. When Miliband, after distributing the population among the various classes, then goes on to raise the question of class consciousness, he can only offer a one-sided, psychological response. The real social processes of capitalism that are constantly remaking the actual, probable and possible dimensions of our consciousness are simply not available at this point to be introduced into the discussion.

Finally, Miliband's sectoral analysis of the capitalist state adversely effects his understanding of the relative autonomy of the state, the subject of much debate among Marxists at the present time. For Marx, the state can be relatively autonomous 1) in relation to actual members of the capitalist class (the case when a majority of high political offices are held by members of other classes), 2) in relation to the influence of the organizations of the capitalist class (the brief periods when this influence is not decisive), and 3) in relation to the structural constraints of the capitalist system (the occasions when the rules of the game can be broken or at least bent). Relative autonomy in this third sense generally indicates a transition period between modes of production, a time when competing rules of the game give political leaders more than the usual room to maneuver. Though these three kinds of relative autonomy can occur together, they also occur apart.

Underplaying as he does the organic connection between the state and the capitalist mode of production, Miliband recognizes only the first two kinds of relative autonomy. Thus, when Marx and Engels say that relative autonomy of the state can come about through a temporary stand-off in the struggle between major classes, Miliband concludes that such a state would have no class connections. This is a conclusion he rightly rejects, but in order to do so he feels he must dispense with the insight that links a stand-off in the class struggle with the relative autonomy of the state. But the state in question may be relatively autonomous only in the first two senses, and—given the structural constraints of capitalism—it would still serve the capitalist class. Or, if the stand-off between major classes occurs in a period of transition between two different modes of production, the relative autonomy of the state could (also) refer to the modest and temporary independence which the state enjoys from constraints coming out of its own past and future. In either case, given the state's identity as the alienated social power in class divided society, it can only function if supported by a class or combination of classes, its leaders will conceive of their role in class determined categories (however disguised in the language of national interest), and—in order to preserve its own existence and avoid economic chaos—it must serve the interests of the ruling economic class (which in capitalism is the capitalist class). The state's ties with the capitalist class, therefore, are far from broken when non-capitalists operate the machinery of Government and the political influence of capitalist organizations has been temporarily eclipsed.

On the contrary, an increasing number of Marxists (including Miliband himself at times) believe that it is in conditions of such relative autonomy—conditions found in both social democracy and fascism—that the modern state can best serve capitalist class interests. With the growing involvement of the state in the production, distribution, exchange and consumption processes of capitalism, its continued acceptance as neutral arbiter and instrument requires at least superficial distancing from the class that it invariably serves.

In sum, the state's ties with the capitalist class are ties which pass through the whole capitalist system, as society, economy and culture, and as illusory community. By restricting his study of the state to a sector of capitalist life, Miliband necessarily misconstrues the state both in its identity with capitalism (as a part which gives expression to the workings of the whole) and in its relative autonomy within capitalism (as a part with a distinct though changing role in the operation of the whole).

All things considered, I have no hesitation in recommending *Marxism and Politics* as an extremely clear and useful introduction to this subject (maybe the best available), though—for reasons given—a fully adequate work on Marxism and politics remains to be written.

8.5

Of Marxism and Universities

The role of Marxism in universities is only slightly less obscure than the role of universities in Marxism, but perhaps some light can be shed on both subjects by examining Marx's little known response to an ancient Roman myth.

Cacus was a Roman mythological figure who stole oxen by dragging them backwards into his den so that the footprints made it appear they had gone out from there. After quoting Luther's account of the story, Marx exclaims, "an excellent picture, it fits the capitalist in general, who pretends that what he has taken from others and brought into his den emanates from him, and by causing it to go backwards, he gives it the semblance of having come from his den."

Capitalists present themselves as producers of wealth, providers of jobs, donors and public benefactors. The press (their press) usually refers to them as "industry." Is this an accurate description of who they are and what they do? What stands out clearly from the example of Cacus is that what Marx and Marxists call bourgeois ideology does not so much falsify the facts as misinterpret them so as to reverse what has taken place:

The footprints are there for all to see, but if we limit ourselves to what is immediately apparent (the subject matter of "empirical" social science) we will arrive at a conclusion that is the exact opposite of the truth.

Only if we examine what led up to the event in question and its surrounding circumstances—that is, its real history and the system of events in which it resides—can we hope to understand what really happened and why.

In the case of the capitalists, only by examining how they got their wealth from the surplus labor of previous generations of workers (history) and how our laws, customs and culture are biased in their favor (structure) can we see it is not the capitalists who are serving society but the rest of society that is serving them.

Though many have criticized Marxism as one-sided because of its emphasis on economic processes, Marxism is really our only all-sided analysis of capitalism as a social system, including its real history, actual workings and future possibilities. Lacking the perspective provided by this analysis, the different events studied by political science, economics, psychology, etc. appear disconnected and arbitrary, and often acquire a meaning that is the exact opposite of how these events function inside capitalism.

Yet some people continue to ask: Should Marxism be taught in a university? If we let our eyes wander away from the footprints left by Cacus's oxen, then we can see the correct question: Does an educational institution that does not teach Marxism deserve to be called a university?

Serious non-Marxist scholars in every field appreciate the contribution Marxism makes in posing the bigger questions, at least. And enough have come to accept its holistic explanations to make Marxism the major alternative to orthodox approaches in history and economics (political science is soon to follow).

And the capitalists, and those Marx called their "ideological handmaidens," who are protesting that teaching Marxism constitutes "indoctrination"...? Well, Cacus, too, had an interest in keeping people from finding out what went on in his cave.

8.6

Review of Henri Lefebvre's Sociology of Marx

In a country where every intellectual worthy of the distinction has written a book on Marxism, Henri Lefebvre is widely regarded as one of the ruling triumvirate of Marx interpreters. The others are Maximilian Rubel and Louis Althusser. *The Sociology of Marx,* which is the first of Lefebvre's works to be translated into English, is an insightful attempt to construct a sociology from the writings of an admitted non-sociologist.

Marx's subject matter, according to Lefebvre, is "a totality in process of becoming and in its present stage of development, a totality comprising levels and aspects which are now complementary, now distinct, now contradictory. As such, his theory is not history, not sociology, not psychology, etc., but comprehends these approaches, these aspects, these various levels of the whole." Marx's approach to studying this totality proceeds through the complex relations between human activity and its various accomplishments in such a way that none of these parts are out of mind when attention is momentarily focused on the other. The rest of this totality finds its way into Marx's writings as the necessary preconditions and results, however, far removed, of these fundamental ties.

Consequently, any attempt to impose academic boundaries on Marx's theories, to particularize Marxism, distorts the real interaction of what has been included. This error is compounded by limiting the definitions of the concepts used to the same discipline to which one has confined the theory, whereas in fact, one must pass through many disciplines to uncover the meaning of any of Marx's major concepts. It was the fruits of such partial and one-sided inquiries into society that Marx, himself, attacked as "abstractions." Still, most studies of Marxism, by friends and foes alike, have led to just such abstractions, to attributing to Marx limited and limiting formulas together with concepts that are too narrowly defined.

Aware of these pitfalls, Lefebvre does not try to build a sociology which lies to the side of Marx's economics, psychology, history, etc. His effort is directed, instead, to locating sociological aspects in Marx's theories and to making one of these aspects a new point of departure for examining the same totality with which Marx was concerned. Serving Lefebvre as the touchstone in this attempt is Marx's treatment of reality on the basis of its social forms and structures. Marx—it is often forgotten (even where it was once remembered)—did not grasp capital as the physical means of production, but as a social production relation or "form" of the relation between people's activities and their product in a particular historical period. Labor, commodity, landed property, profit, money, laws, ethical rules and values, etc., are likewise conceived of as forms of this same relation. As the interaction between activity and its product (viewed in their broadest senses) alters, so, too, do the forms in and through which this interaction manifests itself, requiring either the adoption of new concepts or an extension in the meanings of old ones. Lefebvre would have Marxist sociologists study the current interaction of these forms and how the various manifestations of the relation between activity and its product affect each other, with special attention paid to the practices that undermine them. Working with a cross-section of the present, his emphasis remains on change and development. The sociology Lefebvre finds in Marxism is a sociology of forms that has been weighted to obtain a better understanding of the role of revolutionary practice.

What are the relations between capital and labor, between

commodities and contracts, between values and juridicial principles, between class and ideology, and between all such forms and the daily, often contradictory, activity of humans? In replying to such questions, Lefebvre lays great stress on the unity of social forms as elements that exhibit all the general features of a system. Moreover, he presents each form as being what it is not only by virtue of what the others are, but also by virtue of the no-boundary interaction occurring among the other forms. The relations between parts of a system which possesses no truly separate parts can only be internal relations. Capital and labor, for example, are not only forms of the current relation between people and their activity, but also forms of each other as necessarily interacting components of this relation. The fact that productive activity is alienated is part of the social production relation, capital, just as the fact that the product is alienated from the producers is part of the social production relation, labor. The forms, capital and labor, serve as alternative windows for looking out at the same process.

It is the use Lefebvre makes of Marx's dialectic—for this is where we have arrived—that accounts for both the triumphs and failures of his work; triumphs, because it enables him to offer well-balanced analyses of the forms at issue and to avoid dogmatic definitions. In this regard, we would single out his discussion of ideology as especially illuminating. The same dialectical outlook, however, causes Lefebvre to use terms and a manner of reasoning that most readers will find exceedingly obscure. Though Lefebvre elaborated his views on Marx's dialectic in an earlier study, *Logique formelle, logique dialectique,* the present work offers little aid to the uninitiated. For those unfamiliar with the dialectic (and not potted versions of the same), the value of the *Sociology of Marx* will be limited to the occasional, disconnected, though hardly inconsiderable insights which they can cull. Yet, the chief value of this work is that it does present the sociology of Marx, but as an achievement available only to a few. It is to be hoped that the primers on Marxism with which the Anglo-Saxon world has been deluged has not rendered our intellectuals incapable of studying important though difficult books on this subject. This is one such book.